MEville to WEville

Early Literacy and Communication Supplemental Curriculum

unit 2

my family

RELATIONSHIPS

ablenet™

Real-Life Learning

This program is dedicated to every educator committed to bringing meaningful literacy experiences to students of ALL abilities, and to the students whose lives are enriched by their active engagement in the literacy experience.

Special Thanks to:

Dr. Karen Erickson and her associate, Sally Clendon, who conducted a research study in Spring of 2004 that substantiated the effectiveness of the MEville to WEville: Early Literacy and Communication Supplemental Curriculum. We thank them for their guidance and contributions that ensured quality teaching strategies were embedded in this program.

Dr. Erickson and Sally Clendon are located at the Center for Literacy and Disability Studies at the University of North Carolina, Chapel Hill, N.C.

AbleNet, Inc.
Mpls./St.Paul, MN USA
Toll Free: 1-800-322-0956
(US and Canada only)
Internet: www.ablenetinc.com

Table of Contents

unit 2

my family

Introduction

? What is the MEville to WEville Supplemental Curriculum all about?

Welcome to the MEville to WEville Early Literacy and Communication Supplemental Curriculum. This program is the first of its kind, specifically developed for students with disabilities who have difficulties learning to read and write through traditional instructional methods.

A: Beginning literacy and communication development are addressed while supporting student development of self and a sense of belonging within a community of learners.

This curriculum is the first ever research-based literacy program that meaningfully and systematically integrates reading, writing, speaking, augmentative communicating and listening for elementary students with disabilities in the moderate to severe range of disabilities.

Lesson activities are written based on the understanding of the early literacy learning as described in the reports and additional research readings such as National Reading Panel, National Reading Research Council Project, Reading Difficulties in Young Children and Rand Reading Comprehension Reports.

In addition, these creative lessons were designed to build a classroom community that promotes a true sense of belonging within a network of meaningful relationships. This program supports the development of character education *(having a valued role, acknowledging others, expressing preferences)* and social skills *(turn-taking, responsibility, respect)* by embedding these elements throughout the MEville to WEville program. It's easy to identify the opportunities to work on these skills– just look for the icon adjacent to specific lesson steps.

This resource represents the second of the following three units:

UNIT 1: ME
Students focus on individuality and build a sense of self through a range of lessons about Who I Am, How I Feel and What I Like. Featured book included: Today I Feel Silly *by Jamie Lee Curtis.*

UNIT 2: MY FAMILY
Students build relationships as they participate in theme based lessons including Who Is In My Family?, Things We Do and Living With My Family. Featured book included: "Families" *by Ann Morris.*

UNIT 3: MY SCHOOL
Students cooperate with fellow classmates as they explore themed lessons focused on, Who Is At My School?, Being A Student and What We Do. Featured book included: "My Special Day at Third Street School" *by Eve Bunting.*

Teacher Note: **Additional information on each unit can be found on the Ablenet website at www.ablenetinc.com.**

How is MEville to WEville organized?

A: This Supplemental Curriculum is organized into three parts with five sections, included in each part.

UNIT 2 PARTS:
Part 1: **Who Is In My Family?**
Part 2: **Things We Do**
Part 3: **Living With My Family**

SECTIONS:

Learning New Words:
Students identify new words and develop expressive language skills through saying words, singing songs and using words in high-interest motivational activities.

Vocabulary Activities:
Students practice using the vocabulary words in engaging activities designed with repetition and variety to promote the understanding of each word.

Word Wall Words:
Students learn high frequency words, needed in reading and writing, through activities such as clap/chanting, writing and word identification.

Literacy Lessons:
Students engage in lessons using literature books and real life experiences to practice choice making, direction following and giving a personal response.

Writing Lessons:
Students make decisions about individual and group writings and express themselves through book making and other structured writing projects.

How do I get started using MEville to WEville?

A: It's up to you!

MEville to WEville is flexible enough to meet individual teacher's instructional styles and specific classroom needs. Two lesson planning tools are included.

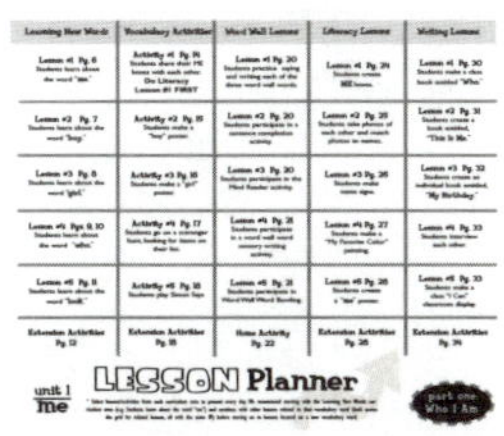

Lesson Planner
Each part begins with a Lesson Planner to assist you in planning your lessons. Select lessons/activities from each literacy area to present every day. We recommend starting with the Learning New Words activity (e.g. Students learn about the word ME) and continue with the other activities related to that vocabulary word before moving on to another word.

Create Your Own Lesson Planner
Create your own daily plans by filling in each day with lessons/activities across the literacy areas. Check each literacy area you select and write the specific name on the line to the right of that literacy area.

How much teaching time does each lesson take?

A: We recommend planning at least 30 minutes of instructional time per lesson, although the time spent on each lesson will differ according to how many students are in your classroom, differing needs of students, and how many teaching assistants and related service personnel are assisting.

Whether you stick to the 75 lessons and 60 extension activities provided or whether you add your own creative ideas, it is recommended you spend time each day providing literacy experiences for your students.

? What will my students be learning when I use MEville to WEville?

A: This resource systematically targets literacy skills that research has shown are critical to literacy learning success while incorporating content area goals and objectives. All lessons support the following areas and are filled with fun and engaging lessons relating to the My Family theme.

Literacy Learning Areas

Vocabulary
Print Concepts
Oral Language
Word Identification
Phonological Awareness

Literacy learning areas are linked to the data collection tools (Part 5).

Content Learning Areas
Unit 2 - My Family

Part 1: Who Is In My Family?:
The student will be able to identify the features, roles, and/or activities of families and family members.

1. Student will be able to accurately identify at least one unique feature of the family to which he/she belongs.
2. Student will be able to accurately name a family member who has a certain role.
3. Student will be able to accurately identify a difference between a game that was played long ago and a game that is presently played.

Part 2: Things We Do:
Student will be able to identify and/or participate in activities that families do.

1. Student will be able to follow a series of one-step directions to complete a task.
2. Student will be able to sort food items into each of the four food groups.
3. Student will be able to name one chore that was done many years ago that is different from chores we do now.

Part 3: Living With My Family:
The student will be able to communicate personal information, family routines, and/or solutions for problem solving within a family.

1. Student will be able to identify and say their city, address and phone number.
2. Student will be able to state one thing they can do if they are upset with a family member.
3. Student will be able to name at least one thing that their family does during a particular time of the day.

A blank data collection chart is provided (Part 5). Enter your students' specific goals/objectives or use those provided above.

Character Education and Community Building Outcomes

- Students will further develop a sense of "Who I Am."
- Students will experience a sense of belonging.
- Students will learn to acknowledge and celebrate accomplishments, contributions, and differences.
- Students will experience a valued role as they learn "What we do for each other is important."
- Every student voice will be heard.

This "character and community" icon will signal a lesson activity that specifically addresses one of the above Character Education/Community Building goals.

View outcomes and gain guidance on how to model and reinforce these skills (Part 5).

say

? How will I be able to include my students with severe disabilities?

A: It's easy, with the *Action Dictionary.*

The *Action Dictionary* (Part 4) references every action verb that is used in the MEville to WEville supplemental curriculum. These action verbs are the words presented in bold throughout the teacher's manual. The *Action Dictionary* describes how student actions may be adapted or modified to enable active participation in the lesson activity.

LIST OF VERBS IN ACTION DICTIONARY

Answer
Ask (Say)
Blow (Dry)
Bring (Get)
Choose
Clap
Clap/Chant
Color
Comment
Count
Cut
Discuss (Say)
Draw
Dry
Get
Glue
Identify
Label
Look
Mark
Match
Mix
Name (Identify)
Paint
Read
Say
Select (Choose)
Show
Sing
Spin
Staple
Take Pictures
Talk (Say)
Tell (Say)
Turn ON/OFF
Turn the page
Vote
Write
Write your name

Action Dictionary Example

This activity requires that the student tells the class what their favorite color is.

The Action Dictionary describes how to adapt this activity for students who are non-verbal or who have limited or unintelligible speech.

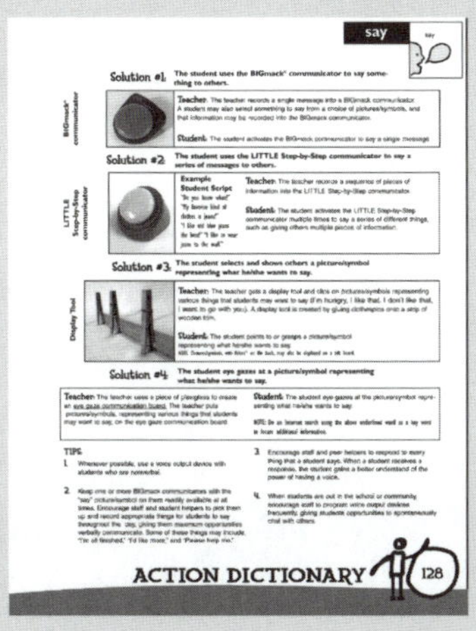
say

ACTION DICTIONARY 128

LESSON ACTIVITY

Students will take turns **telling** the class what their favorite color is.

? What assistive technology products are recommended for MEville to WEville?

A: A complete list of products is in the Assistive Technology Quick Set Up Guide (Part 4).

Also included is the information you'll need to set up assistive technology recommended in the *Action Dictionary.*

? What support materials are included?

A: There are a few materials that you will want to be aware of and create prior to starting the lessons:

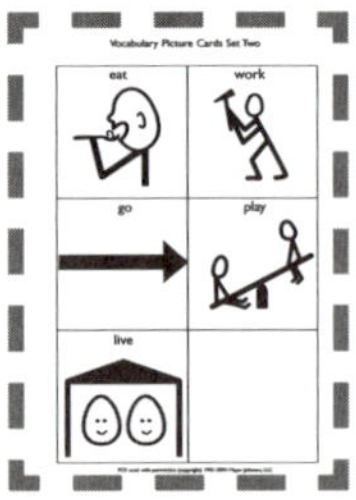

R#58

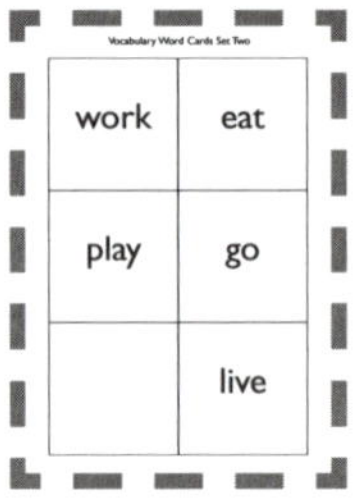

R#59

Vocabulary Cards:

There are two vocabulary word reproducibles provided for each of the Unit parts. These may be copied back to back; creating a card with a word on one side and the corresponding picture/ symbol on the other.

NOTE: Vocabulary words are about comprehension. If you are trying to have students get to the meaning of the word, use the reproducible with the picture/symbol. If the purpose is for the student to read, then use the reproducible with the vocabulary word only.

Unit 1

PART 1 - me, boy, girl, who, look
PART 2 - happy, sad, mad, scared, tired
PART 3 - people, food, place, clothes, book

Unit 2

PART 1 - family, parents, children, cat, dog
PART 2 - eat, work, go, play, live
PART 3 - help, share, give, laugh, celebrate

Unit 3

PART 1 - student, class, teacher, friend, together
PART 2 - school, room, bus, paper, lunch
PART 3 - draw, read, count, sing, write

R#25

Word Wall Words:

Cut out the words from the Word Wall Word reproducible in each part as you get ready to teach each of the Unit parts. Place the words on the Word Wall once they have been introduced.

Unit 1

PART 1 - me, and, who
PART 2 - it, you, I
PART 3 - to, like, what

Unit 2

PART 1 - the, have, we
PART 2 - see, are, do
PART 3 - work, is, help

Unit 3

PART 1 - at, can, big
PART 2 - go, for, want
PART 3 - look, make, will

NOTE: Word Walls contain high frequency words that students will need in their reading and writing. These are the words that are often misspelled and words that are easily confused with other words. Using word wall cards is a strategy for teaching readers frequently used words, such as me, and, who, it, you, I, to, like, what, etc.

Reproducibles:

Many of the lessons are supported with reproducibles for you to use with your students during instruction. Reproducibles can be found in Part 6.

R#49

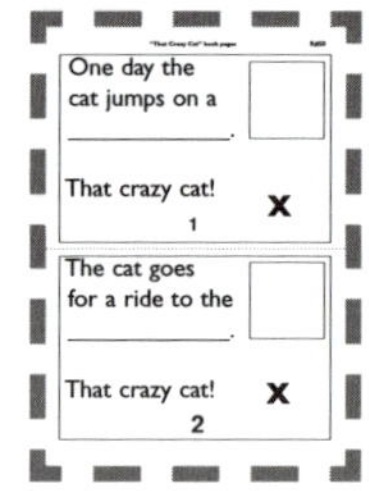

R#50

Class Books:

In the Writing Lessons in each of the parts, your students will be creating books. These book pages should be copied prior to the activity. Have students read and reread these books throughout Unit 2. Send books home when the Unit is complete.

R#109

Family Involvement:

Included are letters to copy and send home to parents. Be sure to familiarize yourself with the letters and when they need to be sent home, as they usually request items from home to be sent to school. For families who may not send in items requested, be sure to have extra items available so the students are able to participate in the lesson/activity.

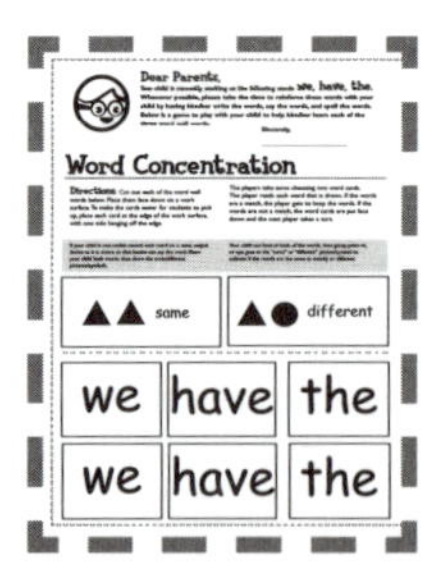

Home Extension Activities:

On the last page in each of the Word Wall sections, a home extension activity has been provided for you to send home. It offers fun and engaging ways for parents to practice identifying, naming, writing, and spelling the Word Wall Words with their child.

Does MEville to WEville provide data collection tools?

A: YES! Student Data Collection Charts are provided (Part 5) for you to easily record and share your students' growth and progress with others. Use these charts to keep track of the ongoing participation and progress of your students. These charts can also be used to capture baseline information prior to starting the program.

Learning New Words/Vocabulary
Word Wall Words
Writing
Literacy
Content Learning

Student Data Collection Chart

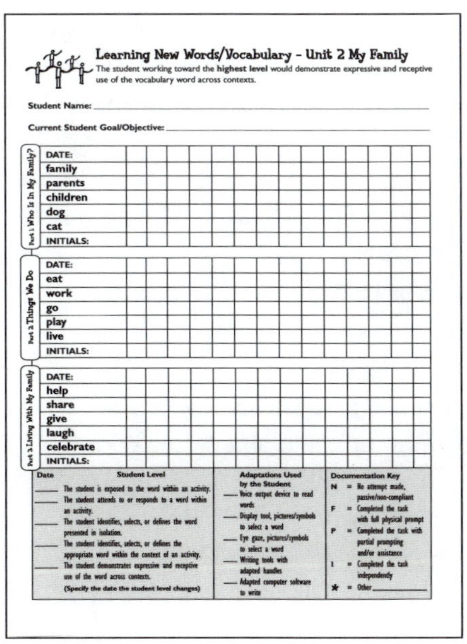

Learning New Words/Vocabulary - Unit 2 My Family
The student working toward the **highest level** would demonstrate expressive and receptive use of the vocabulary word across contexts.

Student Name: __________

Current Student Goal/Objective: __________

Part 1: Who Is In My Family?

DATE:														
family														
parents														
children														
dog														
cat														
INITIALS:														

Part 2 Things We Do

DATE:														
eat														
work														
go														
play														
live														
INITIALS:														

Part 3 Living With My Family

DATE:														
help														
share														
give														
laugh														
celebrate														
INITIALS:														

Date / Student Level	Adaptations Used by the Student	Documentation Key
___ The student is exposed to the word within an activity. ___ The student attends to or responds to a word within an activity. ___ The student identifies, selects, or defines the word presented in isolation. ___ The student identifies, selects, or defines the appropriate word within the context of an activity. ___ The student demonstrates expressive and receptive use of the word across contexts. (Specify the date the student level changes)	___ Voice output device to read words ___ Display tool, pictures/symbols to select a word ___ Eye gaze, pictures/symbols to select a word ___ Writing tools with adapted handles ___ Adapted computer software to write	N = No attempt made, passive/non-compliant F = Completed the task with full physical prompt P = Completed the task with partial prompting and/or assistance I = Completed the task independently ★ = Other_____

Can I use MEville to WEville to enhance character education and community building for my students?

A: YES!

Character education and community building activities are embedded throughout the MEville to WEville program. It's easy to identify when you will have opportunities to work on these skills, with the icon adjacent to the specific lesson steps that promote community building. Remember to take advantage of "teachable moments" where you can incorporate the language of community and key character traits *(e.g. respect, caring, cooperation)* as a way of modeling and reinforcing those outcomes.

View outcomes and see how to model and reinforce these skills (Part 5).

Visit www.ablenetinc.com to download the Reproducibles and Data Collection Tools.

Log in required.
Enter:
User name: unit2
Password: MEville
(all are case sensitive)

How will using MEville to WEville increase the quality of instruction for my students?

A: Lessons are written in a systematic approach providing the repetition and variety that students require for active engagement. Simply teaching these lessons/activities as written will provide your students with the instruction they need to demonstrate measurable gains in achievement. Students are provided with opportunities to actively work on skills generalized across settings. The Vocabulary Words, Word Wall Words and Picture Communication Symbols reoccur throughout all three units of MEville to WEville for ongoing exposure and use to increase comprehension and learning. Reproducible materials are provided to make it easy to include all students in successful completion of activity sheets and student made books.

Can I really make literacy skill development possible for ALL of my students?

A: Absolutely!

MEville to WEville is a comprehensive supplemental curriculum that was specifically created to facilitate the beginning literacy and communication development of students with developmental disabilities, particularly those with complex communication needs. Students within the moderate to severe range of disabilities are at high risk for literacy learning difficulties.

This supplemental curriculum actively combats these difficulties by taking instructional activities and teaching strategies that have proven to be effective at developing the literacy skills of typically developing students, and making them accessible to students across all ability levels.

MEville to WEville incorporates a range of accommodations and technologies to ensure that all students can successfully participate and learn. Students who are able to access written materials, writing tools, and literacy learning activities in traditional ways *(writing with a pencil, verbally reading written materials, holding word cards while playing a word game, etc.)* will be able to participate in this curriculum with zero to minimal adaptations or supports.

Students who have more severe disabilities will be able to access learning materials and activities in alternative ways as listed and explained in the *Action Dictionary*.

Where's the proof?

A: It's in the RESEARCH!

A research group directed by Dr. Karen Erickson from the Center for Literacy and Disability Studies at the University of North Carolina at Chapel Hill, conducted a research study to evaluate the effectiveness of the MEville to WEville supplemental curriculum. A pilot study was completed in spring of 2004 and a large-scale Replication Study took place the summer of 2004.

The pilot study explored how the MEville to WEville program influenced the literacy and communication skills and understandings of 23 children within the moderate to severe range of disabilities, and the attitudes, expectations, and beliefs of their teachers. The children and teachers who participated in the project were from three self-contained special education classrooms in the Piedmont region of North Carolina.

Analysis of the study's findings suggest that the following claims can be made:

Teachers felt valued as teaching professionals because they had access to a curriculum that supported them and that had been specifically designed to meet their students' needs.

Teachers integrated MEville to WEville across the school day.

Teachers spent more time addressing literacy and communication.

Teachers focused on the integration of assistive technology across their school day rather than the creation of instructional activities.

Teachers spent more time focused on meeting individual child needs and less time planning for the whole group.

Related service providers were better able to integrate their services into the classroom.

There were increased opportunities for parent-teacher interaction and collaboration.

Children initiated more communication and interaction during the program.

Children developed stronger social relationships with their peers in special/general education. Children became more socially responsive.

Children made measurable progress as readers and writers.

Visit the AbleNet website to view research methods and the Summer 2004 Replication Study results.

What else would be helpful for me to know?

A: Additional support is available!

If you have questions about MEville to WEville, the lessons/activities, and/or the assistive technology, then the following resources are available to you:

Website
Go to http://www.ablenetinc.com for additional information about the MEville to WEville research methods, answers to frequently asked questions and additional resources. Log-in to download Reproducibles and Data Collection Tools.
User name: unit2
Password: MEville *(case sensitive)*

Email
Send specific questions to customerservice@ablenetinc.com.

Telephone
Call AbleNet at 1-800-322-0956 *(within US or Canada)* or 651-294-2200 *(outside US or Canada)*.

EARLY LITERACY AND COMMUNICATION PROGRAM

Part one

Who Is In My Family?

ablenet™

unit 2

my family

MEville to WEville

In the **Who Is In My Family?** part, students will be able to identify the features, roles, and/or activities of families and family members.

Character Education

Each lesson in this section addresses aspects of character education. Look for the to identify where this occurs.

part one

Who Is In My Family?

Content Learning Objectives

1. Student will be able to accurately identify at least one unique feature of the family to which he/she belongs.

2. Student will be able to accurately name a family member who has a certain role.

3. Student will be able to accurately identify a difference between a game that was played long ago and a game that is presently played.

Overview and Resources

Literature Book to Be Read:
"Families" by Ann Morris

Additional Book Recommendations:
"The Napping House"
by Audrey Wood
"My Family is Forever"
by Nancy Carlson
"My Big Brother"
by Valerie Fisher
"Love You Forever"
by Robert Munsch

Books to Be Created and Read by Students:
My Family book
Thank You book for parents
That Crazy Cat! book
Dog Care book

Songs to Be Sung:
"The Big Dog in the Pet Shop" sung to the tune, "How much is that Doggie in the Window?"

"The Children in this Class" sung to the tune, "The Wheels on the Bus"

Song Recommendations:
"We Are Family" by The Corrs
"Everywhere You Look"
by Jesse Frederick
(Full House television show theme song)

Class Projects and Art Projects:
Family Photo Frame
"Children in Room ____" Poster
Calico Cats
Family Mobile
Dog Painting
Family Chains
Make Cat Cookies
Children's Art Wall

Games:
Is This Your Parent?
Dog Bones
The Parent Says
Parent May I?
Back to the Doghouse

Home/School Activities:
Send in Family Photos
Parent Interview

Learning New Words	Vocabulary Activities	Word Wall Lessons	Literacy Lessons	Writing Lessons
Lesson #1 Pgs. 6-7 Students learn about the word **"family."**	**Activity #1 Pg. 18** Students make a family mobile.	**Lesson #1 Pg. 26** Students practice saying and writing each of the three word wall words.	**Lesson #1 Pg. 30** Students make family chains that connect each family member together.	**Lesson #1 Pg. 36** Students write a book entitiled, **"My Family."**
Lesson #2 Pgs. 8-9 Students learn about the word **"parents."**	**Activity #2 Pg. 19** Students interview their parents about things from their childhood.	**Lesson #2 Pg. 26** Students participate in a Sentence Completion Activity.	**Lesson #2 Pg. 31** Students play the game **"Parent May I."**	**Lesson #2 Pg. 37** Students make a Thank You book for their parent.
Lesson #3 Pgs. 10-11 Students learn about the word **"children."**	**Activity #3 Pg. 20** Students participate in and respond to popular children's activities.	**Lesson #3 Pg. 26** Students participate in the Mind Reader activity.	**Lesson #3 Pg. 32** Students sing the song, **"The Children in This Class."**	**Lesson #3 Pg. 38** Students create a Children's Art Wall.
Lesson #4 Pgs. 12-13 Students learn about the word **"cat."**	**Activity #4 Pg. 21** Students participate in a cat language activity.	**Lesson #4 Pg. 27** Students play the word game **"Dog Bones."**	**Lesson #4 Pg. 33** Students follow recipe directions to make a cat cookie.	**Lesson #4 Pg. 38** Students write a book entitled **"That Crazy Cat!"**
Lesson #5 Pgs. 14-15 Students learn about the word **"dog."**	**Activity #5 Pgs. 22-23** Students learn aboout responsibilities in caring for a dog.	**Lesson #5 Pg. 27** Students participate in the game **"The Parent Says."**	**Lesson #5 Pgs. 33-34** Students play the game Back to the Doghouse.	**Lesson #5 Pg. 39** Students make a Dog Care book.
Extension Activities Pg. 16	**Extension Activities Pg. 24**	**Home Activity Pg. 28**	**Extension Activities Pg. 34**	**Extension Activities Pg. 40**

unit 2

my family

LESSON Planner

part one:
Who Is In My Family?

* Select lessons/activities from each curriculum area to present every day. We recommend starting with the Learning New Words curriculum area (e.g. Students learn about the word "family") and continue with other lessons related to that vocabulary word (look across the grid for related lessons, all with the same #) before moving on to lessons focused on a new vocabulary word.

Create Your Own...

Daily LESSON Planner

Create your own daily plans by filling in each day with lessons/activities across the literacy areas. Check each literacy area that you select a lesson/activity from, and write the specific name on the line to the right of that literacy area.

Monday	___ **Learning New Words** ______ ___ **Vocabulary Activities** ______ ___ **Word Wall Lessons** ______ ___ **Literacy Lessons** ______ ___ **Writing Lessons** ______
Tuesday	___ **Learning New Words** ______ ___ **Vocabulary Activities** ______ ___ **Word Wall Lessons** ______ ___ **Literacy Lessons** ______ ___ **Writing Lessons** ______
Wednesday	___ **Learning New Words** ______ ___ **Vocabulary Activities** ______ ___ **Word Wall Lessons** ______ ___ **Literacy Lessons** ______ ___ **Writing Lessons** ______
Thursday	___ **Learning New Words** ______ ___ **Vocabulary Activities** ______ ___ **Word Wall Lessons** ______ ___ **Literacy Lessons** ______ ___ **Writing Lessons** ______
Friday	___ **Learning New Words** ______ ___ **Vocabulary Activities** ______ ___ **Word Wall Lessons** ______ ___ **Literacy Lessons** ______ ___ **Writing Lessons** ______

EARNING NEW WORDS
ECTION ONE

part one

During each lesson, a new vocabulary word will be introduced and students will participate in activities around that word. In lessons two through five, the previous word learned will be reviewed. Students will participate in an activity involving the previous vocabulary word.

When words are taught in isolation, without repeated use in a variety of activities, students have less opportunities to learn and remember the words and transfer their learning across contexts. For this reason, the words in this section are taught directly, reviewed, and used in a variety of activities.

Included in Part 6 - Reproducibles are optional vocabulary cards R#4 and R#5. These vocabulary cards are additional family members and may be used to support discussions about family.

Teacher Note:

At least two days prior to teaching Learning New Words Lesson #1 and Lesson #2, send home the Parent Letter Reproducible #1. In this section, students will be learning about a cat in Lesson #4. For this lesson, a visit from a cat is a suggested option.

Throughout these **Learning New Words** lessons, students will be learning about what a family is and growing in their understanding of the members that make up a family. Students will have opportunities to share things about their own family. As students share about their own families, ask questions and/or comment about the student's family to communicate that their family is important and of interest to others.

R#1

This "character and community" icon will signal a lesson activity through which a sense of "Who I Am" can be reinforced.

LEARNING NEW WORDS

LESSON #1

Teacher Note: **Parent Letter R#1 needs to be sent home at least two days prior to this lesson.**

MATERIALS:

- **vocabulary cards Set One R#2, R#3**
- **pictures of different families** *(3-5 pictures)*
- **chart paper**
- **construction paper** *(11" x 17")* **one sheet or one sentence strip**
- **black marker**
- **"Families"** *by Ann Morris*
- **student family photos** *(brought in from home)*

NOTE: Keep photos for Writing Lesson#1

- **white card stock** *(one sheet per student)*
- **tempera paint in assorted colors**
- **paintbrushes and/or sponge brushes**
- **glue**
- **Family Labels R#6** *(one copy per student)*
- **scissors**
- **adhesive magnet** *(sold in rolls or strips at most craft departments)*

PREPARATION:

- **Make a sample family photo frame.**
- **Cut a small piece of magnet for each student.**
- **Write the word "family" at the top of the chart paper.**

R#2

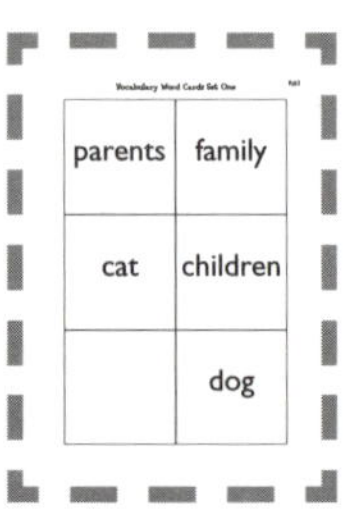

R#3

R#6

Students learn about the word "family."

Students are introduced to the word "family."

- The teacher introduces the "family" vocabulary word. The teacher shows and reads the vocabulary word.
- The teacher leads the students in **saying** the word at least three to five times.
- The teacher asks students to **say** what they think a family is. The teacher may ask students specific questions to help them think about what a family is.
- The teacher writes each student response on the chart paper, exactly as it was expressed by the student. For students who are non-verbal, program all or part of the Student Script into a Step-by-Step communicator, or program one line from the Student Script into a LITTLEmack communicator.
- The students **read** each line that has been written on the chart paper.
- The teacher writes the word "family" on a piece of construction paper or sentence strip with a definition, such as: a group of people who love each other and who live together. The teacher creates the definition to include as many features of the students' definitions as possible.

NOTE: The definition for "family" may vary. Use a definition that will be most clearly understood by your students.

- The teacher shows the students the pictures of families. As each picture is shown, the teacher leads the students in **saying** the word "family," or in **answering** the question, "What is this a picture of?"

OPTION: Ask students to **identify** a picture of a family. The student may then **select** any of the family pictures.

Teacher Script

"What is a family?"
"Who are the people in a family?"
"Are pets part of a family?"
"How do people in a family treat each other?"
"What do families do together?"

Student Script

"The people you live with."
"Your mom. Your brothers and sisters. Your dad."
"A cat and dog are part of a family."
"They love you."
"They come to your birthday parties."

Students do a picture walk through the book, "Families."

- The teacher shows students the book "Families."
- Students **say** what they think the book is going to be about. Students **comment** on the picture on the front cover.
- The teacher gives each student a chance to hold the book. As each student holds the book, the teacher gives the student a directive related to the book.

Teacher Script

"Show us the front of the book."
"Show us the back of the book."
"Show us the first page."
"Show us a picture in the book."
"Can you point to a word in the book?"
(Hand the book to the student upside down.)
"Will you show us the first page of the book?"

- Each student follows the direction given to him/her by the teacher.
- The teacher holds the book and asks students to take turns **turning the pages.**
- On each page, the teacher asks a student to **identify** a family. The student may take the "family" vocabulary card and place it on a picture of a family.
- The teacher asks students to **comment** on the family.

Students share pictures of their own families with each other.

- The teacher explains that everybody is part of a family, and asks if anybody would like to share with the class a picture of their family.
- Students take turns **showing** the picture of their family to the class.
- Students **tell** their classmates about their family, **saying** the name and relation or role of each family member. "This is nanny. She is my grandmother. This is Bob. He is my stepdad. This is Rico. He's our cat."

Students make a special frame (matting) for their family picture.

- The teacher shows students his/her family photo frame. The teacher tells the students about his/her family in the photo.
- Students **select** a color they would like to use to begin painting.
- Students free **paint** on the card stock.
- Students **select** and **paint** with an additional color if preferred.
- Students **dry** their paintings.
- Students **select** family words and/or pictures *(from R#6)* that they would like to have on their family photo frame.
- Students **cut** out the selected words/pictures.
- Students **glue** their family photo in the center of the card stock.
- Students **glue** their selected words/pictures around the photo, creating a frame around the photo.
- Students put the magnet on the back of the frame.
- Students take turns **showing** their family photo frames to their classmates.

"A family is a unit composed not only of children but of men, women, an occasional animal, and the common cold."

OGDEN NASH

MATERIALS:

- **vocabulary cards Set One R#2, R#3**
- **Family Labels R#6** *(bottom half - one per student)*
- **scissors**
- **glue**
- **writing tools**
- **construction paper** *(8 1/2" x 11")* **in assorted colors**
- **"Families"** *by Ann Morris*
- **completed Parent Information sheets R#1**
- **parent photos**
- **note cards** *(3" x 5")*
- **chart paper** *(two sheets)*
- **black marker**
- **white paper**
- **crackers** *(or small snacks that can be counted)*
- **milk and juice**
- **cups and plates**
- **children's books**
- **digital camera**
- **All-Turn-It® spinner** *(optional)*

PREPARATION:

- **Write the word "parents" at the top of the chart paper.**
- **Cut the white paper into strips approx. 8" x 2"** *(one strip per student).*
- **Parent Cards - On each note card, write one of the Parent Card Phrases.**
- **Put the Parent Cards in a stack.**

R#2

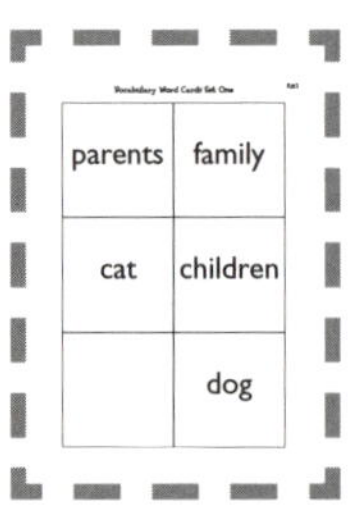

R#3

R#6

Students learn about the word "parents."

Part 1
Students review the word "family."

- The teacher shows each student a different random page of the book "Families" and asks a student to **count** how many people are in that family. Each student **writes** that number on a white board or on chart paper.
- The students **read** the numbers that are on the board.
- The teacher explains to students that families can be made up of many different people, and that families are many different sizes.
- The teacher explains to students that they are each going to make a picture of a family.
- The teacher asks each student to **write** the word "family" on the strip of white paper.
- Students **select** a color of construction paper.
- Students **glue** the word strip on the construction paper.
- Students are instructed to **cut** out the pictures from the Family Labels.
- Students **select** the pictures of the members they want to use to make a family picture.
- Students **glue** those pictures on their paper.
- Students **show** their family picture to each other.
- Students may think of a name for their family and **tell** others the name.
- Each student **counts** up how many members are in the family that he/she created and **tells** the other students.

Part 2
Students learn about the word "parents."

- Show students the "parents" vocabulary card. Lead students in **saying** the word three to five times.
- The students do a picture walk through the book "Families," and **identify** the parent(s) on each page. A student may place the "parent" vocabulary card on the picture of the parent(s).
- Students **comment** on each picture.

Students share with the class the photo of their parent(s).

- Students take turns **showing** each other the photo of their parent(s).
- As students show the photo, they **read** the Parent Information sheet to the class.

NOTE: During these types of activities when students take turns sharing, consider giving special recognition to the child who is sharing, while they are sharing. Some options might include:

- Designate a special chair as the Sharing Chair for the student who is doing the sharing. This could be a unique chair or a decorated chair, or just a regular chair with the label The Sharing Chair on or near it.
- Create a Talking Stick (or talking shell, talking rock, etc.). Decorate this so it's fun and colorful and appealing to students. Make it easy for students to grasp and hold.
- Designate a special hat as the Sharing Hat. This could be a sombrero, a cowboy hat, a Dr. Seuss style hat, or any other fun and colorful hat.

Explain to the other students that when there is somebody in the Sharing Chair, using the Talking Stick, or wearing the Sharing Hat, everybody listens to that person.

- The other students may **ask** the student additional questions about his/her parent(s).
- The student sharing **answers** any questions that are asked of him/her.

Child Script

"I painted today!"
"I read a dinosaur book."
"Pizza."
"Billy was gone.
I played with Sam."
"The swings."

Students learn about the things that parents do.

- Students brainstorm a list of things that parents do. Students take turns **saying** one thing that their parent, or a parent does. The teacher writes each student response on the chart paper.

NOTE: Keep this list for Writing Lesson #2.

- Students take turns **turning the pages** of the "Families" book. On each page, the teacher asks a student to **say** what the parent(s) is doing. The teacher writes this on the chart paper, if it is not already listed.
- Students **read** the list of things that parents do.
- Tell students that they are going to practice doing some of the things that their parents do for them every day.
- Divide students into two teams, Children and Parents. The Parents team draws or **spins** for a Parent Card.
- The Parents team **reads** the card. The teacher models how to do that particular Parent action.

Parent Script

"What else did you do?"
"What was for lunch?"
"Who did you play with today?"
"What did you play outside?"

- The Parents team does the action indicated on the card for the Children team.
- When each of the Parent Cards have been drawn, the Children and Parents change roles.

PARENT CARD PHRASES

Fix a snack for the children
The Parents **count** out three crackers for each of the Children. The Parents **ask** the Children if they would like milk or juice. The Children **name** or **select** the kind of beverage they would like. The Parents pour and serve the requested drinks.

Read a book to the children
Each Parent **asks** one of the Children to **choose** a book. Each Parent **reads** that book to that Child. The Child **turns the pages** of the book and **comments** on the book.

Hug the children
The Parents **ask** the Children if they would like a hug. The Children **say** if they would or would not like a hug.

Take pictures of the children
Each Parent **says** to a child, "Say cheese." The Child **says** "cheese" and the Parent **takes their picture.**

Listen to the children
Each Parent **asks** a Child to **tell** him/her about their day. The Child **tells** the parent about his/her day while the Parent listens and **asks** questions of the child.

MATERIALS:

- **vocabulary cards Set One R#2, R#3**
- **parent photos from Learning New Words Lesson #2**
- **student picture/name cards**
- **pictures of different children** *(include photos of students)*
- **construction paper** *(8 1/2" x 11")*
- **"Families"** *by Ann Morris*
- **black marker**
- **digital camera** *(or school photos of students)*
- **white strips of paper** *(approximately 6" x 3")*
- **writing tools**
- **glue**
- **crayons**
- **drawing paper**
- **children's books**
- **stickers and/or miscellaneous decorations**
- **chart paper**
- **two large sheets of colored poster board**
- **sentence strips** *(one per student)*
- **All-Turn-It® spinner** *(optional)*

PREPARATION:

- **Put the parent photos in a stack or on the large overlay of the All-Turn-It® spinner.**
- **On the top of a sheet of poster board, glue on the "children" vocabulary picture/symbol R#2. Then use a black marker to write the words,** "Children in Room _______."
- **On the top of the other sheet of poster board, write this title at the top:** "Children in Room _______ Like Lots of Things!"
- **On each sentence strip write the sentences:** My name is _______________. I like to____.
- **On the chart paper, write this title at the top:** Things Children Do.

Students learn about the word "children."

Part 1
Students review the word "parents."

Students play the game "Is This Your Parent?"

- Students take turns **spinning** or drawing for a parent photo.
- The student whose turn it is **names,** or **selects** a picture/name card of the student who this is the parent of. The student continues to guess until he/she **identifies** the correct student.

Part 2
Students learn about the word "children."

- Show students the "children" vocabulary card. Read the word.
- Lead the students in **saying** the word at least three to five times.
- Students take turns **selecting** a picture of children and **show** it to the class.

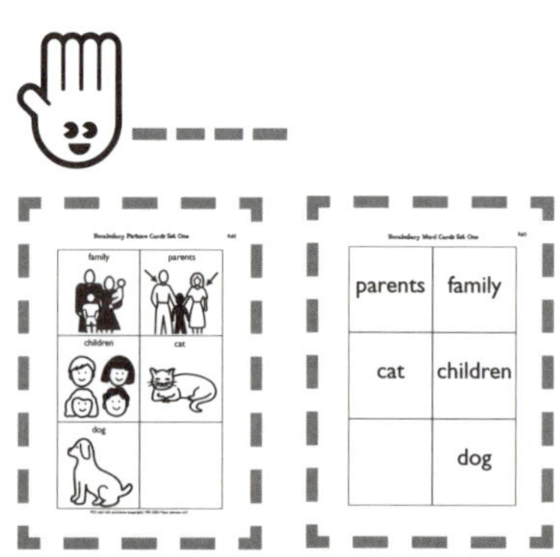

R#2 R#3

- As each picture is shown, put the "children" vocabulary card next to the picture of children and lead students in **saying** the word "children."
- Ask the students to come gather in a group. Show students the "children" vocabulary card and explain to students that they are children.
- Ask small groups of two to three students to come up front. Put the "children" vocabulary card near them and lead the students in **saying** the word multiple times.
- Give directions to the group of children. Students follow the directions.

"Will all the children please come and help me **read** a story?"

"Children who want to turn a page need to **say,** 'please.' "

"All children should take out paper and a box of crayons and **draw** a picture of children."

"The children are going to **sing** 'If You're Happy and You Know It.' Ready? Let's sing!"

NOTE: Add additional directions appropriate to the age, interests, and abilities of your students.

Students make a poster entitled, "Children in Room ________ ."

- Show students the poster board, that says, "Children in Room ______."
- Explain to students that they are going to make a poster of the children in their classroom.
- Students **select** a color of construction paper.
- Students **write** their name on a white slip of paper.
- The names are put on display *(with student pictures if necessary)*, and each student **selects** a name of a student in their class.
- Each student **takes a picture** of their selected student. If a camera is not available, use school photos or have students **draw** pictures of themselves or another student. The photo and name slip are then given to that student.
- Students **glue** their photo, and their name slip, on the construction paper to make a name sign.
- Students decorate their name signs by **coloring** designs, adding stickers, or **gluing** on decorations.
- Students **glue** or **staple** their name signs on the poster.
- Attach the poster to a wall or a bulletin board so it is easily visible.
- Explain to students that their poster has pictures of children from their class on it. Lead students in **reading** the title of the poster, "Children in Room ______."

"There are no seven wonders in the eyes of a child. There are seven million."

WALT STREIGHTIFF

Students make a list of the things that children do.

- Students brainstorm a list of things that children do *(run, play, learn, go to school, paint, hang out together)*. Each student **says** one thing that children do. Write each student response on the chart paper.

NOTE: Keep this list for Vocabulary Activity #3.

- Lead students in a picture walk through the book, "Families." Students take turns **turning the pages** of the book.
- On each page, students **say** what the children on that page are doing *(reading, playing instruments, cooking, singing, camping)*.
- Write each thing on the chart paper if it is not already listed.
- Each student **names** or **selects** one of these things that they like to do.
- Each student fills in the blanks on the sentence strip:
  "My name is ____________ .
  I like to ____________."
  Students **write** their name in the first blank, and **write** the thing they like to do in the second blank.
- Students **glue** their sentence strip on the poster entitled, "Children in Room ____ Like Lots of Things!"
- Put this poster next to the "Children in Room ______" poster or bulletin board.

LESSON #4

Students learn about the word "cat."

MATERIALS:

- **construction paper** *(11" x 17") (two sheets)*
- **black marker**
- **pictures of children** *(from Lesson #3)*
- **pictures of parents from Lesson #3 or pictures of adults**
- **All-Turn-It® spinner** *(optional)*
- **vocabulary cards Set One R#2, R#3**
- **Vocabulary Picture Cards R#2**
- **Cat Description Pictures/Symbols R#7**
- **Cat Body Parts Pictures/Symbols R#8**
- **Calico Cat Direction Script R#9** *(one per student)*
- **pictures of cats or stuffed animal cats**
- **poster board** *(one large sheet)*

PREPARATION:

- **At the top of each sheet of 11" x 17" construction paper, write the word** "children" **on one sheet and the word** "parents" **on the other sheet to make two signs. Glue the corresponding vocabulary picture card R#2 on each sign.**

- **Shuffle the pictures of parents and pictures of children. Put them in a stack, or put them on the large overlay of the All-Turn-It® spinner.**

- **With the black marker, draw an outline of a cat on the poster board, taking up as much of the poster board as possible. See cat example. Write the word "cat" on the poster board.**

- **Copy the Cat Description Pictures/Symbols R#7 and the Cat Body Parts Pictures/Symbols R#8 onto card stock. Cut out each card.**

- **Follow the Calico Cat Direction Script R#9 to make a sample calico cat.**

NOTE: Send a note home with students asking them to bring a stuffed cat from home if they have one.

OPTION: Have a real cat come visit on this day. Be sure and check with parents about allergies students may have. Or share a video clip of a movie about cats, such as Cats and Dogs or The Adventures of Milo and Otis.

MATERIALS FOR CALICO CAT CRAFT

- **Calico Cat Direction Script R#9** *(one per student)*
- **large dinner size paper plate** *(one per student)*
- **small dessert size paper plate** *(one per student)*
- **pom-poms** *(pink, white, red - for the nose)*
- **buttons** *(dark colors - for the eyes)*
- **yarn** *(for the whiskers)*
- **small squares of fabric** *(assorted colors, styles, textures)*
- **clothespins, clamp on style** *(four per student)*
- **pipe cleaners in assorted colors** *(one per student)*
- **one inch construction paper triangles** *(assorted colors)*
- **red felt or fun foam cut into cat tongue shapes**
- **stapler, glue, scissors**

CAT

R#2

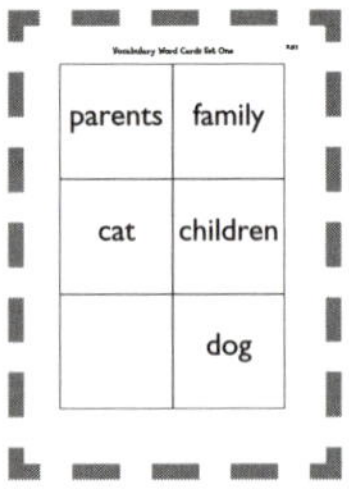

parents	family
cat	children
	dog

R#3

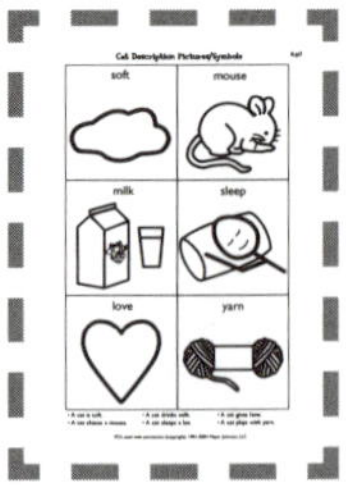

R#7

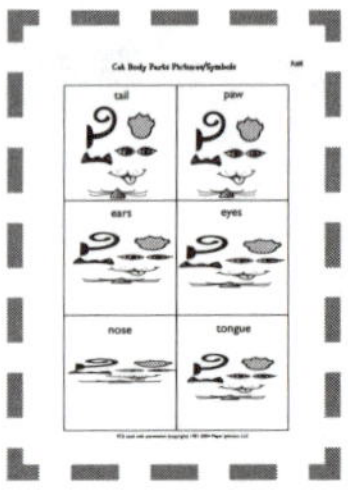

R#8

R#9

> **Teacher Note:** Keep the calico cats that the students create for use in Learning New Words Lesson #5.

Part 1
Students review the words "children" and "parents."

Students categorize pictures of parents and pictures of children.

- Show students the "children" and "parents" signs. Lead students in **saying** each word as the sign is shown.
- Explain to students that they are going to take turns selecting a picture, decide if it's a picture of parents or a picture of children, and put the picture on the "children" or "parents" sign.
- Students take turns drawing or **spinning** for a picture.
- The student, or the class, **says** if it is a picture of parents or a picture of children.
- The student places the picture on the "children" or "parents" sign, or **selects** the sign on which the picture belongs.

NOTE: The pictures may be **glued** on the signs to create "children" and "parents" posters to be put on display.

OPTION: Put the pictures of children and parents on display. Show students a container with a "parents" or "children" vocabulary card attached. Ask the student to **select** a picture of children, or parents, and place it in the matching container.

Part 2
Students learn about the word "cat."

- Show students the "cat" vocabulary card. Read the word.
- Lead the students in **saying** the word at least three to five times.
- Ask students to **say** if they do or do not have a cat.
- Show students the cat pictures, stuffed animal cat(s), or movie clip, or have a real cat visit at this time.
- Ask students to **say** something about the cat - how a cat looks, what a cat does, or what a cat is like. Students may also **select** one of the Cat Description Pictures/Symbols. Write each student response on the poster board, inside the cat outline.
- Students **read** the list of cat characteristics.

NOTE: Keep this list for use in Vocabulary Activity #4.

Teacher Script
"What does the cat look like?"
"How does the cat feel?"
"How does a cat have fun?"
"What does a cat do all day?"
"What does a cat drink?"

Students use assorted materials to make a calico cat.

- Show students a sample calico cat.
- Students take turns **selecting** a Cat Body Parts Picture/Symbol and putting the card on the appropriate part of the sample cat.
- Students **read** the Calico Cat Directions Script.
- Students follow directions to complete each step.

Student Script
"Pretty cat."
"It's furry."
"He chases things."
"Sleeps a lot."
"A cat drinks water."

LESSON #5

Part 1

MATERIALS:

- vocabulary cards Set One R#2, R#3
- Cat Show Award Template R#10
- cat stickers *(optional)*
- bright colored copy paper or card stock
- calico cats *(created in Learning New Words Lesson #4)*
- something with wheels and a flat surface to pull something on, such as a skateboard or scooter board, with a rope attached
- a box with an open front on which to display a calico cat
- white construction paper
- crayons/markers
- writing tools
- duct tape or Velcro®
- black marker or gold marker/pen

PREPARATION:

- Attach the box with the open front to the surface of the skateboard/scooter. Use duct tape or Velcro®.

- Copy the Cat Show Award Template onto various bright colors of copy paper or card stock. Cut them out. Use a black marker or gold pen/marker to write different categories on the awards, such as, "Most Colorful," "Best in Show," "Honorable Mention." The awards can be decorated with cat stickers.

R#2

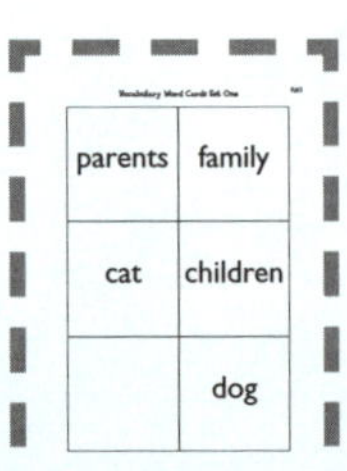

R#3

R#10

Students learn about the word "dog."

Part 1
Students review the word "cat."

Students participate in a cat show in which they display and show off their calico cats.

- Show students the "cat" vocabulary card. Lead the students in **saying** the word three to five times.

- Move the "cat" vocabulary card next to each calico cat. As the card is next to each cat, lead students in **saying** the word, "cat."

- Students **say**, or **select**, a name for their calico cat.

- Students **write** the cat name on a piece of white construction paper to create a name sign.

- Students **color** and decorate the name sign.

- Students are called up by the teacher to show their calico cat.

- As each student is called up, he/she brings their cat, places the cat in the open box on the wheeled platform, attaches the cat name sign, and pulls the calico cat across the front of the room.

- When the student is done showing the cat, he/she **says** at least two things about the cat. Ex: "My cat has a pink nose. My cat has a black tail. My cat's name is Snuggles."

- Other students may **ask** the student questions about and/or **comment** about the cat. For students who are non-verbal, record the Student Script into a LITTLE Step-by-Step communicator.

- When all students have had a chance to show their calico cat, the teacher puts an award on each calico cat. Make certain that every calico cat gets an award.

- As each student and their cat receive an award, the class **claps** for the student and their cat.

Student Script
"What is your cat's name?"
"Your cat has a cool (purple tail)!"
"What color eyes does she have?"
"I like her (pointy ears)!"

"Cats know how to obtain food without labor, shelter without confinement, and love without penalties."

WL GEORGE

Part 2

MATERIALS:

- vocabulary cards Set One R#2, R#3
- Dog Questions R#11
- various pictures or photos of dogs
- chart paper • black marker
- note cards *(3"x5" or larger)*
- All-Turn-It® spinner *(optional)*

PREPARATION:

- Create Dog Question Cards. Write each question from R#11 on a note card. Put the Dog Question Cards in a stack or on the large overlay of the All-Turn-It® spinner.

Students learn about the word "dog."

- Show students the "dog" vocabulary card. Read the word.
- Lead the students in **saying** the word at least three to five times.
- Students take turns **selecting** and **showing** a picture of a dog.
- Students take turns drawing or **spinning** for and **reading** a Dog Question Card.
- The other students **answer** the question.
- As each answer is given, the teacher writes the question and answer as a sentence on the chart paper. *(A dog eats dog food. A dog drinks water.)*
- The class **reads** the sentences.

Part 3

MATERIALS:

- Dog Questions R#11
- The Big Dog in the Pet Shop R#12
- card stock *(four sheets)*
- poster board *(one large sheet)*
- crayons/markers
- adhesive Velcro®
- adult scissors

PREPARATION:

- Copy the Dog Questions R#11 onto card stock *(three copies)*. Color the Dog Picture Cards, two of each of the following colors: brown, black, yellow, orange, white, gray. Cut them out. Put a small strip of rough Velcro® on the back of each card.
- On the poster board, write the title, "The Big Dog in the Pet Shop." Below the title, write out the song text from R#12.
- Put a small piece of soft Velcro® on each blank line.
- Copy R#12 onto card stock. Put a piece of soft Velcro® in the center of the window.

OPTION: Do an internet search for the tune, "How Much is That Doggie in the Window?"

Students sing a song about a dog.

- The teacher shows students each of the different color dogs. As each dog is shown, the teacher asks the student what color the dog is. Students **name** the color and then **name** the animal *(yellow dog, brown dog)*.
- The teacher explains to students that they are going to be singing a song about a dog. The teacher shows the students the pet shop window, and explains that some dogs are sold in pet shops.
- The teacher explains to students that they are going to pretend they are at a pet shop, and ask the pet shop owner about a big dog in the shop.
- The teacher leads the students in **reading** the lyrics to the song.
- After the first stanza is read, the teacher directs a student to **select** a Dog Picture Card. The student places the card in the pet shop window, **shows** the pet shop window to the class, and **says** the color of the dog.
- The teacher leads students in **reading** the second stanza. The teacher places the matching Dog Picture Card on the first blank, then moves it to the second blank. As the students arrive at each blank, they **say** the name of the color.
- The teacher leads students in **singing** the song to the tune of, "How Much is that Doggie in the Window." Each time the song is sung, a new student is chosen to **select** a Dog Picture Card and **show** the card to the students during the second stanza.

R#2

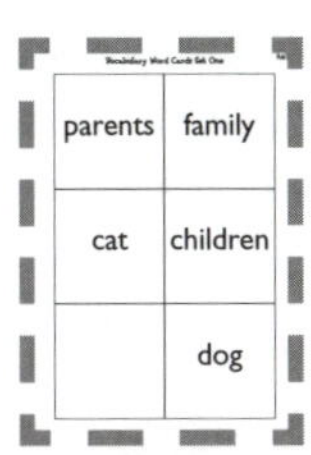

R#3

R#11

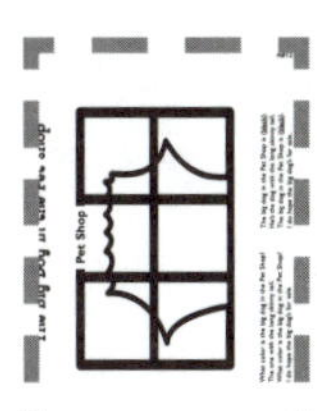
R#12

LEARNING NEW WORDS

EXTENSION ACTIVITIES

FAMILY:

FAMILY JOURNAL ENTRY

Students take turns bringing home a special teddy bear (or other stuffed creature) that the student and their family "adopt" for a day or two, along with a journal and, if possible, a camera. The family and student **write** in a special journal, from the teddy bear's perspective, about the experiences the teddy bear had with the family. *Ex: I ate pizza. I helped with the dishes. I watched "Wheel of Fortune." I went for a walk to the park. I had a bedtime snack.* The student also **takes pictures** of the bear with his/her family. When the teddy bear and journal come back to school, the student **reads** the journal entries from the time the bear was with his/her family. The student **shows** the class any pictures that were taken of the teddy bear with his/her family.

PARENT:

HOST A PARENT TEA, OR A PARENT DESSERT NIGHT

Students make invitations to a special parent tea (during the day) or a special dessert night. Students **color** the invitations and **write** a special note to their parent(s) asking them to come. Students make refreshments for the event. At the event, students do special centers with their parents such as: **painting** a picture together of the child and parent, **writing** about a memory of the parent and child, **taking a picture** of the parent and child, partnering up as parent/child for a special square dance.

CHILDREN:

PLAY "WHO'S WHO?"

Send a note home asking parents to send in a baby picture of their child. Put the baby pictures on the All-Turn-It® spinner, or in a stack. The students take turns drawing, or **spinning** for, a baby picture. The student **show**s the baby picture to the class. The students then take turns **naming,** or **selecting** from a choice of current student photos, the child in the class most resembling that baby picture.

CAT:

WHERE'S THE CAT HIDING?

Explain to students that cats often like to hide in secret places. Divide students up into two teams, the Cats and the Children. Give the Cats a "cat" vocabulary card and the Children a "children" vocabulary card. Cats could also wear cat ear headbands. The Children go out into another room, and the Cats are instructed to go hide from the Children. The Cats find a hiding place. The Children come back into the room and **say,** "Where is that cat?" The Cats all respond in unison by **saying,** "meow." The Children then move around the room, looking for the Cats. When they find a Cat, they **say,** "There's that cat!"

DOG:

WHAT IS IT LIKE TO BE A DOG?

Students make dog ear headbands by **cutting** out a strip of tag board and two dog ears from a template. Students **color** the ears and **glue** them on the strip. A teacher helps the students to adjust the length of the strip and **staple** it together to fit the student's head. The students follow a recipe for people Puppy Chow, found by doing an Internet search for a Puppy Chow recipe. Students put on their dog ear headbands and eat a bowl of people Puppy Chow.

unit 2

my family

The activities in this section provide students with oral language opportunities to actively use vocabulary words and understand their meaning.

Included in Part 6 - Reproducibles are optional vocabulary cards R#4 and R#5. These vocabulary cards are additional family members and may be used to support discussions about family.

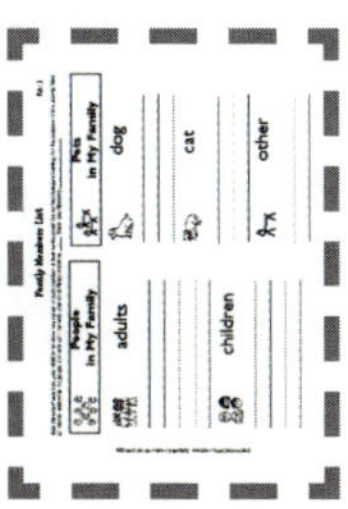

R#13

Teacher Note: **Prior to teaching Activity #1, send home the Family Members List R#13 with each student. In Activity #5, it is also recommended that a real dog come and visit on that day.**

part one

Throughout these **Vocabulary Activities,** students have opportunities to develop meaningful relationships and a sense of belonging as they interact with others in many large group activities.

This "character and community" icon will signal a lesson activity through which the sense of belonging can be reinforced.

ACTIVITY #1

Students make a family mobile.

MATERIALS:

- vocabulary cards Set One R#2, R#3
- pictures of families
- chart paper
- black marker
- Family Members List R#13 *(completed)*
- Family Mobile Templates R#14
- yarn in assorted colors
- crayons or tempera paint
- paint brushes • markers
- misc. decorations *(sequins, glitter, etc.)*
- glue
- small paper strips approximately 2" x 3"
- writing tools
- plastic hanger *(one per student)*
- white card stock
- tape
- stapler
- hole punch *(optional)*

PREPARATION:

- Put the family pictures on display.
- Write the word "family" at the top of the chart paper.
- Cut various colors of yarn into different lengths *(approximately 4", 6", 8")*.
- Make several copies of R#14 on card stock. Cut out each square, and separate the squares by the different family members.
- Make a sample family mobile.

R#2

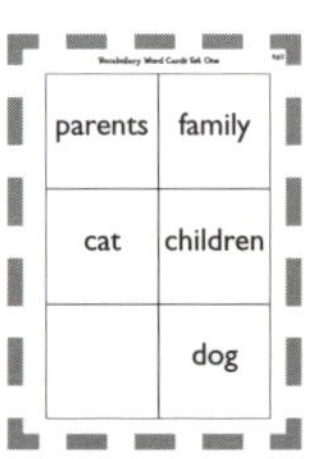

R#3

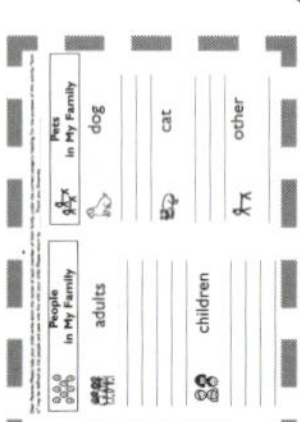
R#13

R#14

Teacher Note: **Prior to this lesson, send home the Family Members List R#13 with each student.**

Students brainstorm a list of different people and pets that could be members of a family.

- Show students the "family" vocabulary card. Lead students in **saying** the word at least three to five times.
- The teacher asks students to **select** and **show** a picture of a family, from the pictures on display.
- The teacher tells students that families are made up of different people, and sometimes pets.
- The teacher asks students to **name** a person or pet that is a part of some families.
- As each family member is named, the teacher, or the student, **writes** the name of each family member on the chart paper.
- When the list is completed, lead the students in **reading** the list of family members. Help students to think of, and **name**, additional family members and add those to the list.

Students make a family mobile.

- Show students the sample family mobile. Read the name of each family member that is part of the mobile.
- Give each student their Family Members List. Students take turns **reading** the name of each person and pet that is part of their family.
- Students bring their Family Members List to the area where the Family Mobile Templates are displayed. For each family member, a student takes a corresponding Family Mobile Template square.
- Students **select** the name of one family member on their list, and **select** the appropriate template.
- The student **writes** that family member's name on a strip of paper.
- The student **colors** or **paints** the template.
- The student **glues** on additional decorations to make the paper template look like that family member.
- As each template is decorated, the student **staples** the family member's name somewhere on the template, so it is hanging off of the bottom or side, and not covering the template.
- Students **select** a color of yarn to use to hang their decorated templates from the hanger.
- Students tape, **glue**, or **staple** one end of each length of yarn to the back of each template.
- Students help the teacher tie each strip of their yarn to the hanger. A hole punch may be used to put a hole in the template, and the yarn may be tied through that hole.
- Students **show** their completed mobile to each other, and **read** the name of each family member.

Students interview their parents about things from their childhood, and write a report from the interview.

Students learn about the parent interview they are going to do.

- Show students the "parent" vocabulary card. Lead the students in **saying** the word at least three to five times.
- Show students the "children" vocabulary card. Lead the students in **saying** the word at least three to five times.
- Explain to students that although their parents are grown-ups now, they were once children too.
- Explain to students that they are going to find out what their parents were like when they were children.
- Give each student a Parent Interview. Explain to students that these are the questions they are going to **ask** one of their parents.
- Lead students in **reading** each question on the Parent Interview.

Students interview a parent.

- Students bring home the Parent Interview.
- Students **ask** their parent the questions on the Parent Interview.
- Students **write** the answers on the Parent Interview.
- Students bring the Parent Interview back to school.

Students read their Parent Reports to the class.

- The teacher or student completes the Parent Report from the Parent Interview, to use as a guide in sharing with the class.
- Students take turns **reading** their Parent Reports to the class.
- The student **shows** pictures he/she has brought of his/her parent.

"There is a garden in every childhood, an enchanted place where colors are brighter, the air softer, and the morning more fragrant than ever again."

ELIZABETH LAWRENCE

Teacher Note: This lesson will need to be completed over at least two days.

MATERIALS:

- **vocabulary cards Set One R#2, R#3**
- **Parent Interview R#15** *(one per student)*
- **Parent Report R#16** *(one per student)*
- **parent photos** *(sent in from home)*
- **writing tools**

R#2

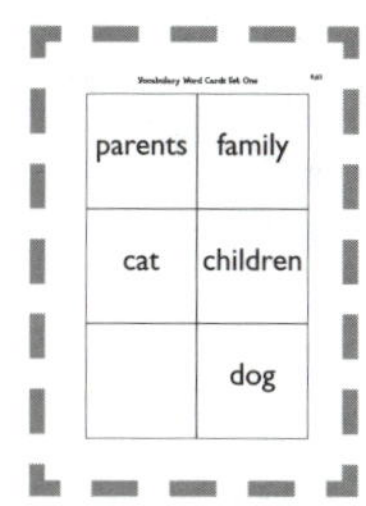

R#3

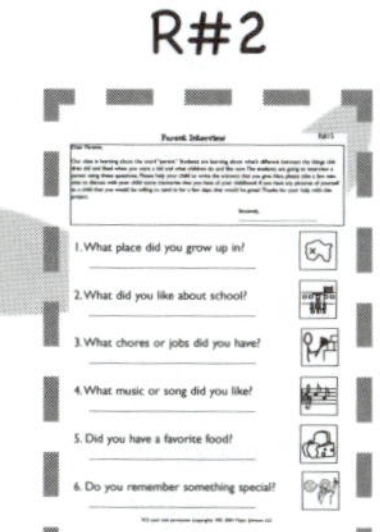

R#15

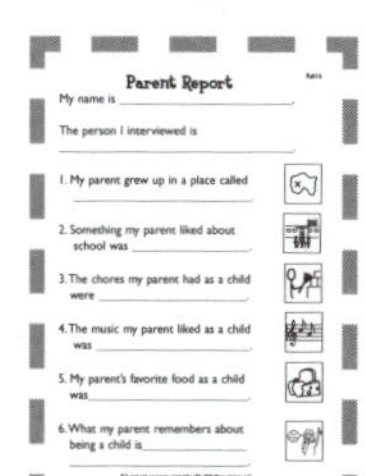

R#16

Students participate in and respond to popular children's activities.

MATERIALS:

- **list of things children like to do** *(from Learning New Words Lesson #3)*
- **Children's Activity Centers materials**
  - puzzles - colorful, fun picture books
  - games *(board games, card games)*
  - CD or tape player with children's albums
  - Play-Doh® with cookie cutters - drawing paper
  - paintbrushes, tempera paint - dress up clothes
  - snack - balls *(Koosh balls, texture balls, etc.)*
  - building blocks *(Bristle Blocks, Legos®, wooden blocks)*
  - toy cars, trucks, etc.
  - make believe *(plastic figurines, house, etc.)*
- **table or area to set up each center**
- **Children's Activities Plan R#17** *(one per student)*
- **Children's Activities Pictures/Symbols R#18** *(one per student)*
- **Children's Activities Response Sheet R#19** *(one or more per student)*
- **writing tools**
- **scissors**
- **glue**
- **crayons/markers**
- **construction paper**
- **drawing paper**

R#17-R#19

PREPARATION:

- **Decide what centers you will be using and set up those centers. Make each center student accessible.**

- **Write the name of each activity center on a piece of construction paper and glue the corresponding picture/symbol (R#18) on the paper to make activity center signs.**

- **Create a children's activities picture/symbol sheet from which students can select activity centers. Use your own symbols** *(2" size)* **or R#18.**

- **Assign a staff or peer helper to each activity center.**

Teacher Note: Complete **Learning New Words Lesson #3** before teaching this lesson.

Students talk about things children like to do.

- Lead students in **reading** the list of things children do *(from Learning New Words Lesson #3).*

- Explain to students that today they are going to practice being "children" and will do some of the things that most children like to do.

Students learn about the different Children's Activity Centers.

- The teacher gives each student a Children's Activities Pictures/Symbols sheet and Children's Activities Plan.

- The teacher leads the students to each activity center and leads the students in **reading** the activity center sign.

- The teacher explains to students about that center.

- The students **identify** that picture/symbol on their Children's Activities Pictures/Symbols sheet.

- When all the activity centers have been explained, students **select** three children's activities that they want to do.

- Students **color** and **cut** out the three pictures/symbols that match their chosen activities.

- Students **select** the activity they want to do first and **glue** that picture/symbol on the first box of the Children's Activities Plan.

- Students **select** the activity they want to do next and **glue** that picture/symbol on the second box.

- Students **select** the activity they want to do last and **glue** that picture/symbol on the last box.

Students participate in their selected Children's Activity Centers.

- Direct students to **read** their first sentence on their Children's Activities Plan.

- Direct students to go to that first Children's Activity Center and do the activity. Direct students to **match** the picture/symbol on their Children's Activities Plan to the picture/symbol on the activity center sign.

- Students participate in the activity. After five to ten minutes, signal students to go to their next center.

- Students repeat this process for sentences two and three on their Children's Activities Plan.

Students respond to the children's activities.

- A student or the teacher **reads** the Children's Activities Response Sheet Directions at the bottom of the response sheet.

- Students follow directions to complete the response sheet.

Students participate in a cat language activity.

Students participate in a language activity with a stuffed animal cat.

- Explain to students that the "cat" is going to take turns sitting with the students.
- Lead the students in **reading** the sentence, "The cat is sitting with ___________________."
- Students take turns drawing or **spinning** for a student picture.
- When the picture is selected, it is placed (using double sided tape) on the blank line in the written sentence.
- Students **read** that sentence with the student's name. The student with the cat **brings** the cat to that student.
- The activity continues until every student has had a turn at holding the cat.

Students learn about and use the Cat Activities Language Boards.

- Show students the "cat" vocabulary word. Lead students in **saying** the word at least three to five times.
- Lead students in **reading** the list of things that describe cats, from Learning New Words Lesson #4.
- Show students the cat cutout and explain that they will each have a picture and a cat cutout of their own, and will need to make the cat do what the sentence that is read says the cat is doing.
- Read an example sentence from the Cat Activities Script and show the cat doing that on the language board.
- Give each student a Cat Indoor Activities Language Board and a cat cutout.
- Give one student the Cat Activities Script and ask the student to **read** the first sentence.
- After the student has read the sentence, the other students pick up their cat and move their cat to the appropriate location.
- When all sentences involving the Cat Indoor Activities Language Board have been read, switch to the Cat Outdoor Activities Language Board.

Students write sentences about a cat doing different things.

- Give each student a Cat Activity Sentences page.
- Lead students in **reading** the first sentence together.
- Tell students to **look** at the picture next to that sentence and **say** where the cat is.
- Tell students to **select** and **write** the missing word to complete the sentence.
- Continue this process for each sentence on the page.

R#2-#3 R#20-R#23

First complete Learning New Words Lesson #4.

MATERIALS:

- **vocabulary cards Set One R#2, R#3**
- **stuffed animal cat**
- **large sheet of poster board**
- **black marker**
- **student pictures**
- **tape**
- **paper clips**
- **Cat Activities Script R#20**
- **Cat Indoor and Outdoor Activities Language Boards R#21, R#22**
- **Cat Activity Sentences R#23**
- **card stock**
- **adult scissors**
- **writing tools**
- **All-Turn-It® spinner** *(optional)*
- **list of things that describe cats** *(from Learning New Words Lesson #4)*

PREPARATION:

- **Write the sentence, "The cat is sitting with _______" on the sheet of poster board, or on a white board.**
- **Put the student pictures in a stack, or on the large overlay of the All-Turn-It® spinner.**
- **Copy the Cat Indoor and Outdoor Activities Language Boards** *(R#21 and R#22)* **onto card stock** *(one per student)*.
- **Cut on the dotted line at the top strip of each language board. Cut out the cat picture on the strip. Paper clip the cat cutout on the board.**

ACTIVITY #5

Students learn about responsibilities in caring for a dog.

MATERIALS:

• vocabulary cards Set One R#2, R#3
• photos of various dogs, and photos of people with dogs
• dog - real dog, stuffed animal dog, a staff or student in a dog costume/headband

NOTE: If possible, invite a dog owner to come in with their dog, show the dog, and talk about what it's like to have a dog for a pet.

• card stock
• note cards 3" x 5"
• chart paper • black marker
• Dog Responsibility Cards R#24
• dog care materials and supplies
• adult scissors • tape
• white drawing paper • tempera paints *(darker, "dog" paint colors)*, paintbrushes
• All-Turn-It® spinner *(optional)*

PREPARATION:

• Copy the Dog Responsibility Cards onto card stock. Cut out the ten cards and put them in a stack, or place them faceup on the large overlay of the All-Turn-It® spinner.

• Create a VET sign by writing the word on card stock.

R#2

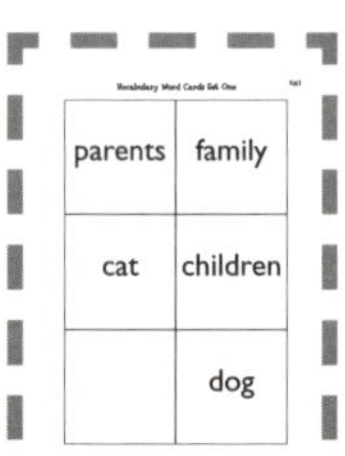

R#3

R#24

Students brainstorm a list of things that are good about having a dog for a pet.

- Ask students to **say** if they have a dog.
- Show students pictures or photos of people with their dogs. Students **comment** on the pictures, or **tell** the class about their dog.
- Students **say** the good things about having a dog for a pet.
- As each student response is given, the teacher writes the response on the chart paper.
- When the list is completed, students **read** the entire list together.

OPTION: Create Boardmaker pictures/symbols of good things about having a dog for a pet (love, fur, fun, exercise). Students **select** a symbol and the word on the symbol can be programmed into a voice output device. The student then **reads** the word to the class.

Students practice the responsibilities involved in taking care of a dog.

- Show students the "dog" vocabulary word. Lead students in **saying** the word at least three to five times.
- Refer to the list that students just made of good things about having a dog for a pet.
- Explain to students that there are lots of good things about having a dog for a pet.
- Explain to students that there are also many responsibilities in taking care of a dog.
- Ask students to **name** some of those responsibilities.
- Bring out the dog that will be used for this activity. Students may **vote** on the name of the dog.
- Explain to students that there are lots of things they will need to help them take care of the dog.

DOG CARE MATERIALS AND SUPPLIES

• bag
• dog leash
• dog brush
• dog food and food dish
• water and water dish
• ball
• VET sign

- Bring out the bag of dog supplies. Have students take turns pulling out one supply at a time. Ask the student to **say** what the dog supply is. Write down the name of the item on a 3" x 5" note card and tape it to the item to label it. Do this for each item that is pulled out of the bag. If appropriate, demonstrate how this item is used in caring for a dog *(brush, leash, water dish)*.

NOTE: After this activity, put the VET sign up in a visible place.

- Students take turns drawing or **spinning** for a Dog Responsibility Card.

- Students **name** the picture and **show** it to the class.

- Students **read** the sentence(s) on the card, and do what is written.

Students paint a picture of the kind of dog they would have for a pet.

- Students **look** at pictures of different kinds of dogs.

- Students **choose** their favorite dog from the pictures on display and **say** what they like about that kind of dog.

- Give students a sheet of drawing paper and explain that they are going to paint a picture of a dog - the kind of dog they would want to have, or a picture of the dog they already have.

- Ask students to **name** some different colors they may use in painting their dogs. As each color is named, get out that color of tempera paint to show the students.

- Students **paint** a dog on their paper.

OPTION: Cut out a dog template and let students apply paint to that.

- Students think of a name for their dog and **write** the name somewhere on their dog painting.

- Students **show** their dog paintings to their class after they **dry**.

"One reason a dog can be such a comfort when you're feeling blue is that he doesn't try to find out why."

AUTHOR UNKNOWN

VOCABULARY EXTENSION ACTIVITIES

FAMILY:

PLAY-DOH® FAMILY

Set out various colors of play-doh, and the following cookie cutters: person *(big and little)*, cat, dog, other pet animals. Tell students that they are going to make a family by cutting out different family members from play-doh. Students **select** the cookie cutters they want to use. Students **select** the color or colors of play-doh they want to use. Students use the cookie cutters to cut the shapes out of the play-doh. Students **tell** the other students about their play-doh families.

PARENT:

HOST A PARENT/CHILDREN SOFTBALL GAME

Invite parents from several classes or a grade level to come challenge the children in a softball game. Students make a T-shirt or ball cap for themselves and a parent. Students create banners for each team by **writing** the word PARENTS on one banner and the word CHILDREN on the other. Students **paint** the banners. Make a scoreboard for use during the game. Write the word PARENTS on one side and the word CHILDREN on the other side of the scoreboard. Students and parents cheer and **clap** for their team.

CHILDREN:

CHILDREN COLLAGE

Students **turn the pages** of various catalogs, newspapers, and magazines **looking** for pictures of children. When students **identify** pictures of children, they **cut** them out. Students gather back together and **show** their pictures to the other students. Each student **tells** the other students about the pictures. The students **discuss** the differences between children. Students **glue** their pictures on the poster board. A teacher, or a student, **writes** the word "children" on the top of the poster board.

CAT/DOG:

DO A JOKE SURVEY

Look up cat and dog jokes on the Internet or in joke books. Students divide up in teams - a cat team and a dog team. Each team **reads** several jokes about their animal and **votes** on their three favorite jokes. The students **write** those jokes on paper. The student teams go out in the school and **read** the jokes to others. They **ask** the people if they like each joke. Students tally the votes and **identify** which cat and dog jokes were the favorites.

CAT/DOG:

TIC-TAC-TOE

Make a large Tic-Tac-Toe board using a piece of construction paper or card stock. Make a set of about six cat and six dog pictures/symbols, sized so they will fit on the Tic-Tac-Toe board. Two students play. One student places the "cat" picture on their selected spot, and the other student places the "dog" picture on their selected spot. The board may be numbered with squares #1 - #9, and then students may **select** a square on which they would like somebody to help them place their cat or dog.

SECTION THREE

unit 2

my family

In these Word Wall Lessons, students will have opportunities to practice identifying, reading, spelling and writing the words.

part one

Throughout **The Word Wall Lessons**, students will have active roles as they read the word wall words, lead activities, and provide directions to other students.

As students engage in these roles of reader, leader, and teacher, look for opportunities to communicate to them the importance of what they are doing.

This "character and community" icon will signal a lesson activity through which students can have a valued role and learn to understand the importance of their role.

LESSON #1, #2, #3

LESSON 1

Students practice saying and writing the word wall words.

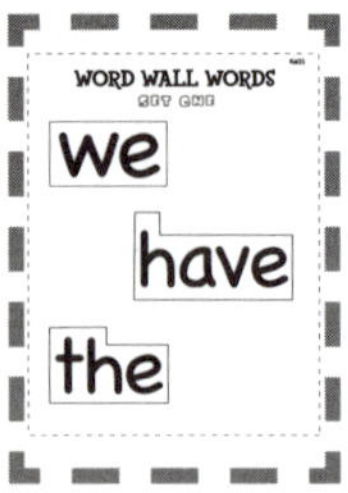
WORD WALL WORDS

we

have

the

R#25

MATERIALS:

- **Word Wall Words Set One R#25**
- **writing tools**
- **construction paper**
- **craft sticks or wooden dowels**
- **tape**

PREPARATION:

- **Make a letter sign for each letter in the word wall words. Write the letter in bold marker on the piece of construction paper and tape on a wooden dowel or craft stick.**

- The teacher names each word wall word and uses it in a sentence.

- As a class, the students shout the letters to each word.
  - Select one student for each letter of the word and give the student that letter sign.
  - Position students in a row in letter order. Each student holds up their letter sign and leads the class in **saying** or shouting out that letter.

- The students **write** each word wall word several times.

LESSON 2

Students participate in a Sentence Completion Activity.

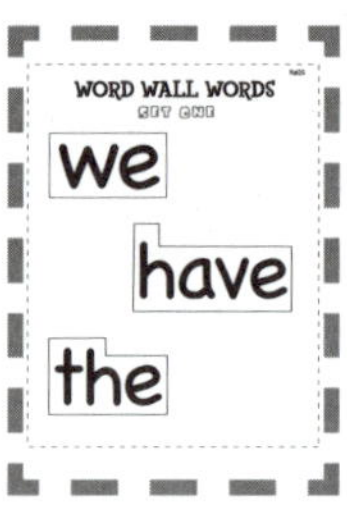
WORD WALL WORDS

we

have

the

R#25

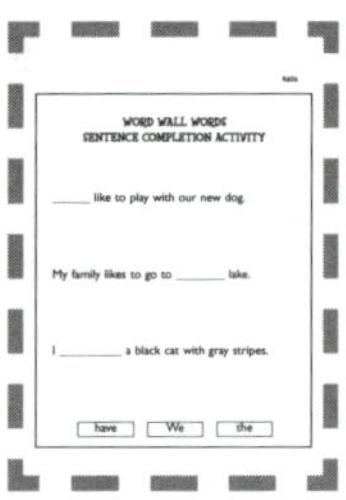
R#26

MATERIALS:

- **Word Wall Words Set One R#25**
- **flashlight**
- **writing tools**
- **Sentence Completion Activity R#26** *(one per student)*

PREPARATION:

- **Put each of the three word wall words up on the word wall.**

- The teacher names a word, and the student **identifies** the word by shining the flashlight beam on that word. The student leads the other students in **reading** that word.

- The teacher leads students in **reading** one sentence aloud and directs the students to **select** the word wall word that fits in the blank.

- The teacher assists each student in **identifying** and **writing** the correct word on their Sentence Completion Activity.

- Students **clap/chant** each word.

LESSON 3

Students participate in the Mind Reader activity.

MATERIALS:

- **Word Wall Words Set One R#25**
- **writing paper**
- **writing tools**
- **Mind Reader Script R#27**

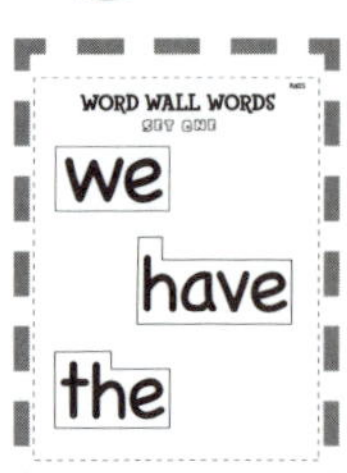
WORD WALL WORDS

we

have

the

R#25

R#27

- A student, or the teacher, **reads** the clues from the Mind Reader Script to the class.

- Students **select** the word which they think is being described. The teacher affirms the choice of word or redirects if needed.

- Students **write** the word on paper.

- As a class, students **clap/chant** the word wall word in any of the following ways:
  - Flap your wings like a chicken while you chant each letter.
  - Jump up and down like a frog, one jump per letter.
  - Use a whisper voice to **say** each letter while you **clap** the letter.

LESSON #4

PREPARATION:

- **Cut out a dozen bone shapes out of the sandpaper** *(to make them feel like dog biscuits)* **or use real dog bone biscuits.**
- **On each bone, write one of the three word wall words. The word wall words from Unit One** *(me, who, and, it, you, I, to, like, what)* **can also be used for review.**
- **Put the dog bones in a pile. Put the number cards in a stack, in a container to draw from, or faceup on the large overlay of the All-Turn-It® spinner.**

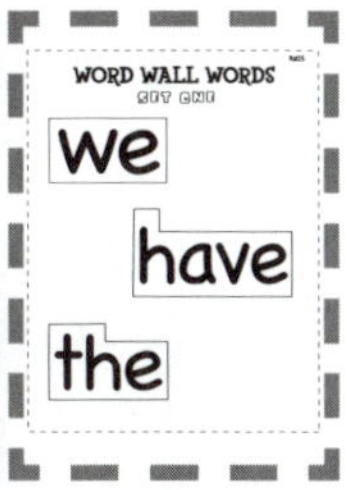
WORD WALL WORDS
we
have
the

R#25

- Students take turns drawing or **spinning** for a number card.
- The student takes that many bones and **reads** each word. The student then **shows** each bone to the class and leads the class in **reading** each word.
- After the words are read, the student feeds each bone to the dog puppet by grasping the bone by one end and pushing the other end of the bone through the dog puppet's open mouth. The dog puppeteer should grab the bone in it's mouth, make a happy, yippy barking sound, then quickly disappear and spit out the bone before reappearing for another bone.
- The bones may be recycled until all students have had multiple turns.

LESSON 4

Students play the word game, "Dog Bones."

MATERIALS:

- **Word Wall Words Set One R#25**
- **adult scissors**
- **sandpaper or 12 bone shaped dog biscuits**
- **black marker**
- **dog puppet** *(could be a brown paper bag puppet with floppy ears, a nose, a tongue, and google eyes)*
- **12 note cards** *(3" x 5")* **with number one, two or three written on each card**
- **All-Turn-It® spinner** *(optional)*

LESSON #5

MATERIALS:

- **Word Wall Words Set One R#25**
- **paper, pencils**
- **"The Parent Says" Script R#28**
- **crayons**
- **parent clothes such as suit, tie, dress, etc.** *(optional)*

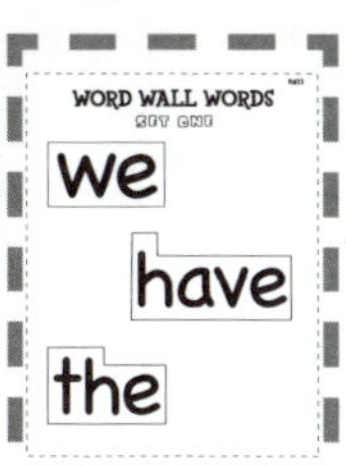
WORD WALL WORDS
we
have
the

R#25

"The Parent Says" Script

R#28

- Students take turns being the parent. For fun, the student playing the role of the parent can dress up in parent clothes.
- The parent **reads** a line from "The Parent Says" Script. If the parent **says**, "The parent says," then the other students do what the parent says to do. If the parent does not say, "The parent says," then the students should not do as told.
- Students take turns being the parent until everyone has had a turn.

LESSON 5

Students participate in the game "The Parent Says."

NOTE:
This is played like Simon Says.

Dear Parents,

Your child is currently working on the following words: **we, have, the.**

Whenever possible, please take the time to reinforce these words with your child by having him/her write the words, say the words, and spell the words. Below is a game to play with your child to help him/her learn each of the three word wall words.

Sincerely,

____

Word Concentration

Directions: Cut out each of the word wall words below. Place them face down on a work surface. To make the cards easier for students to pick up, place each card at the edge of the work surface, with one side hanging off the edge.

The players take turns choosing two word cards. The player reads each word that is drawn. If the words are a match, the player gets to keep the words. If the words are not a match, the word cards are put face down and the next player takes a turn.

If your child is non-verbal, record each word on a voice output device as it is drawn so that he/she can say the word. Show your child both words, then show the same/different pictures/symbols.

Your child can look at both of the words, then grasp, point to, or eye gaze at the "same" or "different" picture/symbol to indicate if the words are the same (a match) or different.

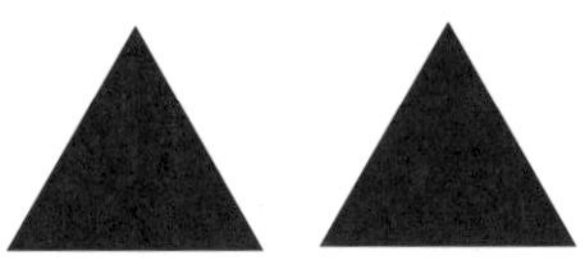

same

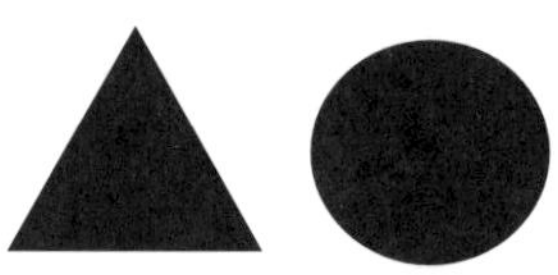

different

we	have	the
we	have	the

MEville to WEville

unit 2

my family

part one

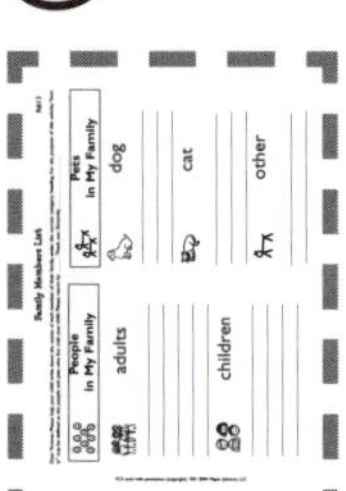

R#13

Teacher Note:

Several days before teaching Lesson #1, send home the Family Members List R#13.

Throughout these **Literacy Lessons**, students and teachers will have frequent opportunities to acknowledge individual names, preferences, and responses.

This "character and community" icon will signal a lesson activity that provides an opportunity for students and teachers to acknowledge each other.

Students make family chains that connect each family member together.

MATERIALS:

R#2

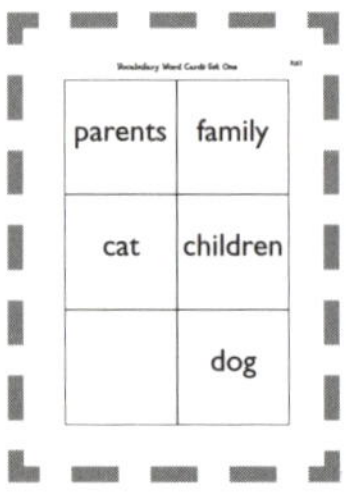
parents | family
cat | children
dog

R#3

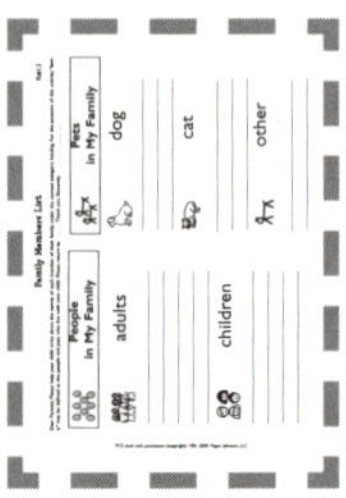
R#13

R#29

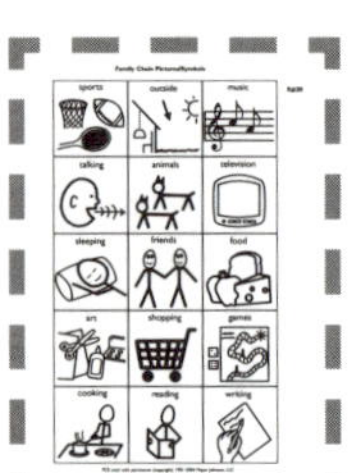
R#30

- vocabulary cards Set One R#2, R#3
- writing paper
- writing tools
- Family Members List R#13 *(completed)*
- Family Chain Sentences R#29 *(at least ten copies) (cut into thirds)*
- Family Chain Pictures/Symbols R#30
- black marker
- poster board *(one large sheet)*
- construction paper 11" x17" *(cut into thirds, lengthwise)*
- paper cutter
- note cards *(3" x 5")*
- crayons/markers
- glue
- stapler

PREPARATION:

- Cut out the Family Chain Pictures/Symbols. Put a selection of the symbols on display.
- Make a sample family chain, using your own family members.
- Use the black marker to write on the poster board, in large letters, the words, "Families Stick Together."
- Decide on a place to hang the family chains where students and staff can easily read them. Mount the poster board sign near this place.

Students write a list of people and pets in their family.

- Show students the "family" vocabulary card. Call out the name of different students and have them lead the class in **saying** the word "family" several times.
- Explain to students that they are going to make an art project that shows and tells about all the members of their family.
- Give each student a sheet of writing paper. Students **write** a list of the names of all of their family members *(can be those people and pets that live with the child, or may be expanded to people that are close to the child).*

NOTE: If students are unable to name the people, or are not able to spell the names, use the Family Members List for the names of family members. Say the name of each family member and encourage students to **say** the name. Write out the name of the family member as a model for the student, and assist the student in **writing** that name on their paper.

- Students **count** up the number of names they have.
- Students **count** out that number of Family Chain Sentences.
- Students **select** a color of construction paper.
- Give each student that same number of construction paper strips as family members.

Students make a family chain.

- Direct student to **look** at the first name on their list, and **write** that name on the first blank line on a sentence strip.
- Direct students to think about one thing that family member likes, and **write** it on the line. Students may also **select** a Family Chain Picture/Symbol and **write** that word on the blank line on a sentence strip. The student may **glue** the corresponding picture/symbol next to the sentence.
- Students **draw** a picture of that family member on a 3" x 5" note card.
- Students **glue** the sentence strip and the picture card on the construction paper strip.
- When all strips have been completed, students **staple** the strips together in rings to make a paper chain.

Students share their family chains with each other.

- Students take turns **reading** the sentences on the links of their chain, and **showing** each picture.
- Hang the family chains up near the sign that says, "Families Stick Together."

"We cannot destroy kindred: our chains stretch a little sometimes, but they never break."

MARQUISE DE SEVIGNE

Students play the game "Parent May I."

Students brainstorm a list of questions that children ask a parent(s).

- Show students the "parent" vocabulary card.
- Point out different parent pictures in the book "Families" and ask different students, "Who is this?" The student will **say**, "This is a parent" or "These are parents."
- Explain to students that there are many questions that children ask their parents, and that they are going to make a list of those questions. *(See Teacher Script.)*
- Write each student question on a sentence strip.

Teacher Script

"Remember what a question is? It's when we ask somebody for information, ask them for something, or ask them to do something."

"Let's see how many questions we can think of that children ask their parents!"

"What are some things that you want that you ask your parents for?"

"We'll write out those questions first."
Example: Can I have a snack?
Will you buy me a toy car?

"What are some things you ask your parents if you can do?"
Example: Can I play a video game?
Can I go over to (John's) house?

"What are some questions you ask your parents about things you want to know?"
Example: Are we there yet?
What are we having for dinner?

Students role play being children and parents. The children ask questions and the parents answer them.

- Divide students into two teams of "parents" and "children." Students from the "children" team take turns **reading** a question on a sentence strip to the "parents."
- The students on the "parents" team take turns **answering** the "children" with an appropriate response. Students on the "parents" team can be given two or more options of appropriate answers and **select** one to give to the "children."
- When all students on the "children" team have had an opportunity to ask a question, and all students on the "parents" team have had an opportunity to give an answer, the teams reverse roles.
- As students role play by **asking** and **answering** questions, look for opportunities for students to **discuss** different answers that parents may give and possible reasons for giving those answers.

Students play the game, "Parent May I."

- Break the students up into at least two teams, and assign one student to be the parent.
- The teacher or a student gives game directions to the other students. *(See "Parent May I" Direction Script.)*
- Students follow directions to participate in the game.

MATERIALS:

- **vocabulary cards Set One R#2, R#3**
- **sentence strips**
- **black marker**
- **"Families" book by Ann Morris**
- **masking tape, colored electrical tape, or yarn**
- **All-Turn-It® spinner with dice overlay or dice to roll**
- **two large sheets of poster board or construction paper**

PREPARATION:

- **On each of the pieces of poster board or construction paper, write one of these sentences:** - Parent, how many steps may we take? - Children, you may take _______ steps.
- **Put both papers on display.**
- **Use the tape or yarn to create a START line and FINISH line on the floor, and to make lines in between showing how far forward students may move for each step.**

R#2-R#3

"Parent May I" Direction Script

- "We are going to play a fun game called, 'Parent May I.' "
- "See this line? This is the START line. The line way up here is the FINISH line."
- "The first team to cross the FINISH line wins the game."
- "(Josh) is going to play the role of the parent and sit near the FINISH line."
- "The rest of you will play the role of the children."
- "When I point to your team, you may **ask** the parent, 'Parent, how many steps may we take?' "
- "The parent then rolls/**spins** for a number and **says** to your team, 'Children, you may take (three) steps.' "
- "For each step, move to the next line on the floor."
- "Your team takes that many steps toward the finish line. Then the next team gets a turn."
- "The first team to the FINISH line wins the game."

NOTE: Direct the children and the parent to the two sentence papers to guide them in what to say to the parent or children.

MATERIALS:

- vocabulary cards Set One R#2, R#3
- poster board *(one large sheet)*
- Children's Activity Cards R#31
- black marker
- paper and writing tools
- cardstock
- paper and crayons/markers
- children's book
- CD or tape player with music
- All-Turn-It® spinner *(optional)*

R#2

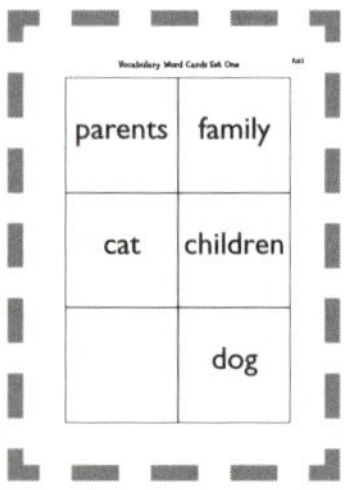

R#3

R#31

PREPARATION:

- Copy onto card stock the Children's Activity Cards R#31. Cut them out. Place them in a stack or on the large overlay of the All-Turn-It® spinner.
- Use the black marker to write the words to the song on the poster board.

The children in this class will

_______ _______ _______

_______ _______ _______

_______ _______ _______

The children in this class will

_______ _______ _______

All, through, the room.

Students sing the song, "The Children in This Class."

(sung to the tune of "The Wheels on the Bus.")

Students review pictures of activities that children do.

- Show students the "children" vocabulary card. Ask students to **name** some children in the class.
- Students take turns drawing or **spinning** for a Children's Activity Card.
- The student **shows** the activity card to the class and the class **reads** the word on the card.
- As each activity card is named and shown, demonstrate what everyone will do when they sing about that activity in the song.
  - shout: **Say** "Yee-ha!" in a really loud voice.
  - dance: Move around the room and dance to the music.
  - read: We'll take turns **reading** the pages of a book.
  - write: **Write** your name in big letters on the paper.
  - spell: Together we'll **say**, in order, the letters in the word "cat" while I write the letters on the board.
  - color: Use crayons or markers to **color** a picture of anything you like.
  - laugh: On the count of three, laugh or giggle as loud as you can. Stop when I say "Children, please stop."
  - jump: When I say, "Ready, set, jump!" jump up and down like a frog.
  - count: Together we'll **count** aloud from one to ten.

Students sing and participate in the actions to the song.

- Explain to students that they are going to sing a song about things that children do.
- Students take turns drawing or **spinning** for a Children's Activity Card and **say** the word on the card.
- The teacher leads the students in **singing** the song, moving the activity card to each blank as it's being sung.
- After each verse is sung, the teacher demonstrates the activity and the students do the activity.

"The real magic wand is the child's own mind."

JOSE ORTEGA Y GASSET

LESSON #4

Students follow recipe directions to make a cat cookie.

Students review the word "cat."

- Show students the stuffed animal cat or the cat picture.
- Ask students, "What is this?" Wait for students to **answer**.
- Show students the sample cat cookie and tell them that they are going to make their own cat cookie.

Students follow the recipe cards to make their own cat cookies.

- Students take turns **selecting** an ingredient card. They **read** the name of the ingredient, and **identify** the ingredient that matches that name. The student puts the ingredient card on or near the ingredient.
- After each ingredient is identified, students open the ingredient and put it in a small bowl with a spoon.
- The teacher shows each recipe card in order to the students.
- Students **read** each recipe card, and follow the directions to make a cat cookie.
- Students **show** their cat cookies to each other.

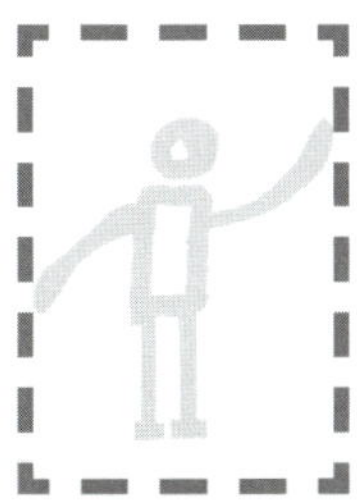
R#2–R#3

R#32–R#34

MATERIALS:

- **vocabulary cards Set One R#2, R#3**
- **cat picture or stuffed animal cat**
- **Cat Cookie Ingredient Cards R#32**
- **Cat Cookie Recipe Cards R#33, R#34**
- **cupcakes or sugar cookies** *(one per student)*
- **paper plates** *(one per student)*
- **small bowls**
- **plastic spoons**
- **white frosting**
- **spatula**
- **Hershey chocolate kisses**
- **small colored candies**
- **small pretzel sticks**

PREPARATION:

- **Copy the Cat Cookie Ingredient and Recipe Cards onto card stock. Cut out each ingredient and recipe card.**
- **Make a sample cat cookie.**

LESSON #5

Students play the game Back to the Doghouse.

PREPARATION:

- **Cut out the park and doghouse pictures/symbols. Glue each picture/symbol in a different corner of the poster board.**
- **Copy the Game Space Templates onto brown paper** *(multiple copies)* **and cut them out.**
- **Create a game board.** *(See R#35)*
- **Copy the "people" and "dog" game cards onto card stock. Put them in separate containers with the corresponding picture/symbol on the outside.**
- **Create a game playing marker for each student by copying the "dog" game piece pattern onto card stock and cutting it out. Color each a different color.**

OPTION: Put a small square of soft Velcro® on each paw print game space and a small piece of rough Velcro® on the bottom of each game piece.

MATERIALS:

- **dog pictures or photos** *(three to five)*
- **poster board** *(one large sheet)*
- **card stock**
- **brown construction paper**
- **Game Patterns R#35**
- **Game Space Templates R#36**
- **People Game Cards R#37, R#38**
- **Dog Game Cards R#39, R#40**
- **dice or All-Turn-It® spinner with dice overlay**
- **adhesive Velcro®** *(optional)*
- **chart paper**
- **black marker**

R#35–R#40

Students participate in a discussion about lost dogs.

- Show students pictures of dogs. As each picture is shown, ask students, "What is this?" Students **answer**.
- Ask students to **tell** about what happens when a dog gets lost.
- Ask students to **say** how they would feel if their dog, or other pet, was lost.
- Ask students to **say** things that people can do if they lose a dog. Write every idea on the chart paper.
- Lead students to ideas they have not thought of and write them down.
- **Read** the entire list together as a class.

Students play the Back to The Doghouse Game.

- Students **select** a game marker.
- Students put their game marker at the park.
- Students roll or **spin** for a number.
- Students **count** as they move their marker that many spaces.
- If a student lands on a "dog" or "people" symbol he/she **selects** and **reads** the corresponding game card.
- The student follows the direction on the game card.
- The first student to the doghouse wins the game.
- The students **clap** for the winner.

Literacy EXTENSION ACTIVITIES

FAMILY:
FAMILY SCRAPBOOK

Ask parents to send in four to six photos of the student and his/her family. Students **glue** each photo on a separate piece of construction paper or tag board. Students **write** one sentence about that photo. Students **select** die-cuts or other decorations and **glue** them on the page. Students may **draw** or **color** additional designs on the page. Students **show** and **read** their completed scrapbooks to the other students.

PARENT:
THANK YOU GIFT

Students **paint** a clay flower pot. Students **dry** the pot. Students **glue** decorations on the flower pot. Students follow directions to put dirt in the pot and plant a flower or other plant in the pot. Students make a card to go with the gift. Students **select** a sheet of construction paper and **write** the words, "Thank you for helping me grow." Students bring the flower pot gift and the card home to their parent(s).

CHILDREN:
CHILDREN SURVEY

Students do a survey of children in the school to see what their favorite food, color, game, sport, and/or subject is. Students in the class **name** some of their favorite things in certain categories. Students then go into the school and **ask** students to tell them which of those things is their favorite. Students go back to the room and **count** up the number of votes that each choice in a category received. Students then **say** which item in each category was the school's favorite.

CAT:
RECIPE BOOKS

Give each student a set of recipe cards from Lesson #4. Students **cut** out and **read** each recipe card. Students put the recipe cards in order and **staple** them together to make a cat cookie recipe book.

DOG:
EDIBLE DOGHOUSE

Students follow directions to make a doghouse snack. Students each start out with an empty, dried-out, individual serving milk carton. Students then spread softened cream cheese on the outside of the milk carton. Students take turns **spinning** or drawing for a number card. Students **read** the number to the class. All students **count** out that many cheese crackers, and place them on the cream cheese on the milk carton as shingles on the doghouse. When the cream cheese is covered, students may choose to take apart their doghouses by dipping the cheese crackers in the cream cheese and eating them!

SECTION FIVE

MEville to WEville

part one

Throughout these **Writing Lessons**, students will be making choices as to what elements they want on the pages of the books they are creating. Give all students opportunities to let their own voice be heard as they communicate individual selections and read their completed books to the class.

unit 2

my family

In Lesson #5, students make Dog Care Books. Students will be reading their books to a class of younger students on the day of this lesson or the day or two following this lesson.

It is also recommended that a real dog come and visit on that day.

This "character and community" icon will signal a lesson activity in which students will have an opportunity to express their preferences and let their own voice be heard.

LESSON #1

Students write a book entitled, "My Family."

MATERIALS:

- **vocabulary cards Set One R#2, R#3**
- **construction paper** *(8 1/2" x 11")*
- **family photos** *(previously sent from home in Learning New Words Lesson #1)*
- **Family Description Picture Cards R#41** *(one per student)*
- **"My Family" book page R#42**
- **card stock**
- **crayons**
- **writing tools**
- **black markers** *(for student use)*
- **glue**
- **scissors**
- **stapler**

PREPARATION:

- **Make multiple copies of the "My Family" book page R#42.**
- **Cut each page in half along the dotted lines.**
- **Copy the Family Description Picture Cards R#41 onto card stock. Cut out each picture.**
- **Make a sample "My Family" book.**

R#2

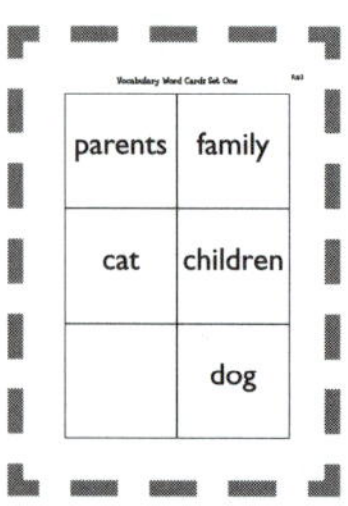

R#3

R#41

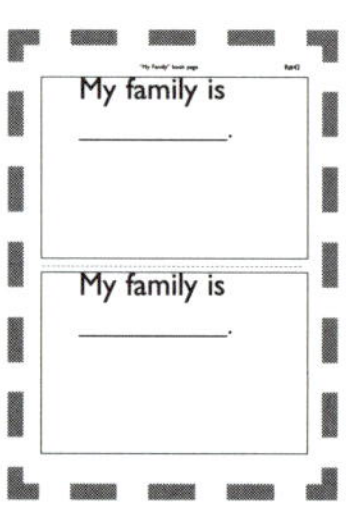

R#42

Students discuss words that describe families.

- Show students the "family" vocabulary card. Lead students in **saying** the word several times.
- Ask students to **name** words that may describe a family. Show students the Family Description Picture Cards for each word named, then all other Family Description Picture Cards.
- Lead students in **discussing** what each word means in relation to families.

Teacher Script

Silly - Is your family ever silly? Does your family like to tease each other and laugh a lot?

Curious - Is your family curious? Does your family like to try new things and go new places?

Loving - Is your family loving? Maybe your family gives each other hugs or asks each other how they are doing.

Fun - Is your family fun? Do you and your family have a good time together?

Healthy - Is your family healthy? Do you and your family do things to stay healthy, like going for walks or bike rides?

Busy - Is your family busy? Are people in your family always doing something and going places?

Students select words that describe their family.

- Give each student the Family Description Picture Cards R#41.
- Students **select** and **color** each word/picture box that describes their family. Students may **write**, in a blank box, any other word that describes their family and **color** in that box.
- Students **cut** out the selected pictures that they colored.
- Students **count** the number of pictures they have.
- Students **ask** the teacher for that many book pages.

Students make a "My Family" book.

- On each book page, students **look** at one of their Family Description Picture Cards and **write** that word, or **glue** that Family Description Picture Card, on the blank line.
- On each book page, students **draw** a picture of their family acting as the sentence describes them or **color** the page however they want.
- Students put each of their book pages on top of each other and **staple** them to the lower half of a sheet of construction paper.
- Students **glue** their family photo on the top of the construction paper and **write** the words "My Family" above the photo.
- Students take turns **reading** their "My Family" books to each other.

Students make a Thank You book for their parent.

'tudents discuss the different 'hings that their parents do.

Students take turns **reading** one line from the list of things that their parents do for them. *(From Learning New Words Lesson #2.)*

Show students the "Things Parents Cook" chart.

Ask students to **name** a favorite thing that their parents cook for them.

Write this on the chart in large letters.

Help students think of additional things that parents cook/prepare for them (*toast, oatmeal, sandwich, spaghetti, cookies, green beans*).

Repeat this process for each of the four charts.

'tudents make a Thank You 'ook for their parent(s).

Show students the sample Thank You book. Read the book to them.

The teacher, or a student, **reads** the Thank You book Direction Script to the others.

Students follow directions to complete each page of the book.

OPTION: For each page of the book, students **select** a picture/symbol representing their choice of word to fill in the blank. The student then **glues** that picture/symbol on the page, and a helper assists the student in **writing** that word on the line.

NOTE: For students who are non-verbal, send home a voice output device with their book pre-recorded so that they can **read** their Thank You book to their parent.

Students read their books.

- Students **read** their Thank You books to each other to practice before reading to a parent.
- Students bring their book home and **read** it to their parent.

"If the family were a fruit, it would be an orange, a circle of sections, held together but separable – each segment distinct."

LETTY COTTIN POGREBIN

R#2

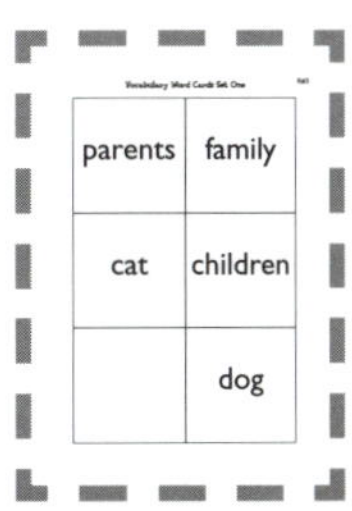

R#3

R#43

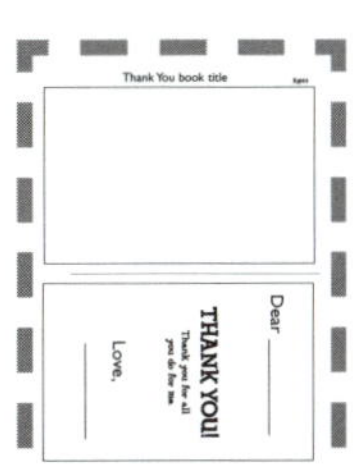

R#44

MATERIALS:

- **vocabulary cards Set One R#2, R#3**
- **chart paper** *(four large sheets)*
- **black marker**
- **Thank You book Direction Script R#43**
- **Thank You book title R#44**
- **Thank You book pages R#45, R#46** *(one set per student)*
- **writing tools**
- **card stock**
- **crayons, markers**
- **stapler**
- **scissors**
- **list of things parents do** *(from Learning New Words Lesson #2)*

PREPARATION:

- **At the top of each of the pieces of chart paper, write one of the following titles, in large black letters.**
  - **Things Parents Cook**
  - **Chores Parents Do**
  - **Places Parents Take Children**
  - **Things Parents Do with Children**
- **Make a sample Thank You book.**
- **Copy the Thank You book title onto card stock** *(one per student)*.

OPTION: Create Boardmaker symbols representing the following:
- Things Parents Cook: breakfast, spaghetti, macaroni and cheese, pizza, cookies, soup
- Chores Parents Do: mow the lawn, take out the trash, wash the clothes, do the dishes, clean the bathroom, do grocery shopping
- Places Parents Take Children: doctor, dentist, school, restaurant, store, park
- Things Parents Do with Children: read, play games, walk, watch TV, go outside, talk, cook

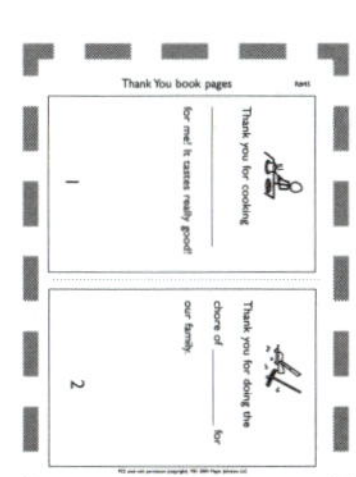

R#45

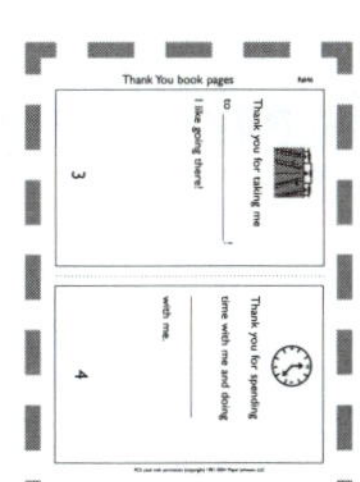

R#46

LESSON #3

Students create a Children's Art Wall.

MATERIALS:

- paintings or drawings or real art
- tempera paint and paintbrushes
- poster board, one large sheet
- Artwork Description R#47
- construction paper
- drawing paper
- mounting tape
- writing tools
- black marker
- glue

R#47

PREPARATION:

- Use the black marker to write the words Children's Art Wall on the poster board and place on a wall.
- Make copies of the Artwork Description R#47.

Students learn about the Children's Art Wall.

- Show students the artwork and lead students in **discussing** what they like about it.
- Explain to students that they are each going to create an art piece to put on the Children's Art Wall.

Students make their own art to be displayed on the Children's Art Wall.

- Students **select** a color paint and **paint** on the drawing paper.
- Students **tell** an adult when they would like another color of paint and continue **painting** until they are finished.

Students write about and share their artwork.

- Students **read** each sentence on the Artwork Description R#47.
- Students **look** at their artwork and **write** the information about their artwork.
- Students **glue** their Artwork Description in the center of a sheet of construction paper.
- Students take turns **showing** their artwork and **reading** their description.
- The students help the teacher mount the paintings and the Artwork Descriptions on the Children's Art Wall.

LESSON #4

Student write a story book entitled "That Crazy Cat!"

MATERIALS:

- vocabulary cards Set One R#2, R#3
- "That Crazy Cat!" Book Direction Script, title and book pages R#48, R#49, R#50, R#51 *(one set per student)*
- book pictures R#52, R#53 *(one set per student)*
- construction paper • glue • scissors
- writing tools • stapler • crayons
- white card stock • Velcro® *(small pieces)*

PREPARATION:

- Make a sample "That Crazy Cat!" book.
- Cut out each set of "That Crazy Cat!" book pictures and have them ready to put on display.
- Copy each title page onto card stock.

Students listen to directions for the book making project.

- Show students the "cat" vocabulary card. Lead students in **saying** the word at least three to five times.
- Explain to students that they will be making a book about a cat who does some crazy things.
- Show students the sample book. Demonstrate how to move the cat from page to page.

R#2-R#3

R#48-R#53

Students follow directions to make their own Crazy Cat book.

- The teacher, or a student, **reads** the "That Crazy Cat!" Book Direction Script.
- Students follow directions to create the "That Crazy Cat!" book.
- Students then **color** and **cut** out their cat, put a piece of rough Velcro® on the back of the cat, and place the cat on the front cover.
- Students **read** their book to others.

"A cat is a puzzle for which there is no solution."

HAZEL NICHOLSON

Students make a Dog Care book.

Students review pictures of things that dogs need.

- Show students the "dog" vocabulary card. Lead students in **saying** the word three to five times.
- Explain to students that they are going to be talking about how to take care of a dog.
- Students take turns drawing or **spinning** for a Dog Care Picture Card.
- The student **shows** the card to the class and the class **reads** the word on the card.
- As each card is named and shown, ask students to **say** why a dog needs that thing.

Students make a cover for their book.

- Explain to students that they are going to be making books that tell others how to take care of a dog.
- Students **select** a color of construction paper and fold it in half, short side to short side.

NOTE: The book will open from the bottom, not from the side.

- Students **read** the words "Dog Care" on the board and **write** them on the front cover.
- Students **look** through the magazines, **identify** pictures of dogs, **cut** them out, and **glue** them on the book cover.

Students put together their dog care book.

- Students **cut** each of the three pages on the dotted line, separating each page into two book pages.
- Students follow teacher directions to put their pages in the correct order.
- Students **staple** all the pages together at the fold.

Students complete each page of the book.

- As students **read** each page they **look** at the Dog Care Picture Cards and **identify** the picture/ word that best fits in the blank in that sentence.
- Students **write** that word on the blank and **turn the page**.
- The above process continues until every page is completed.

Students go to another classroom, preferably a class of younger students.

- Each student sits with one or more students from that class.
- The students **read** their Dog Care book to the other student(s).

"Scratch a dog and you'll find a permanent job."

FRANKLIN P. JONES

Teacher Note: Be sure you have arranged for your students to read their books to a younger class.

MATERIALS:

- **vocabulary cards Set One R#2, R#3**
- **card stock** *(one sheet)*
- **black marker**
- **construction paper** *(8 1/2 x 11)*
- **Dog Care Picture Cards page R#54**
- **Dog Care book pages R#55, R#56, R#57** *(one set per student)*
- **magazines with dog pictures**
- **scissors**
- **writing tools**
- **glue**
- **stapler**
- **All-Turn-It® spinner** *(optional)*

PREPARATION:

- **Copy onto card stock the Dog Care Picture Cards R#54. Cut them out. Put them in a stack, or place them facedown on the large overlay of the All-Turn-It® spinner.**
- **Write the words "Dog Care" on the board.**
- **Arrange with another class, preferably younger students, to go into their room after the books have been completed and have your class read the Dog Care books to their class.**

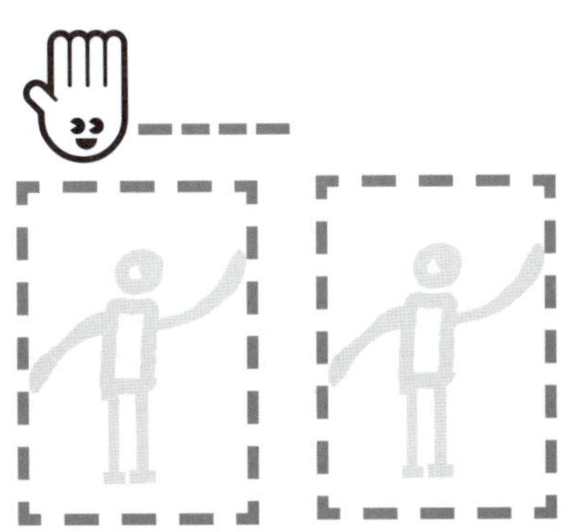

R#2-R#3 R#54-R#57

EXTENSION ACTIVITIES

WRITING LESSONS

FAMILY:

Family Memory

Students bring home a note asking their family to help them write about a memory they have of a special family time, such as a birthday party, a family game night, or a family vacation. The student can **write** about what they did, who was there, and how they felt. The student can **write** about their favorite part of the memory, and why it's special to them. Students can then **read** their memory writings to their classmates and **show** any pictures that go along with the memory.

PARENT:

A Letter to My Parent

Students **write** a letter to their parent telling the parent about their day. The student can **select** certain things that they want to tell their parent, such as what they learned, what special activities they did, what they had for lunch, who they spent time with, etc. The student can then **write** about each of the things they selected. The student can also **select** certain things to ask their parent(s) about in the letter, which could include questions about how the parent's day was and what they did at work or at home.

CHILDREN:

Children Observe Children

Students go into the school, or the community, and take time to observe other children. Before students start this assignment, they **read** questions about children they might see, questions they will have to answer. Some questions might include: *What are the children doing? Are the children having fun? How do you know? Who are the children with? What are the children wearing? How old do you think the children are? What else do you know about these children?* The students **write** down the answers to these questions on their observations sheets and **read** them to each other.

CAT:

E-mail a Vet

Speak to a local veterinarian and ask if your class can e-mail him/her with questions they have about cats. Students think about different things they want to know about cats. Students each **say** one question they have about cats. The teacher writes down each question, and the class **reads** them as a whole group. The students then take turns typing each question into the computer and together creating an e-mail to send to the veterinarian. When the e-mail reply is received, students together **read** the reply.

DOG:

Research Your Favorite Breed

Students **look** at pictures of different breeds of dogs, or go to the pet store or humane society and actually visit and observe different breeds. Students **select** a breed of dog that they like. Students research this breed on the Internet, in the library, and through any other methods that may prove helpful. Students gather as much information as possible and **write** it down in a report format. Students **read** their reports.

EARLY LITERACY AND COMMUNICATION PROGRAM

Part two

Things We Do

ablenet

unit 2

my family

MEville to WEville

In the **Things We Do** part, students will be able to identify and/or participate in activities that families do.

Character Education

Each lesson in this section addresses aspects of character education. Look for the ☺ to identify where this occurs.

part two

Things We Do

Content Learning Objectives

1. Student will be able to follow a series of one-step directions to complete a task.
2. Student will be able to sort food items into each of the four food groups.
3. Student will be able to name one chore that was done many years ago that is different from chores we do now.

Overview and Resources

Literature Book to Be Read:
"Families" by Ann Morris

Additional Book Recommendations:
"Grandpa's Garden" by Shea Darian
"Owl Moon" by Jane Yolen
"When I Was Young in the Mountains" by Cynthia Rylant
"Winners Never Quit" by Mia Hamm
"The Relatives Came" by Cynthia Rylant
"Rattletrap Car" by Phyllis Root

Books to Be Created and Read by Students:
Sack Pack
Laundry Toss
Let's Go to the Store
Where Do You Live?

Songs to Be Sung:
"I've Been Working with My Family" sung to the tune,
"I've Been Working on the Railroad"

Song Recommendations:
"Home on the Range"
by Brewster Higley

Class Projects and Art Projec
"Ways to Go Places" poster
Make placemats
Treasure Hunt
Make home models
Make butter

Games:
Work Charades
Follow the Leader
Family Chore Olympics
Old Fashioned Children's Games
The Word Find Game
The Question Exchange activity
Name That Place
Catch a Rhyme
Crazy Rules game

Home/School Activities:
Make a menu to bring home

unit 2

my family

unit 2 LESSON Planner

my family

Learning New Words	Vocabulary Activities	Word Wall Lessons	Literacy Lessons	Writing Lessons
Lesson #1 Pg. 46 Students learn about the word **"eat."**	**Activity #1 Pg. 52** Students learn how to set the table for a meal that they eat together.	**Lesson #1 Pg. 58** Students practice saying and writing the word wall words.	**Lesson #1 Pg. 62** Students learn about and practice proper table manners.	**Lesson #1 Pg. 68** Students write a menu to bring home to their family.
Lesson #2 Pg. 47 Students learn about the word **"work."**	**Activity #2 Pg. 53** Students participate in Family Chore Olympics.	**Lesson #2 Pg. 58** Students participate in a Sentence Completion Activity.	**Lesson #2 Pg. 63** Students sing and act out the song **"I've Been Working With My Family."**	**Lesson #2 Pg. 69** Students make butter and write about the experience.
Lesson #3 Pg. 48 Students learn about the word **"go."**	**Activity #3 Pg. 54** Students participate in a treasure hunt and "go" different places.	**Lesson #3 Pg. 58** Students participate in the Mind Reader activity.	**Lesson #3 Pg. 64** Students participate in the game, **"Name That Place."**	**Lesson #3 Pg. 70** Students make a class big book entitled, **"Let's Go to the Store!"**
Lesson #4 Pg. 49 Students learn about the word **"play."**	**Activity #4 Pg. 55** Students play old fashioned children's games.	**Lesson #4 Pg. 59** Students participate in The Word Find Game.	**Lesson #4 Pg. 65** Students make and play a rhyming game.	**Lesson #4 Pg. 71** Students write rules to the game, **"Crazy Rules."**
Lesson #5 Pg. 50 Students learn about the word **"live."**	**Activity #5 Pg. 56** Students create a model of their home where they live.	**Lesson #5 Pg. 59** Students participate in The Question Exchange activity.	**Lesson #5 Pg. 66** Students participate in reading the book, **"Families."**	**Lesson #5 Pg. 71-72** Students make a book entitled **"Where Do You Live?"**
Extension Activities Pg. 50	**Extension Activities** Pg. 56	**Home Activity** Pg. 60	**Extension Activities** Pg. 66	**Extension Activities** Pg. 72

* Select lessons/activities from each curriculum area to present every day. We recommend starting with the Learning New Words curriculum area (e.g. Students learn about the word "eat") and continue with other lessons related to that vocabulary word (look across the grid for related lessons, all with the same #) before moving on to lessons focused on a new vocabulary word.

Create Your Own...

Create your own daily plans by filling in each day with lessons/activities across the literacy areas. Check each literacy area that you select a lesson/activity from, and write the specific name on the line to the right of that literacy area.

Daily LESSON Planner

Monday	__ Learning New Words ____ __ Vocabulary Activities ____ __ Word Wall Lessons ____ __ Literacy Lessons ____ __ Writing Lessons ____
Tuesday	__ Learning New Words ____ __ Vocabulary Activities ____ __ Word Wall Lessons ____ __ Literacy Lessons ____ __ Writing Lessons ____
Wednesday	__ Learning New Words ____ __ Vocabulary Activities ____ __ Word Wall Lessons ____ __ Literacy Lessons ____ __ Writing Lessons ____
Thursday	__ Learning New Words ____ __ Vocabulary Activities ____ __ Word Wall Lessons ____ __ Literacy Lessons ____ __ Writing Lessons ____
Friday	__ Learning New Words ____ __ Vocabulary Activities ____ __ Word Wall Lessons ____ __ Literacy Lessons ____ __ Writing Lessons ____

ECTION ONE

MEville to WEville

Teacher Note:

Throughout these lessons, student picture/name cards will be frequently used. If you do not already have these in your classroom, create a set by gluing a picture of each student on a 3" x 5" note card and writing the student's name on the card.

part two

R#60

Several days prior to beginning teaching the lessons in this section, send home Parent Letter R#60. This letter asks parents to send in information/materials that will be used in various lessons throughout this section.

Throughout these **Learning New Words** lessons, students will be learning about themselves and growing in their understanding of "**Who I Am.**" Students will share about the things that they do with their families, and the role that they play in their family.

This "character and community" icon will signal a lesson activity through which this sense of "Who I Am" can be reinforced.

LESSON #1

Students learn about the word "eat."

MATERIALS:

- **vocabulary cards Set Two R#58, R#59**
- **food items: at least four foods from three or more of the letter categories below** *(empty containers can be used)*

NOTE: Select three or more foods (preferably one from each letter category) that students will taste (or smell if unable to eat). Have enough of that food for each student to have a small taste.

C - cake, cookies, corn, cucumber, carrot, candy bar, cauliflower

P - popcorn, pepper, potatoes, pudding, peas, pickles, pancakes, pie, pepperoni

M - mushrooms, macaroni, mayonnaise, mustard, muffin

T - tuna, turkey, tomato, tortilla, toast

- **non-food items - crayons, books, cup, etc.**
- **grocery bag**
- **plates**
- **sentence strips** *(one per student)*
- **black marker**

PREPARATION:

- **On each sentence strip, write the sentence, "People eat _________________."**
- **Notify parents of the foods that students will be tasting to assure that there are no allergies or concerns.**

OPTION: Create Boardmaker pictures/symbols of each of the food items you have selected to show to students.

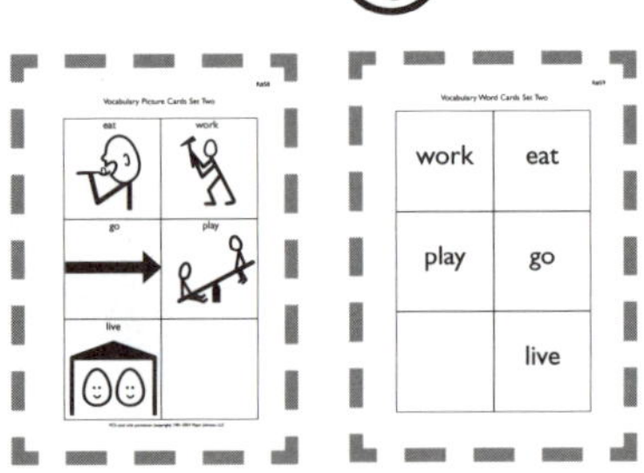

R#58 R#59

Students are introduced to the word "eat."

- Show students the "eat" vocabulary card. Read the word.
- Lead the students in **saying** the word at least three to five times.
- Put on display a combination of things we do eat and things that we don't eat.
- Students take turns **selecting** a food item, something that people eat.
- The student **names** the food item and the teacher, or student, **writes** the food name on the blank line on the sentence strip.
- After each student has had a turn, students take turns **selecting** a sentence strip and leading students in **reading** it.

Students pack a grocery bag with things that people eat.

- Tell students that they are going to fill up a grocery bag with things that people eat.
- Lead students in **selecting** particular foods and putting them in a grocery bag. *(See Teacher Script.)*

Students select and eat various foods.

- Put on a separate plate each of the food items that students will be able to taste.
- Show and name each food item. Explain to students that they may eat a sample of any, or all, of the food items.
- Students **select** the food items they want to eat and the teacher puts a sample of those items on the student's plate.
- Students eat the selected food.
- Ask each student, "What food did you eat?"
- Each student **names**, or **shows** a picture/symbol of the food(s) he/she ate.

Teacher Script

"Here is a potato. Do people eat potatoes? 'Potato' starts with the 'p' sound." (Make the 'p' sound instead of saying the letter name.)

"Here is some popcorn. Do people eat popcorn? Popcorn also starts with the 'p' sound."

"(<u>Stephen</u>), find something else people eat that starts with the 'p' sound. Put that food in the grocery bag."

"(<u>Rebekka</u>), find another thing people eat that starts with the 'p' sound and put it in the grocery bag."

"Here is some mustard. Do people eat mustard? Mustard starts with the 'm' sound."

"Here is some macaroni. Do people eat macaroni? That also starts with the 'm' sound."

"(<u>Mikala</u>), find something people eat that starts with the 'm' sound. Put that food in the grocery bag."

"(<u>Jerome</u>), find another food that starts with the 'm' sound and put it in the grocery bag."

Continue this format for foods of different letter categories.

Students learn about the word "work."

Part 1

Students review the word "eat."

- Students **select** a color of construction paper.
- Direct students to **look** at the board and **read** the words, "People eat food."
- Direct students to **write** those words on their paper.
- Students **look** through magazines and **select** pictures of things people eat.
- Students **cut** out the pictures and **glue** them on the construction paper.
- Students **show** their food collages to the class, **read** the title, and **name** one or more food items on the paper.

Part 2

Students learn about the word "work."

- Show students the "work" vocabulary card. Read the word.
- Lead the students in **saying** the word at least three to five times.
- Lead students in **discussing** what it means to "work."
- Students go on a walk throughout the school with the clipboard and **identify** people who are doing work. Students **ask** the people, "What work are you doing?"
- A teacher, or student, **writes** the response down on the clipboard paper.
- When students return, they take turns **reading** each written response from the clipboard.
- Ask students to think about, and **say,** work that they, or the teachers do in their classroom. Write each response on chart paper.

Students practice doing various household work tasks.

OPTION: An alternative to setting up Work Stations (centers) would be to choose a few of the work tasks and lead the class in doing them as a group.

- Students **name** work (a chore) that they do at home or see others doing at home.
- Lead students in **discussing** the importance of a family working together to complete chores.
- Explain to students that they are going to practice being a family and doing some chores.
- Show students each Work Picture Card. Lead students in **saying** the name of the work.
- Model for students how to do each work task.
- Divide students into small groups. The groups take turns drawing or **spinning** for a Work Picture Card.
- The group goes to that Work Station and **labels** the location/activity, then does the work task. *(See R# 61)*

The class writes about their work experiences.

- For each work task, show the students the Work Picture Card and ask the students, "Who did this work?"
- The students who did the work **say** "me."
- On chart paper, the teacher **writes** a sentence following this format: (James and Desmond) (washed the dishes).
- Students **comment** on the experience.
- The teacher writes the comments on the paper in the following format: They said (it was fun!)

MATERIALS:

- **vocabulary cards Set Two R#58, R#59**
- **Work Picture Cards R#61**
- **construction paper**
- **glue**
- **scissors**
- **magazines, grocery ads** *(containing food pictures)*
- **chart paper and black marker**
- **clipboard with paper**
- **All-Turn-It® spinner** *(optional)*
- **Work Station Materials** *(see R#61)*
- **Talking Symbol® notepad** *(optional)*

PREPARATION:

- **Copy the Work Picture Cards onto card stock** *(two copies)*. **Cut them out. Put one set in a stack or on the large overlay of the All-Turn-It® spinner. Have the other set ready to show students.**
- **Set up the different Work Stations** *(see Preparation on R#61)*. **Right before students begin the work tasks, place each Work Picture Card or Talking Symbol® notepad near the matching Work Station.**
- **On the board, write the words, "People eat food."**

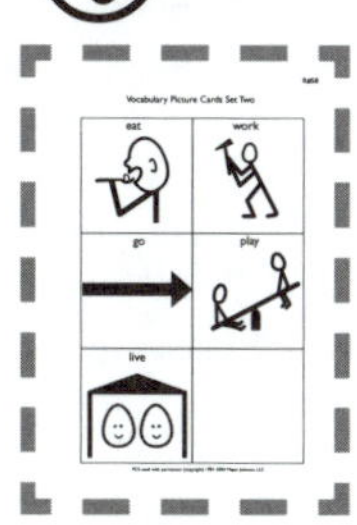

R#58

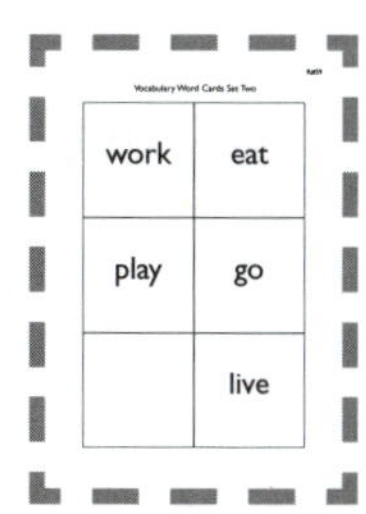

R#59

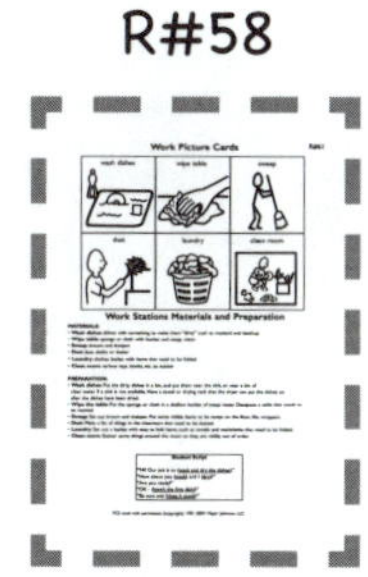

R#61

Students learn about the word "go."

MATERIALS:

- vocabulary cards Set Two R#58, R#59
- Work Picture Cards R#61
- All-Turn-It® spinner *(optional)*
- Place Picture Cards R#62, R#63
- Transportation Picture Cards R#64
- Parent Letter R#60 *(returned from home)*
- card stock
- chart paper and black marker
- note cards *(3" x 5")*
- clipboard
- writing tools

PREPARATION:

- Put the Work Picture Cards in a stack or facedown on the large overlay of the All-Turn-It® spinner.
- Copy the Place Picture Cards and Transportation Picture Cards onto card stock. Cut out each card.

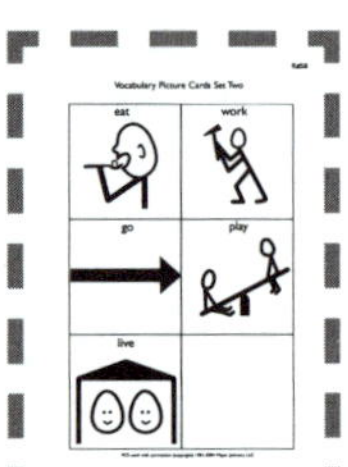
R#58

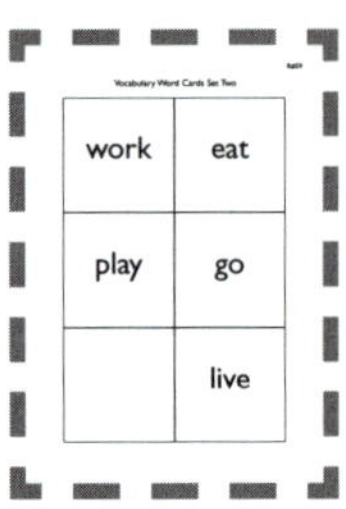

R#59

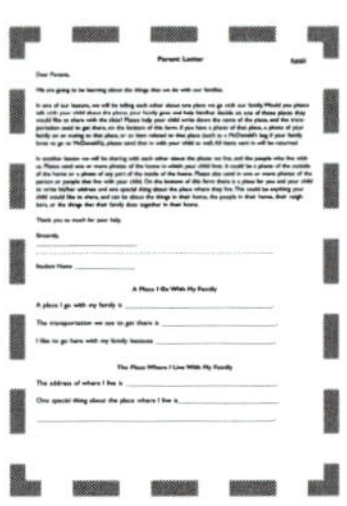
R#60

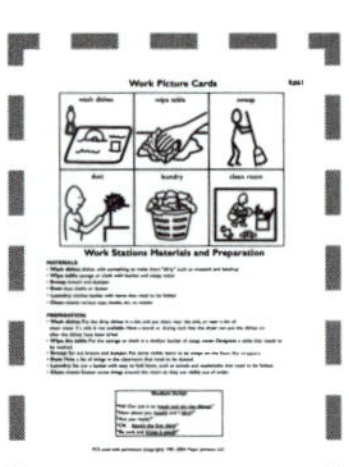
R#61

R#62

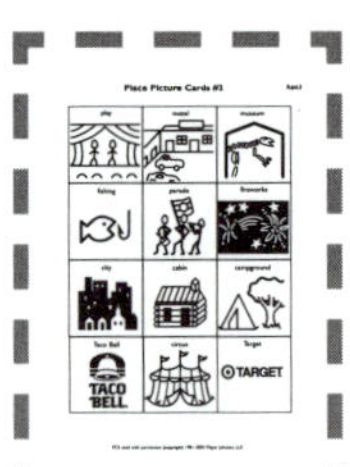
R#63

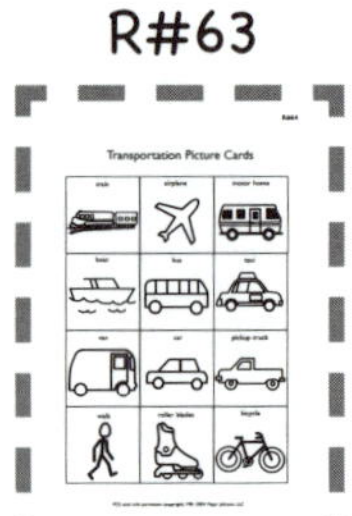
R#64

Part 1
Students review the word "work."
Students play the game Work Charades.

- Student pairs or teams take turns drawing or **spinning** for a Work Picture Card.
- The student team **looks** at their card without saying the name of the work task.
- The group works together to act out that work task, without talking.
- The other students take turns **naming** or **selecting** a Work Picture Card representing the work task they think it is.
- Play continues until every team has had a turn to act out a work task.

Part 2
Students learn about the word "go."

- Show students the "go" vocabulary card. Lead students in **saying** the word three to five times.
- Students follow directions to go different places in the room.

Teacher Script

"Everybody, go to the teacher's desk."
"If you are a boy, go to the classroom door."
"If you are a girl, go to the chalkboard/white board."
"Everybody, go to your chair."
"Everybody, go to the calendar."

Students play "Follow the Leader" to go different places in the school.

- Students take turns **naming** different places in the school that they can go. Write down each place on a note card.
- Students take turns **selecting** one of those places *(from a choice of three to five of the note cards)* they want to go.
- The student brings the clipboard *(with the place note cards attached)* and leads the students to that place, "Follow The Leader" style. Explain to students that they must follow the leader and do whatever the leader is doing as they go to that place *(flapping arms like a chicken, singing a song, clapping, etc.)*.
- When students arrive at the destination, another student **selects** a place *(from the place note cards)* to go and leads the students in going there.
- When they return to the classroom, ask students to **name** the places they went.

Students discuss different places that families go.

NOTE: See bottom of R#60 for information about a place that the student goes with their family.

- Students **name** or **select** *(from Place Picture Cards)* different places that families go.
- Students **name** or **select** *(from Transportation Picture Cards)* different ways that families can go to those places *(walk, roller-blade, bike, car, truck, etc.)*.
- Students take turns **naming** or **selecting** a picture card of a place their family goes and the transportation they use.
- Students **tell** the class why they like going there with their family.

Students learn about the word "play."

Part 1

Students review the word "go." Students make a poster entitled, "Ways to Go Places."

- Students take turns **selecting** a Transportation Picture Card, **showing** it to the class, and leading the class in **reading** the card.
- Direct students to **look** through magazines, **select** pictures of people going places or a method of transportation used to go places, **cut** them out, and **glue** them on the poster board.
- When the poster is complete, ask students to take turns **naming** one way of going places that they see on the poster.

Part 2

Students learn about the word "play."

- Show students the "play" vocabulary card. Lead the students in **saying** the word at least three to five times.
- Students take turns **turning the pages** of the book "Families."
- On each page, ask students if they see a picture of a family playing. Students **answer** "yes" or "no."
- On pages where a family is playing, ask students to **say** how the family is playing, or what they are doing to play.

Students learn about different play materials and play activities.

- Show students each Play Activity Card, and demonstrate how to engage in that activity.
- While demonstrating the activity, instruct students on how to participate. *(See Teacher Script.)*

Students participate in playing at different activity centers.

- Put each set of play materials in a separate area and place the matching Play Activity Sign or Talking Symbol® near the activity.
- Students **select** a Play Activity Card representing something they would like to play.
- Students **match** that Play Activity Card to the Play Activity Sign or Talking Symbol® at the center.
- Students go to that center, **label** the center, and follow activity instructions to play with the materials at the center.
- At the sound of a special signal, students **select** a different Play Activity Card and go to that center.

Teacher Script

catch - Throw the ball in the basket, or play with others and take turns throwing the ball to each other.

cards - Play a card game with one or more people.

game - Play a game with one or more people. Everybody has a game piece and takes a turn.

puzzles - Put together a puzzle by yourself, or work with others to find pieces that fit together.

play-doh - Make your own play-doh creation, or share the play-doh with others and make something as a group.

blocks - Build your own tower, or play with others and take turns putting a block on top of another block to build something.

MATERIALS:

- **vocabulary cards Set Two R#58, R#59**
- **Transportation Picture Cards R#64**
- **Play Activity Cards R#65** *(two copies)*
- **poster board** *(one large sheet)*
- **black marker**
- **magazines** *(likely to contain pictures of transportation)*
- **scissors**
- **glue**
- **"Families"** *by Ann Morris*
- **construction paper and tape**
- **play activity materials: balls and basket, card game, board games, puzzles, building blocks, play-doh**
- **Talking Symbol® notepad** *(optional)*

PREPARATION:

- **Use the black marker to write the title, "Ways to Go Places" on the top of the poster board.**
- **Cut out both sets of Play Activity Cards. Put one set aside, to be used by students to select activities. With the other set, glue each Play Activity Card on a separate piece of construction paper to make Play Activity Signs.**

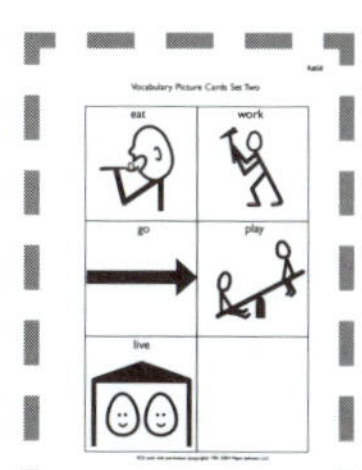
R#58

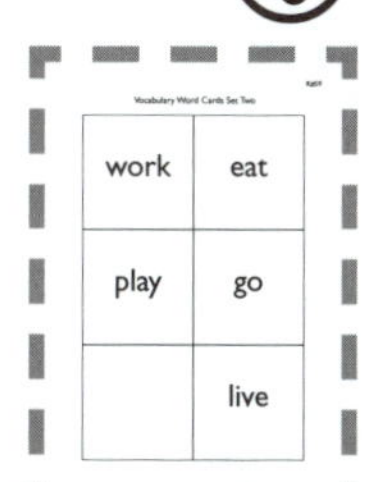

R#59

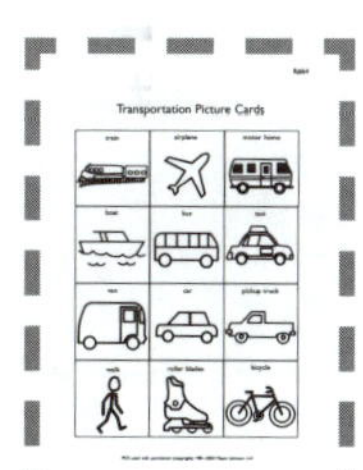
R#64

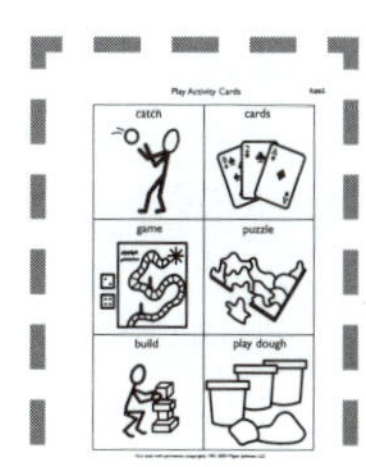
R#65

Students learn about the word "live."

R#6

R#58-R#60

MATERIALS:

- **Family Labels R#6** *(bottom half)*
- **vocabulary cards Set Two R#58, R#59**
- **Parent Letter R#60** *(returned from home)*
- **play items from classroom**
- **photos of students' homes and families** *(sent from home)*
- **pictures of homes**
- **construction paper**
- **card stock**

PREPARATION:

- **Copy the Family Label R#6 onto card stock. Cut out and display each of the family member pictures/symbols.**
- **Trim the corners off of a sheet of construction paper to form a house shape.**

Part 1

Students review the word "play." Students tell others about their favorite play activities.

- Students take turns **selecting** a play item/activity of their choice.
- Students **tell** the class why they like that play item/activity.

Part 2

Students learn about the word "live."

- Show students the word "live" and lead them in **saying** the word at least three to five times.
- Show students the pictures of homes and tell students that people live in homes with their family.
- Show students the "family" vocabulary card and the construction paper house. Tell students that some families live in houses.
- Show students the family member pictures/symbols and lead students in **naming** each of the pictures/symbols.
- Tell students, "A (cat) lives in this house." Direct a student to **identify** the "cat" picture/symbol and place it in the house. Continue this process for each family member picture/symbol.

Students share with their class photos of the home where they live and the people who live with them.

- Ask students, one at a time, "Where do you live?"
- Direct students to **show** the class the picture of their home, **tell** the class, "I live here," and **read** their address. *(See Parent Letter.)*
- The student also **tells** the class one special thing about where they live *(see Parent Letter information).*
- Ask that student, "Who lives with you?"
- Direct the student to **show** the class the picture of their family and **tell** the class, "I live with my family" or, "I live with (my mom)."

EXTENSION ACTIVITIES

LEARNING NEW WORDS

EAT: Menu Mania!

Gather up some menus from various restaurants. Some restaurants, like McDonald's, will offer picture and/or Braille menus. Students **look** at the various things to eat and **say** the things they like and don't like. Students then role play being customers and servers. The servers **ask** the customers what they would like to eat, and the customers **select** what they would like and tell the server. The server may **write** down the customer's choices.

WORK: Family Interview!

Interview a person, or preferably one or more members of a family *(such as a retired couple)* about the work they need to do at home. Before the interview, students **write** out questions they will ask about different work chores:

What chores do you do at home?
Who does which chores?
How much time do they take?
What happens if you don't do them?
What chores do you like?
What chores do you not like?

Students **select** a question they want to ask. During the interview, the students take turns **asking** their question. Students either **write** down the answers or record the answers and **discuss** them later.

GO: Where Will We Go Today?

Students **look** at their schedule for the day. Direct students to **say,** in a complete sentence, the first place they will go, the next place, etc. Students will **answer** *(Ex. "We will go to music. Then we will go to math.")* Write out each sentence on a sentence strip. Mix them up and have students **read** each one, then put them in the order of when they will do things that day.

PLAY: Rate the Games!

Select three different games that all of your students are able to play. They may be familiar games or new games. Students play each of the three games, either as a whole group, or in small group centers through which they rotate. When each of the games have been played, students **select** and **name** the game that is their number one choice, and **tell** others what they like about that game.

LIVE: Where Does the Teacher Live?

The teacher tells students about where he/she lives. The teacher brings in photos of different things in his/her home, and photos of people or pets that may live with him/her. The teacher tells students about who the neighbors are. Students **ask** the teacher questions about where he/she lives, and the teacher answers. The teacher then asks the students similar questions about where they live and the students **answer.**

SECTION TWO

MEville to WEville

VOCABULARY ACTIVITIES

part two

unit 2
my family

The activities in this section provide students with oral language opportunities to actively use vocabulary words and understand their meaning.

Throughout these **Vocabulary Activities** students have opportunities to develop meaningful relationships and a sense of belonging as they interact with others in many large group activities.

This "character and community" icon will signal a lesson activity through which this sense of belonging can be reinforced.

ACTIVITY #1

MATERIALS:

- vocabulary cards Set Two R#58, R#59
- Tableware Picture Cards page R#66
- Tableware Templates page R#67
- construction paper *(11" x 17")* in assorted colors
- table settings *(see R#66) (one per student)*
- breakfast or lunch food and beverage for class
- chart paper
- card stock
- black marker
- scissors
- glue

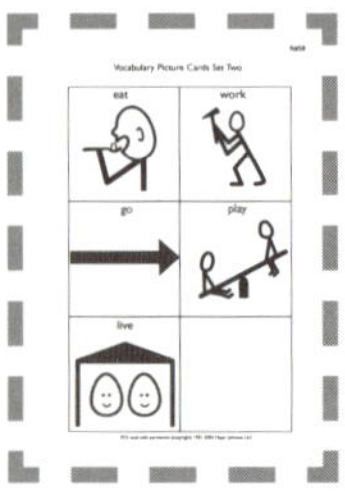
R#58

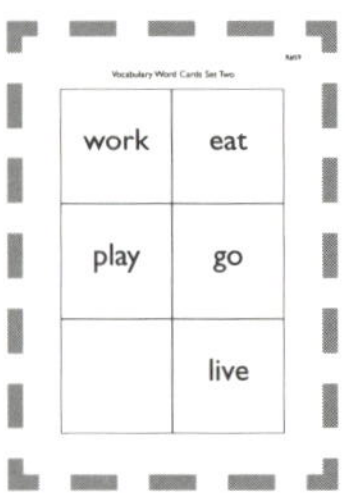

R#59

R#66

R#67

NOTE: If possible, serve items that require the use of all silverware, such as a breakfast of French toast, scrambled eggs, and peaches or a lunch of spaghetti, green beans, applesauce.

PREPARATION:

- Write the title, "Places Families Eat Meals" at the top of the chart paper.
- Copy the Tableware Picture Cards onto card stock. Cut them out.
- Create a plate and glass template page. Trace a regular size plate and the bottom of a glass onto a sheet of copy paper. Make a copy for each student.
- Make a sample place mat.
- Clear off a table that can be used to practice setting a table, and will seat all of the students.

OPTION: Create Boardmaker pictures/symbols of different places families might eat meals together (kitchen/dining room table, picnic table, campfire, restaurant, living room).

Students learn how to set the table for a meal that they eat together.

Students discuss different places where families eat meals.

- Show students the "eat" vocabulary card. Lead students in **saying** the word at least three to five times.
- Ask students to **name** or **select** different places where a family could eat a meal.
- Write each student response on the chart paper.
- Students **read** the list of places a family may eat a meal.
- Students **name,** or **select** a picture/symbol of one place their family eats meals.

Students learn about the items used to set a table.

- Explain to students that when their family eats a meal at the table, it is important to first set the table with the items they will need during the meal.
- Students take turns **selecting** a Tableware Picture Card.
- The student **identifies** the actual tableware item that matches the Tableware Picture Card and places it on that card.
- The student **tells** or demonstrates the use of the tableware item *(holding food, drinking, eating, scooping)*.
- After all tableware items have been discussed/demonstrated, the teacher asks students to **identify** the tableware item that has a particular use. Ex: "Susie, what do we use to cut food?"

Students make place mats.

- Students **cut** out each of the templates.
- Students **select** a color of construction paper.
- Show students the plate picture card. Direct students to **identify** the plate template and **glue** it in the center of the paper.
- Show students each of the other Tableware Picture Cards, one at a time. As each picture card is displayed, direct students to **identify** the matching template and **glue** it on that place. *(See place mat illustration on R#67.)*

NOTE: Send home these place mats with a note suggesting parents use this place mat at family meals and encourage their child to set their own place at the table, following the templates on their place mat.

Students set the table using their place mats.

- Give each student an individual place setting and their place mat.
- Show students a Tableware Picture Card. Begin with the plate, and then the napkin.
- Students **identify** that tableware item from the items in their set.
- Students place that tableware item on the appropriate place on their place mat.
- Continue this process for each tableware item.

Students use their utensils to prepare and eat a meal.

- Serve each student, or instruct students to serve themselves. Ask students to hand you their plate, cup, etc. when you are serving them, or direct them to put certain foods on their plate.
- Students use their tableware to eat and drink their meal and wipe their hands and face.

NOTE: Continue working on these skills in the cafeteria on a regular basis. Ask students to think about what silverware they need, identify that silverware, put it on their tray, and use it appropriately.

Students participate in Family Chore Olympics.

Students review the importance of chores within a family.

- Show students the "work" vocabulary card. Lead the students in **saying** the word multiple times.
- Students **discuss** the work that needs to be done in our homes.
- Explain to students the importance of all members of a family working together to do the household chores.

Student teams actively participate in the Family Chore Olympics.

NOTE: If time is a major constraint, choose one of the games and follow directions to participate in the Family Chore Olympics.

- Explain to students that they are going to break up into two teams, and each team will be considered a "family" for the games they are going to play.
- Call out the name of each student. The student identifies himself/herself by **saying**, "That's me!"
- Direct each student to move to one of the family tables.
- Students take turns **reading** a part of the directions for each game from the Family Chore Olympics Directions Script.
- Students follow directions to participate in their family groups, in a practice round and real round of each game.
- Take a picture of each team actively participating in each game *(four pictures total)*.
- Students cheer their team members on during the games.
- At the end of each game, the students **clap** for the winning team.

Students make language experience class books about the Family Chore Olympics.

- Show students the cover for the class book, Sack Pack.
- Show students the first page and together **read** the words, "We put food in the bag."
- Put the photos from the Family Chore Olympics on display. Ask one student from each team to **identify** the picture of their team putting food in the bag.
- Both students **show** the picture to their team.
- One student from each team **glues** the photo on one of the two rectangular boxes on the first page (R#70).
- Show students the next page (R#71), "We put ______in the bag."
- Ask students to **name** or **select** a food that they put in the bag.
- The teacher, or a student, **writes** that food name on the blank line.
- Lead the students in **reading** that sentence.
- Continue this process for each page, until all food items have been named and written.
- Show students the cover for the class book, Laundry Toss.
- Complete the above step-by-step process for creating the pages of the Laundry Toss book.
- Give a page, from either book, to each student. Each student **reads** their page.
- Students illustrate their page by **drawing** or **coloring** a picture of the food or clothes that they put in the bag or basket.
- Collect the book pages and ask a student to **staple** the books together.
- Students **read** each book.

MATERIALS:

- vocabulary cards Set Two R#58, R#59
- Family Chore Olympics Directions Script R#68
- construction paper
- black marker
- two large tables
- Family Chore Olympics Materials
  - Grocery/Laundry List R#69 *(two)*
  - grocery items *(two of each)* on R#69
  - clothes *(two of each item)* on R#69
  - two paper grocery sacks
  - two laundry baskets
- digital camera
- book page 1 R#70 *(two copies)*
- book page 2a R#71 *(six copies)*
- book page 2b R#72 *(six copies)*
- markers/crayons
- glue
- stapler

PREPARATION:

- Prior to each game, put one set of Family Chore Olympics Materials on each table.
- Cut both copies of the Grocery/Laundry List R#69 down the center, cutting on the dotted line.
- On one copy of book page 1 R#70, fill in the blanks so that the sentence reads, "We put food in the bag" and on the other copy, fill in the blanks so that the sentence reads, "We put clothes in the basket."
- Write the titles Sack Pack and Laundry Toss on separate sheets of construction paper to create book covers.

R#58-R#59

R#68-R#72

ACTIVITY #3

MATERIALS:

- vocabulary cards Set Two R#58, R#59
- Treasure Hunt Place Pictures/Symbols R#73
- Treasure Hunt Clue Sheets R#74, R#75, R#76
- construction paper *(8" x 11") (six sheets)*
- glue
- magazines and newspapers
- scissors
- legal size envelopes *(six)*
- scotch tape
- props for the treasure hunt
  - soda can
  - book
  - pair of shoes
  - loaf of packaged bread
  - stuffed animal bear *(teddy bear)*
  - box of treasure, such as candy or Hershey® Treasures

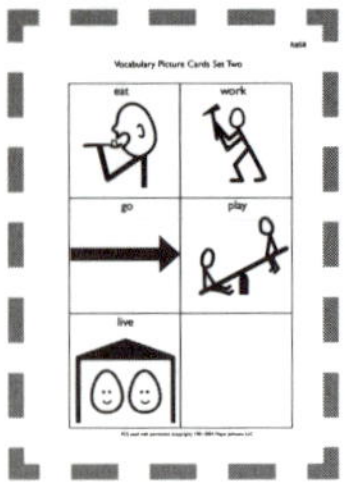

R#58

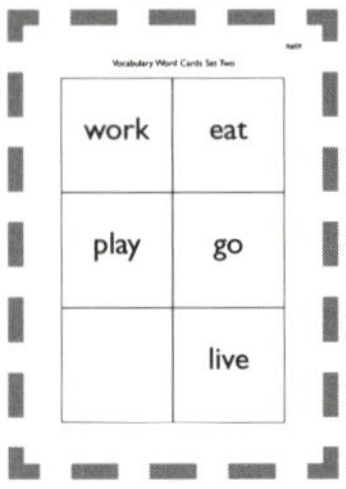

R#59

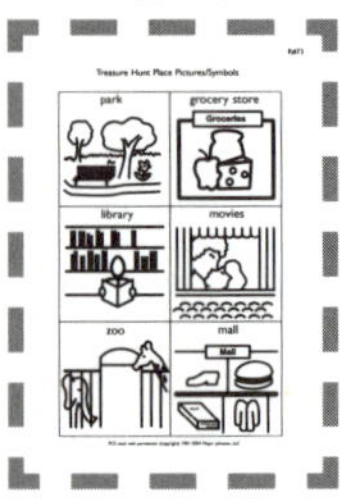

R#73

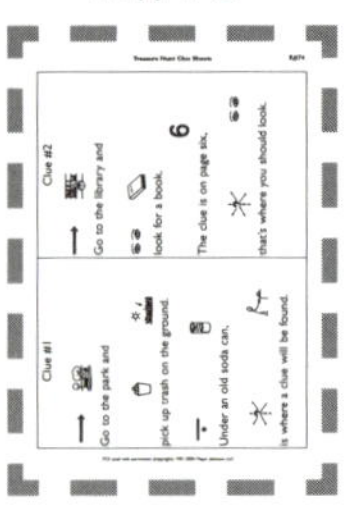

R#74

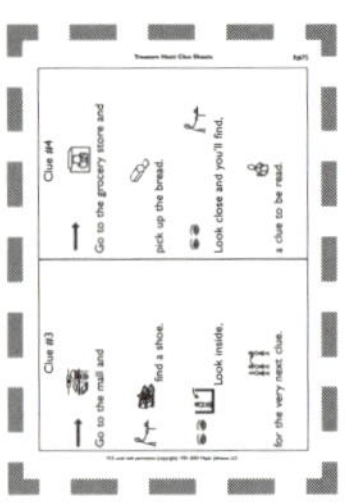

R#75

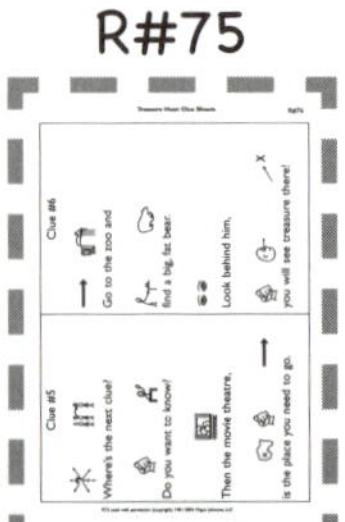

R#76

PREPARATION:

- Designate an area that will be used for the treasure hunt.
- Cut each of the three clue sheets in half, creating a total of six clue sheets.
- Put each clue in an envelope and write the clue number on the outside of the envelope.
- Cut out each of the Treasure Hunt Place Pictures/Symbols and place one in the center of each of the six sheets of construction paper, to create place signs.
- Follow the directions on the Treasure Hunt Clue Set-Up.

Students participate in a treasure hunt and "go" different places.

Students prepare for the treasure hunt.

- Show students each of the place signs. Lead students in **saying** the name of each place.
- Explain to students that they are going to be working in small groups, and each group will make a poster of a different place.
- Split the class in six groups and have each group make one poster, or in three groups and have each group make two posters. Give each group a place sign, magazines and newspapers, scissors, and glue.
- Direct students to **look** through the magazines and newspapers and **select** pictures of things representing their place: park - trees, library - books and words, mall - clothes, movie theatre - newspaper movie ads, grocery store - food, zoo - animals.
- Students **cut** out the pictures and **glue** them on the place sign to create a place poster.

NOTE: For the next part of the activity, the actual treasure hunt, the clues and clue props need to be set up without students watching.

Students follow directions to "go" different places by participating in a treasure hunt.

- Show students the "go" vocabulary card. Lead students in **saying** the word multiple times.
- Explain to students that they will go on a treasure hunt.
- Tell students that they will be reading clues that tell them to go different places and look for new clues.
- Hand clue #1 to a student. The student opens the envelope and leads the class in **reading** the first clue.
- The students follow the clue. The students find the next clue, and one student opens it and leads the class in **reading** the clue.

  NOTE: Each clue envelope may be opened by ripping it open or by **cutting** it open.
- This process continues until the students arrive at the zoo sign, locate the bear, and find and share the treasure.

TREASURE HUNT CLUE SET-UP

Put each place poster up in a different location and lay out the clues with the clue props:

1. Have Clue #1 ready to give to a student.
2. Put Clue #2 under a soda can near the park poster.
3. Put Clue #3 in page 6 of a book near the library poster.
4. Put Clue #4 inside a shoe underneath the mall poster.
5. Tape Clue #5 on a loaf of bread. Place by the grocery store poster.
6. Put Clue #6 near the movie theatre poster.
7. Put the stuffed animal bear near the zoo poster. Place the treasure box behind the bear.

Students play old fashioned children's games.

Students learn about children's games.

- Show students the "play" vocabulary card. Lead the students in **saying** the word several times.
- Tell students about the games they are going to play.

Teacher Script

"We're going to play some fun games today!"
"These are games that your parents and grandparents probably played when they were kids."
"The games are called Red Light Green Light, Musical Chairs, and Drop the Handkerchief."
"One person will read the directions for each game."
"Listen closely to the directions, then we'll play each game."
"After each game, we'll talk about what we liked and didn't like about that game."
"After we play all three games, we're going to vote on our favorite game."

Students play and respond to each game.

- One student **reads** the directions to the first game from that Game Direction Card.
- The students follow the directions to participate in the game.
- A teacher or other adult takes pictures of the students playing the game.
- The students **clap** for the winner of the game.
- The teacher writes the game title at the top of the chart paper.
- The teacher asks students to **tell** the class what they liked or didn't like about the game.
- The teacher writes each student response on the chart paper.
- The students **read** the responses.
- This process is repeated for each game.

  OPTION: These games are all action games requiring movement. Consider pairing each child with a peer and playing each game as a pair or mini team to accommodate students in wheelchairs.

Students vote on their favorite game.

- The teacher shows the students a Game Direction Card and leads the students in **reading** the game title.
- The students take turns **saying** how they played the game, and anything else about the game.
- This process is repeated for each game.
- Students then **vote** on which game was their favorite game to play.
- For each game, the teacher marks one tally per vote. Students **count** up the number of votes for each game.
- Students **identify** the winning game, and may play that game again.

"Wheresoever you go, go with all your heart."
CONFUCIUS

MATERIALS:

- **vocabulary cards Set Two R#58, R#59**
- **Game Direction Cards R#77** *(cut out)*
- **prizes** *(optional)*
- **black marker**
- **chart paper** *(three sheets)*
- **individual game materials**

RED LIGHT GREEN LIGHT

- **construction paper** *(one red sheet, one green sheet)*
- **ruler or paint stirrer stick** *(two)*
- **masking tape**

MUSICAL CHAIRS

- **tape player/CD player with music**
- **chairs or construction paper and Scotch tape**

DROP THE HANDKERCHIEF

- **handkerchief or bandana**
- **masking tape**

PREPARATION:

RED LIGHT GREEN LIGHT

Cut two large, equal circles out of the construction paper. Write the word STOP on the red circle and the word GO on the green circle. Tape a ruler or paint stick to the back of each circle, creating a handle. Make a START line and FINISH line on the floor, using masking tape.

MUSICAL CHAIRS

Set up chairs in a circle. If students in wheelchairs will be participating, tape large sheets of construction paper to the floor in a circular shape. Put the music in the tape player or CD player.

DROP THE HANDKERCHIEF

Use masking tape to make a large circle on the floor.

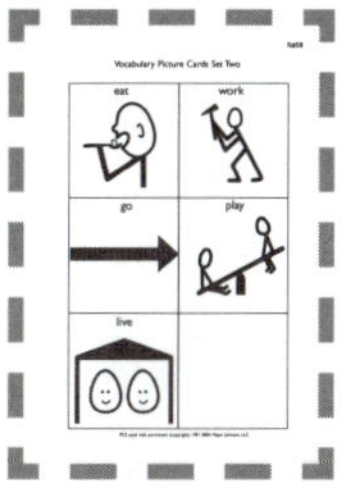
R#58

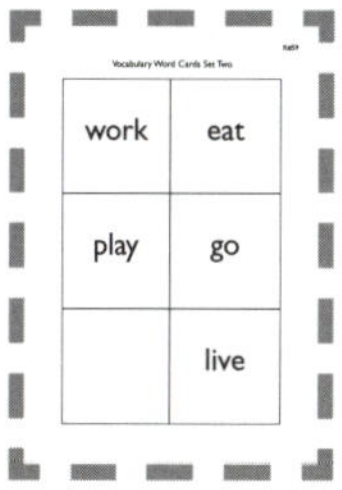

R#59

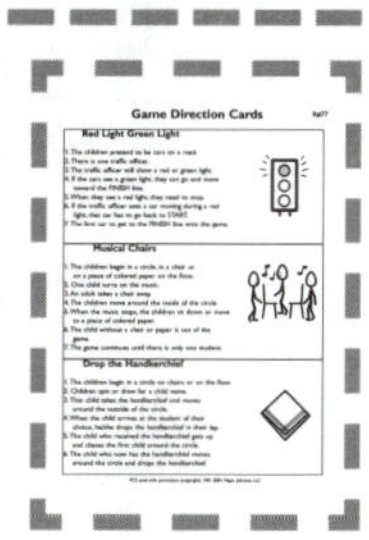
R#77

ACTIVITY #5

Students create a model of their home where they live.

MATERIALS:

- vocabulary cards Set Two R#58, R#59
- paper shapes in a variety of sizes and colors
- white drawing paper
- glue
- writing tools
- note cards *(3" x 5")* *(one per student)*
- crayons/markers
- magazines and department/ furniture store flyers
- scissors
- envelopes

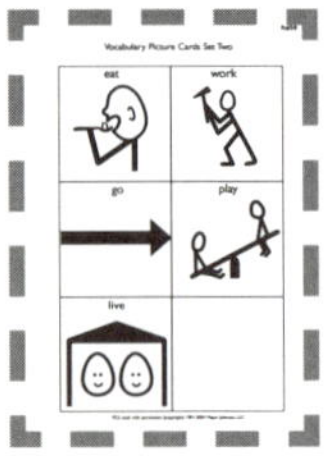

R#58

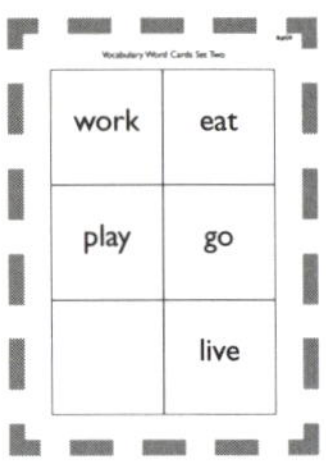

R#59

PREPARATION:

- Make a sample home model.
- Write a short note to each student. Put each note in an envelope and seal it. Write the student's address on the outside of the envelope.

Students build a two dimensional model of their home.

- Show students the "live" vocabulary card. Lead the students in **saying** the word several times.
- Show students the sample home model and the shapes they can use to build their home model.
- Students **glue** the shapes on their paper to create a home model.
- Students use crayons or markers to **draw** a background scene on their paper, such as roads and trees.
- Students **look** through magazines and **select** pictures of things that are in the home in which they live. Students **cut** out the pictures and **glue** them on their home model.

Students label their home model with their address.

- Students **write** their address on the note card.
- Students **glue** the address card on their home model.
- Students **show** their home model to others and **read** their address.

Students receive mail at their home address.

- Take out each envelope and ask the students, "Who lives at (1552 Randolph Rd.)?"
- Students **look** at the address card on their home model. If it matches the one being read, they **say,** "I live there!"
- The teacher brings the mail to that student. The student opens the envelope and **reads** the teacher note.

VOCABULARY EXTENSION ACTIVITIES

EAT: TASTE TEST!

Students **select** a food with which they would like to do a taste test. Students follow directions to make two variations of a certain recipe, such as cookies with or without frosting. Or, purchase two different brands of a food item at the grocery store. Students invite another class to come sample the food, and **ask** the other students to **say** which of the two food options they liked better. Students **mark** Choice A or Choice B for each person who does the taste test. Students then **count** up how many votes each choice got and announce the food that more students like to eat!

WORK: CHORE CHART

Send a note home to parents asking them to send in a list of three different chores or jobs that their child is responsible for at home, or that they would like their child to begin to do at home. Give each student a chart that has a place to write the name of each chore, with at least five boxes after each chore in which students may place a sticker when they do that chore at home. Students **read** and **write** the name of each chore. Students bring the Chore Chart home to use.

GO: DREAM VACATION ITINERARY

Gather as much information as possible on a fun place that most of your students would love to go if they could, such as Disney World. Tell students that they are going to go on a pretend vacation to this place. Show students all of the different information and pictures/ brochures of places to go and things to do on this pretend dream vacation. Students then take turns **selecting** a particular place they would like to go while at this vacation place. The teacher writes the name of this place on their Vacation Schedule, as a complete sentence. *(Ex: We will go to the water park. We will go to the pizza place.)* Students then **read** the list of places and **discuss** what they think they would like about each of those places.

PLAY: MAKE MUSIC!

Explain to students that one fun way some families like to play together is to play music, and sometimes to make music! Bring in an assortment of different instruments, and different styles of music. Students **select** an instrument they would like to play and all students make music together! Record the music and play it back. Students **say** how they think the music sounds, and if they like the sound of the music! Students also **select** different types of recorded music to play and **say** if they do or do not like that music. Students may **tell** the others about music they like to play or listen to with their family.

LIVE: WHERE DO YOU LIVE?

Students learn about the state in which they live. Show students a United States map and help them **identify** their state on the map. Read one or more books to students about the state in which they live. Students **answer** teacher questions about their state. Students may **color** in an outline map of their state.

SECTION THREE

MEville to WEville

unit 2

my family

In these Word Wall Lessons, students will have opportunities to practice identifying, reading, spelling and writing the words.

part two

Throughout **The Word Wall Lessons,** students will have active roles as they read the word wall words, lead activities, and provide directions to other students. As students engage in these roles of reader, leader, and teacher, look for opportunities to communicate to them the importance of what they are doing.

This "character and community" icon will signal a lesson activity through which students can have a valued role and learn to understand the importance of their role.

LESSON #1, #2, #3

LESSON 1

Students practice saying and writing the word wall words.

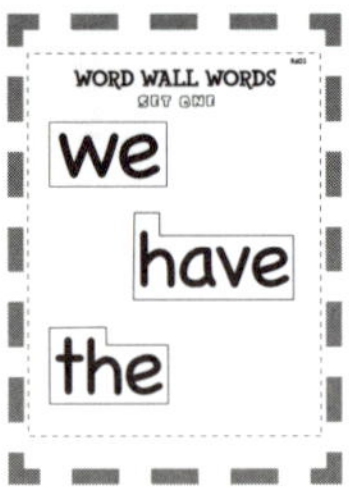

R#25

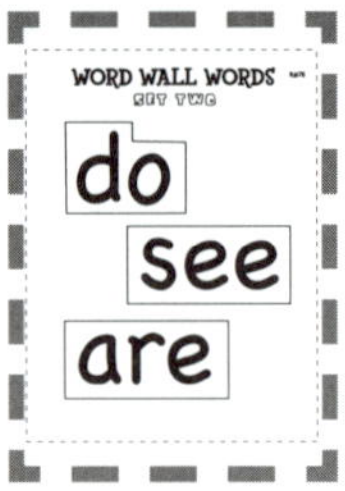

R#78

MATERIALS:

- **Word Wall Words Set One R#25 and Set Two R#78**
- **writing tools such as: pencils, crayons, gel pens, markers, chalk**
- **writing paper**
- **wooden dowel, stick, or other letter pointer**

PREPARATION:

- **Set out the different writing tools.**

- The teacher writes a word on the board in large, bold letters.
- A student comes to the board and uses the pointer to point out each letter of the word and lead the students in chanting out, or loudly **saying**, each letter.
- Each student takes a turn leading the class in chanting the words. Include words from Part 1 *(we, have, the)* and Part 2 *(see, do, are)*.
- The students **write** each word wall word several times using one or more writing tools.

LESSON 2

Students participate in a Sentence Completion Activity.

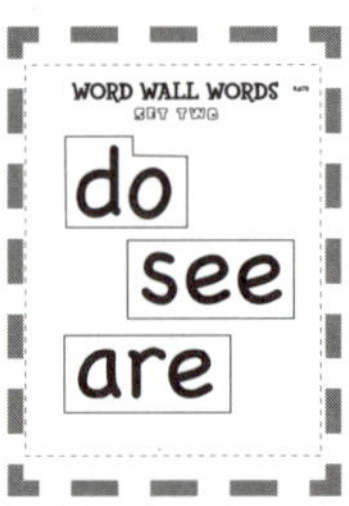

R#78

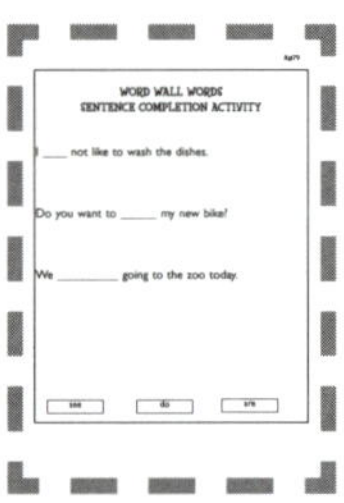

R#79

MATERIALS:

- **Word Wall Words Set Two R#78**
- **writing tools**
- **Sentence Completion Activity R#79** *(one per student)*
- **white board or chalk board with dry-erase markers/chalk**

PREPARATION:

- **Put double-sided tape on the back of each word wall word. Put the word wall words on the board.**

- The teacher writes the first sentence from R#79 on the board.
- The teacher leads the students in **reading** the sentence.
- The teacher asks a student to come to the board, **identify** the correct word, and place it in the correct spot in the sentence on the board.
- That student leads the others in **reading** the entire sentence.
- Students **identify** the word on their paper.
- Students **write** the correct word in the blank.

LESSON 3

Students participate in the Mind Reader activity.

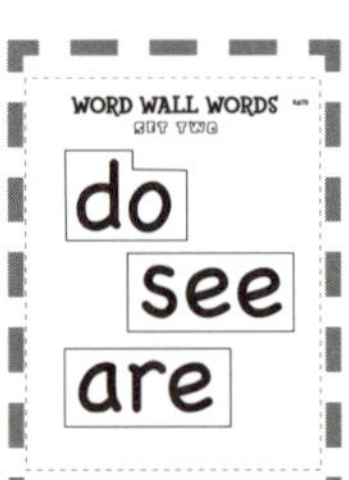

R#78

R#80

MATERIALS:

- **Word Wall Words Set Two R#78**
- **writing tools**
- **note cards** *(3" x 5")*
- **Mind Reader Script R#80**
- **coin or other small object** *(one per student)*

- The teacher shows students each word wall word and directs them to **write** each word on a 3" x 5" note card.
- Students place their word cards on the desk or table surface in front of them.
- A student, or the teacher, **reads** the clues from the Mind Reader Script to the class.
- Students **select** the word wall word which they think is being described and place their object on that word card.
- The teacher affirms or redirects each student's choice.
- Students **say** the word together as a class.

LESSON #4

Students participate in The Word Find Game.

Students prepare for the Word Find Game.

- Students take turns **selecting** one of the word signs.
- The student **shows** the word to the class and leads the class in **reading** the word several times.
- The student **chooses** a place in the room to put the word sign, and uses tape to attach the sign to that location.

Students participate in The Word Find Game.

- The teacher selects a word and tells students, "Go to the word (see)."
- Students look at the word signs around the room and **identify** the word that was said.
- Students move to that sign.
- The teacher shows students the word and leads the students in **clap/chanting** the letters to the word.
- This process continues until all words have been called at least once.

LESSON 4

MATERIALS:

- **Word Wall Words Set One R#25 and Set Two R#78**
- **construction paper**
- **black marker**
- **tape**

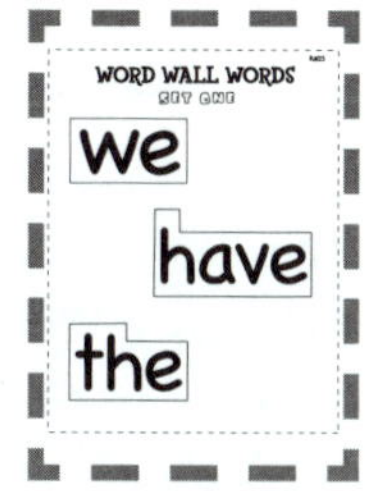

R#25

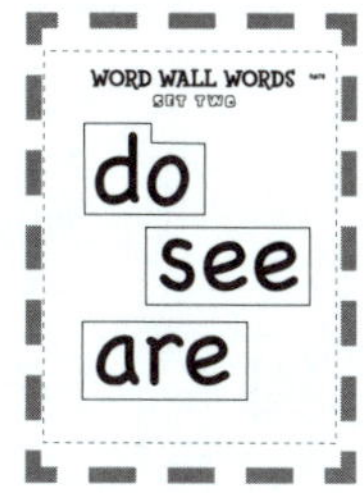

R#78

PREPARATION:

- **Write each word wall word on a sheet of construction paper in large letters to create word signs.**

LESSON #5

Students participate in The Question Exchange activity.

Students prepare for The Question Exchange activity.

- The teacher shows students each of the word wall words and leads students in **saying** each word several times.
- The teacher shows students each of the questions, and leads students in **reading** each question.
- The teacher puts the word wall words on display so that they are highly visible to all students.
- The teacher explains to students that they are going to use Word Wall Words to write questions that they will ask students later.
- The teacher gives each student two to three note cards and a writing tool.
- The teacher reads one of the questions, and directs students to **write** that question on their note card.
- Continue this process for each question you'd like to have the students asking each other.

Students ask each other the written questions they created.

- Divide students into two groups. Assign Group A to ask the questions and Group B to answer the questions.
- Each student in Group A **selects** a student from Group B and **reads** the question on each of their cards.
- The student in Group B **answers** each question.
- Students switch groups. Students who did the asking now do the answering.

LESSON 5

MATERIALS:

- **Word Wall Words Set One R#25 and Set Two R#78**
- **note cards** *(4"x 6")*
- **writing tools**
- **Unit 1 Word Wall Words - Use word cards from Unit 1 or create word cards by writing each of the following words on a note card:** me, who, and, I, it, you, like, to, what

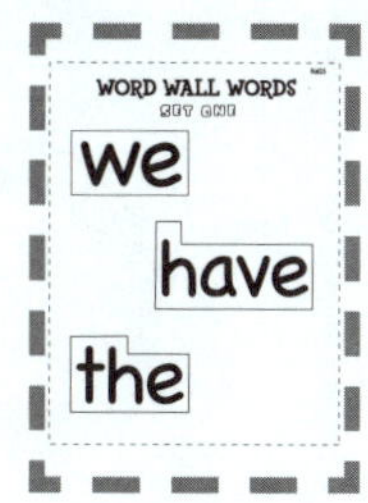

R#25

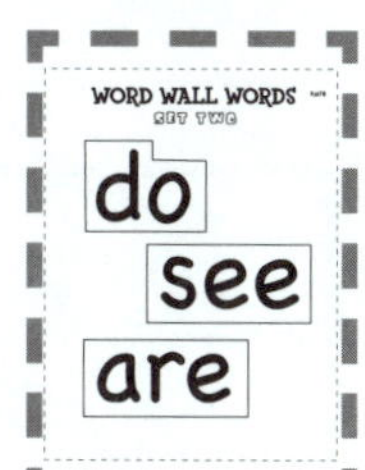

R#78

PREPARATION:

- **Write each of the following questions on a separate piece of paper, in bold letters.**
  - What do you see?
  - Who do you see?
  - What do you like?
  - Who do you like?
  - What do you do?
  - Do you see me?
  - What do you have?

Dear Parents,

Your child is currently working on the following words: **are, see, do.**

Whenever possible, please take the time to reinforce these words with your child by having him/her write the words, say the words, and spell the words. Below is an activity to do with your child to help him/her learn each of the three word wall words.

Sincerely,

____

Word Writing

Directions:

Cut out each of the word cards below. You may want to tape down the word card so that it does not slip when your child is writing on it.

Let your child select a writing tool they want to use to trace each letter of the word, such as a marker, crayon, piece of chalk, pencil, colored pencil, pen, or paintbrush with paint. Direct your child to start with the first letter of the word and trace each letter, saying the letter name. The word may be traced multiple times.

If your child is able to form letters, give your child a piece of blank paper and their choice of writing tool to write the word, making their own letters.

If your child is not able to grasp a writing tool, consider tracing each letter with fabric paint or glue and letting it dry. Then bring the word card up to your child's hand and help him/her run their hand along the card, feeling each raised letter as you and your child say each letter name.

are

see

do

MEville to WEville

unit 2

my family

part two

Several days before teaching Literacy Lesson #2, send home the I've Been Working With My Family home song sheet R#82.

R#82

Teacher Note: Complete Vocabulary Activity #1 before teaching Literacy Lesson #1.

Throughout these **Literacy Lessons**, students and teachers will have frequent opportunities to acknowledge the contributions and accomplishments of others. When student responses are given, acknowledge the person who contributed it and acknowledge the value of that response.

This "character and community" icon will signal a lesson activity that provides an opportunity for students and teachers to acknowledge each other.

LESSON #1

Teacher Note:

Complete Vocabulary Activity #1 before teaching this lesson. Consider inviting another class to join you in eating a meal.

MATERIALS:

- **Table Manners Picture and Scenario Cards R#81**
- **chart paper**
- **card stock**
- **All-Turn-It® spinner** *(optional)*
- **place mats** *(created in Vocabulary Activity #1)*
- **place setting** *(plate, cup, knife, fork, spoon, napkin) (one set per student)*
- **breakfast or lunch food and beverage for class** *(ask for food from cafeteria or make together as a class)*
- **serving utensils**

PREPARATION:

- **Copy the Table Manners Picture and Scenario Cards R#81 onto card stock. Cut out each card.**
- **Put the Table Manners Picture Cards on display.**
- **Place the Table Manners Scenario Cards facedown in a stack or on the large overlay of the All-Turn-It® spinner.**

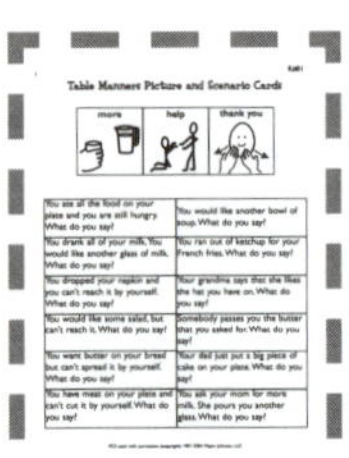

R#81

- **Put the serving utensils on or near each food item.**

Students learn about and practice proper table manners.

Students read and respond to scenarios about eating a meal at a table.

- Explain to students that when people eat a meal at the table, it is important to use good table manners and ask for what you need.
- Show students the Table Manners Picture Cards and lead them in **saying** each of the words. Put them on display.
- As each word is named, explain to students when you would use that word.

  more: When you want more of something to eat/drink, use the word "more" to ask for more.

  help: When you can't do something by yourself even after you try, use the word "help" to ask for help.

  thank you: When somebody does something nice for you, serves you, or helps you, use the words "thank you" to thank them for their help.
- Tell students that they are going to read about situations that happen when eating at a table, and decide what to say.
- Students take turns drawing or **spinning** for a Table Manners Scenario Card. The student **reads** the card to the class.
- The student **selects** and **reads** the Table Manners Picture Card that shows an appropriate response.
- The teacher leads the students in **saying** a complete sentence in response to the question, "What do you say?"

  Ex. Question - "You ran out of ketchup for your French Fries. What do you say?"

  Answer - Student **selects** the "more" Table Manners Picture Card and **says**, "More ketchup, please."

Students discuss situations in which they would use each of the table manners words/phrases.

- Ask a student to **select** a Table Manners Picture Card and **show** it to the class.
- Lead the students in **reading** the word/phrase on the card.
- Ask students to **tell** the class why somebody might say this to somebody else when eating at a table.
- Suggest to students additional reasons why somebody may use this word/phrase when eating at a table.
- Write the word/phrase on the chart paper, and write all responses underneath.
- Continue this process for each of the three Table Manners Picture Cards.

Students practice communicating appropriately to others while eating a meal at a table.

- Students put their place mat down on the table and set their place mat with the dishes and utensils.
- The teacher puts the food items on the table, family style, with serving utensils.
- Students use the appropriate words and phrases *(more, help, thank you)* to **ask** for what they need and respond to what they are given.

  NOTE: Continue working on these skills in the cafeteria on a regular basis. Remind and/or prompt students to use appropriate words when interacting with others at the cafeteria.

THINK ABOUT! Think about leading students in discussing and identifying the differences between a snack and a meal. Identify the types of food you have at each, when they are eaten, who you would eat with at each, and the silverware you would need for each.

Students sing and act out the song "I've Been Working With My Family."

Teacher Note: **Consider having students practice this song for a week or more and then perform it for another class or for parents. Schedule a performance at least a week prior to the big day!**

Students learn about the song, "I've Been Working With My Family."

- Students **look** at and **read** each of the Song Picture Cards *(except family)*. Explain that these are different places in a home where families do chores.
- Put the different song props on display, excluding the work rags and chore clothes. Students take turns **selecting** a prop and **showing** it to the class.
- Students **say** the purpose of that item and **select** the Song Picture Card showing where it would be used.
- Direct students to place each item near the matching sign on the prop table.
- Put the "family" sign on the table. Put the work rags and chore clothes on the table by the sign. Explain to students that family members need to wear chore clothes and use work rags for any family chores they do.
- Follow Teacher Directions #1 - #5 (R#84) to prepare students for singing the song.

Students sing and act out the song, "I've Been Working With My Family."

- Students follow the "I've Been Working With My Family" Teacher Directions #6 - #9 (R#84) to **sing** and act out the song, "I've Been Working With My Family."
- When the song is completed, students may **select** a Song Picture Card representing a stanza they want to sing again.

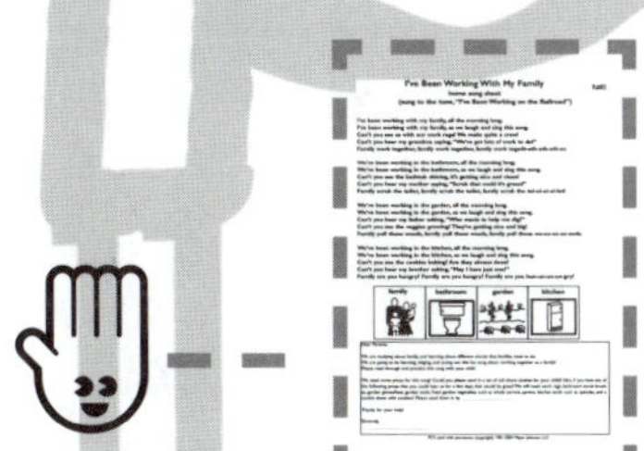

R#82

R#83

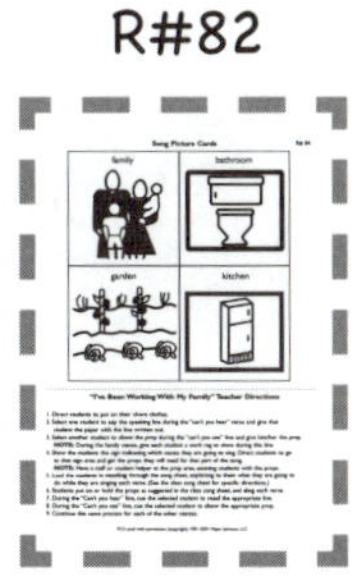

R#84

Teacher Note: **Send home the I've Been Working With My Family home song sheet several days before doing this lesson so that parents will have time to send in the necessary props.**

MATERIALS:

- **I've Been Working With My Family home song sheet R#82 and class song sheet R#83**
- **Song Picture Cards R#84** *(two copies)*
- **poster board** *(four large sheets)*
- **black marker**
- **construction paper**
- **glue**
- **prop table**
- **song props -**

  Family Chores: work rags, chore clothes *(sent in from home)*
  Bathroom: cleaning supplies *(scrub brushes)*, flashlight
  Garden: garden gloves and garden tools, real vegetables
  Kitchen: aprons and kitchen tools, cookie sheet with cookies

PREPARATION:

- **Glue each Song Picture Card on a piece of construction paper to create signs, and put these signs, except the "family" sign, on the table. Cut out the other set of Song Picture Cards.**
- **Write out the verses to each stanza, one stanza per poster board.**
- **Write each of the following sentences on a separate sheet of construction paper:**
  "We've got lots of work to do!"
  "Scrub that mold, it's green!"
  "Who wants to help me dig?"
  "May I have just one?"

OPTION: Do a search on the Internet using the words, "I've Been Working on the Railroad" music to access a recording of the tune.

Students participate in the game, "Name That Place."

MATERIALS:

- Place Picture Cards R#62
- "Name That Place" Game Directions Script R#85
- "Name that Place" Game Questions Script R#86
- hand-held bells *(two)*
- construction paper *(11" x 17")*
- card stock
- black markers
- sport coat and tie from the 70's *(optional)*

PREPARATION:

- Copy the Place Picture Cards R#62 onto card stock. Cut them out.
- Divide the students into two teams.

Place Picture Cards #1

R#62

"Name That Place" Game Directions Script

R#85

"Name That Place" Game Questions Script

R#86

Students prepare for the game, "Name That Place."

- Show students each of the Place Picture Cards and lead them in **reading** the name of each of the places.
- Put three to five Place Picture Cards on display.
- Students take turns **reading** the "Name That Place" Game Directions Script.

Students participate in playing the game, "Name That Place."

- Instruct students to **say** some ideas for a name for their team. If students have difficulties independently generating and/or agreeing on a team name, give the team some name options and have them **vote** for their name choice.
- The students **write** their team name, and their own individual names, on a sheet of construction paper to make team signs.
- Write each team name on the board in large letters. Points will be recorded here.
- Each team name sign is hung or placed near the area where the team will be participating in the game.
- Students take turns being the host and **reading** a question from the "Name That Place" Game Questions Script.
- Students follow the game directions to participate in the game.

NOTE: The host may choose to dress up as a game show host from the 70's.

"We don't stop playing because we grow old; we grow old because we stop playing."

GEORGE BERNARD SHAW

Students make and play a rhyming game.

Students discuss games they play with their families.

- Show students the "play" vocabulary card. Lead students in **saying** the word at least three to five times.
- Ask students to **name** some games that they like to play with their family.
- Write each of those games on the chart paper.
- Ask students to **say** why they like playing games with their families.
- Explain to students that they are going to make a game to take home and play with their family.

Students follow directions to make the "Catch a Rhyme" game.

- Show students the sample "Catch a Rhyme" game.
- Students open up their file folder. Students **glue** a sheet of blue construction paper on each side of the file folder, completely covering both sides.
- Students **cut** on the dotted line on the "Catch a Rhyme" Game Directions sheet.
- Students close the file folder and **glue** the "Catch a Rhyme" Game Directions on the lower front of the folder.
- Students **cut** fish shapes out of the colored construction paper and **glue** them on the front of the file folder.
- Students **glue** the clasp envelope on the back of the folder, with the clasp side facing out.
- Students **cut** out each of the picture cards, paper clip them together, and put them in the envelope.
- Students **cut** out each of the Fish Cards, paper clip them together, and put them in the envelope.
- Students put their mini fishing pole in the envelope.

Students play the rhyming game with a classmate.

- Students **select** a classmate with whom they want to play their "Catch a Rhyme" game.
- The students follow the game directions to play the "Catch a Rhyme" game.
- When students have completed one game, they may play again using the other student's game board.

Students bring the game home to play with their family and respond to that experience.

- Students bring their "Catch a Rhyme" game home, with the Family Game Response Sheet.
- Students play the game with their family. Students **write** and **mark** their responses on the sheet.
- Students return the sheets to school and take turns **reading** their family responses to the class.

MATERIALS:

- **vocabulary cards Set Two R#58, R#59**
- **chart paper**
- **black marker**
- **"Catch a Rhyme" Game Directions R#87**
- **Fish Cards R#88, R#89**
- **Family Game Response Sheet R#90**
- **file folder** *(one per student)*
- **manila 5" x 7" clasp envelope** *(one per student)*
- **blue construction paper** *(11" x 17") (two sheets per student)*
- **colored construction paper** *(any size)*
- **paper clips**
- **scissors**
- **glue**
- **tongue depressor or craft stick** *(one per student)*
- **felt or rubber grip mat** *(1/2" square per student)*

R#58-R#59

R#87-R#90

PREPARATION:

- **Make a sample game.**
- **Make a mini fishing pole for each student by cutting a small piece of rubber grip mat or felt, and gluing it on the very end of the tongue depressor or craft stick.**
- **Make one copy of R#87-R#90 per student.**
- **Trace the rhyme fish onto construction paper for students to cut out and use to decorate their "Catch a Rhyme" game.**

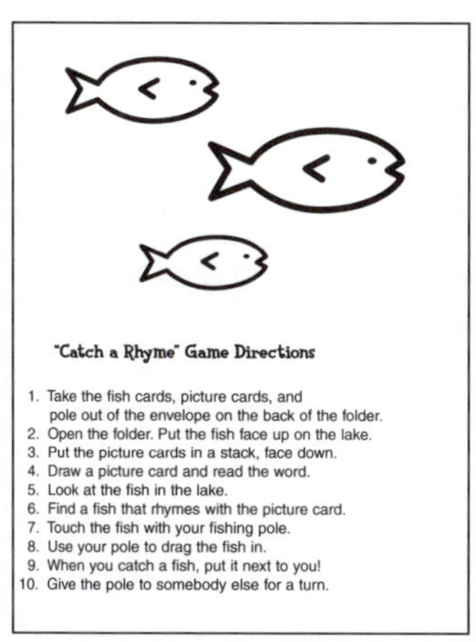

"Catch a Rhyme" Game Directions

1. Take the fish cards, picture cards, and pole out of the envelope on the back of the folder.
2. Open the folder. Put the fish face up on the lake.
3. Put the picture cards in a stack, face down.
4. Draw a picture card and read the word.
5. Look at the fish in the lake.
6. Find a fish that rhymes with the picture card.
7. Touch the fish with your fishing pole.
8. Use your pole to drag the fish in.
9. When you catch a fish, put it next to you!
10. Give the pole to somebody else for a turn.

LESSON #5

Students participate in reading the book, "Families."

MATERIALS:

- "Families" by Ann Morris
- "What Families Do" book page R#91 *(multiple copies per student)*

R#91

- writing tools
- chart paper
- black marker
- stapler
- glue
- scissors
- construction paper *(two sheets)*
- magazines, newspapers, and catalogs *(likely to contain pictures of families)*

PREPARATION:

- Write the title, "What Families Do" on one sheet of construction paper, to create the class book title page.
- Cut out pictures of families doing things together to use as example pictures.

Students read the book "Families" by Ann Morris.

- Lead students in **reading** the title of the book "Families" by Ann Morris.
- Tell students that they are going to read the book, and listen for three things that families do together.
- Students take turns **turning the pages** of the book and **reading** each page.

Students discuss what they read in the book.

- Ask students to **tell** the class three things that families did together in the book.
- Write each student response on the chart paper. Lead students in **reading** each of the responses.

Students make a class book called, "What Families Do."

- Lead students in **reading** the "What Families Do" book page.
- Students follow teacher directions to complete one or more pages of the class book. *(See Teacher Script.)*
- Students put the book pages inside the title page and back page, and **staple** the book together.
- Students **read** the book to others.

Teacher Script

"**Choose** a magazine, catalog, or newspaper. Look through it and **identify** pictures of Families doing things together."
"**Cut** out each of those pictures."
"**Choose** your favorite picture and **glue** it on the box above the words on the book page."
"Now fill in the blank in the sentence, 'This family is _____ together' by **writing** on the line what the family is doing together."
"**Choose** another picture and make another book page."

EXTENSION ACTIVITIES part two LITERACY LESSONS

EAT:

FAMILY RECIPES!

Send a note home asking families to send in a special family recipe. Read each recipe to students. Students **vote** on one recipe they would like to make. Students **write** a list of the ingredients and kitchen utensils they will need. Students go to the store to buy what they need. Students follow the recipe directions to make the food.

WORK:

CHORE SUPPLIES

Students **name** as many household chores that they can think of. Write the name of each chore on a piece of paper, and ask students to **name** different supplies that they would need to complete that chore. Write each supply on the paper. Bring the papers to the grocery store. Students find those chore supplies in the store and **write** down different varieties/brands of supplies that could be used.

GO:

TRAVEL SCRAPBOOK

Students follow directions to make a special Travel Scrapbook in which they can collect photos, souvenirs, and written memories of different places they go with their family. To make a scrapbook, students follow step-by-step directions: 1. **Select** a color of construction paper and take two sheets of it. 2. Use a marker to **write** the words, "My Travels" on one of the sheets. 3. **Look** through magazines and **select** pictures of places you like. 4. **Cut** out those pictures and **glue** them on the front cover. 5. **Count** out ten sheets of white paper. 6. Put the white paper between the two sheets of construction paper, with the title in front. 7. **Staple** the pages together and now you have your own travel scrapbook to fill up!

PLAY:

TEAM PLAYERS

Students watch part of a movie about a team who plays together, such as Airbud by Disney. Before watching the movie clip, tell students to watch for how the players treat each other, things the players do together, and how the players work together. After the movie, ask students one or more of these questions. Students **answer** each question. Students then play a team game such as kickball with another class. Remind students of the ways the team members in the movie worked together and **discuss** ways that they should treat each other during their game.

LIVE:

DECORATE WITH ART

Tell students that they are going to make a special piece of artwork to bring home and decorate where they live. Give students paint and paper and let them **paint** anything they want. Students **dry** the painting, and **select** a color of construction paper to **glue** it on. Students **write** a title for their artwork on a small slip of white paper and **glue** that on the construction paper, under or above the painting. Students **select** a room in their home where they would like to display their artwork.

SECTION FIVE

unit 2

my family

part two

Throughout these **Writing Lessons**, students will be making choices as to what elements they want on the pages of the books they are creating. Give all students opportunities to let their own voice be heard as they communicate individual selections and read their completed books to the class.

This "character and community" icon will signal a lesson activity in which students will have an opportunity to express their preferences and let their own voice be heard.

WRITING LESSONS

5

LESSON #1

Students write a menu to bring home to their family.

MATERIALS:

- **Large Food Group Picture Cards R#92** *(one per student, plus two additional)*
- **Small Food Group Picture Cards R#93** *(one per student)*
- **Menu R#94** *(one per student)*
- **construction paper** *(11" x 17")*
- **writing tools**
- **foods that fit into each of the four food groups** *(several foods, or containers of foods, from each group)*
- **legal size envelopes** *(four per student)*
- **large manila clasp envelope** *(one per student)*
- **scissors**
- **glue**

PREPARATION:

- **Cut out the picture cards on two copies of the Large Food Group Picture Cards. Glue one set of cards on construction paper, at the top, one card per sheet, to create food group signs.**

R#92

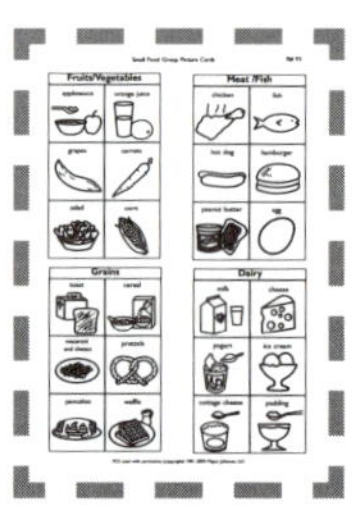
R#93

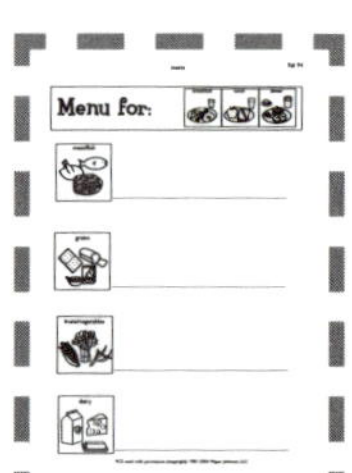
R#94

Students learn about the four food groups.

- Show students each of the four Large Food Group Picture Cards. Lead students in **reading** each card.
- As each Large Food Group Picture Card is shown, ask students to **name** different foods that belong in that group. Confirm that food group, or tell students the correct group that food belongs in and why.
- Write each of these foods on the appropriate food group sign.
- Lead students in **reading** each food group name and the list of foods on that food group sign.

Students categorize foods according to the four food groups.

- Place each of the four food group signs on a table or other work area, slightly apart.
- Put the real food items on display in an area that is accessible to all students.
- Put the four Large Food Group Picture Cards on display.
- Students take turns **selecting** a real food item.
- The student **shows** the food item to the other students and **says** the name of the food.
- The student **identifies**, or **selects**, the food group to which the food belongs and places the food on that food group sign.

Students prepare for making a menu.

- Students **discuss** the importance of eating foods from each of the four food groups.
- Explain to students that they are going to make a menu to bring home to their family that has food from each of the four food groups.
- Explain to students that they are going to make a special envelope for each of the four food groups, to hold food picture cards they can use for making menus.
- Direct students to **cut** out each of the four Large Food Group Picture Cards and **glue** one on the front of each envelope.
- Direct students to **cut** out one group of Small Food Group Picture Cards at a time and place them in the corresponding food group envelope.
- Direct students to fold down the flap of each envelope, and place all four envelopes in the large manila envelope.

Students make a menu to bring home.

- On a blank menu, students **mark** the picture/symbol of the meal for which they would like to **write** a menu.
- Ask students to **name** the first food group they see on their menu *(meat/fish)*.
- Direct students to take out their four envelopes and **identify** the envelope that matches that food group.
- Direct students to **select** a picture card from that envelope that they would like to put on the menu.
- Direct students to **write** that word on the line next to the food group.
- Continue this process for each of the food groups on the menu.
- Students take turns **reading** their menus to each other.
- Students take home their menu to their family.
- Have students keep their envelopes at school. Make extra copies of the blank menus and use them frequently to give students practice in making balanced menus.

LESSON #2

Students make butter and write about the experience.

Students learn about the butter making activity they are going to do.

- Explain to students that the chores their family does today are very different than some of the chores their grandparents and great grandparents did.
- Show students the butter, and tell students that many years ago, families that lived on farms made their own butter.
- Tell students that they are going to make butter, and find out what it was like to do that chore many years ago.

Students participate in the butter making activity.

- Show students each Butter Making Materials Picture Card. Lead students in **naming** the material. Ask a student to **identify** that material and place the card on the material.
- Lead students through the steps of making butter. Students, or teachers, **take pictures** throughout the activity.
- Give each student a small amount of butter, a slice of bread, and a plastic knife. Direct students to spread the butter on the bread and eat the bread.
- Students eat the bread and **tell** the other students if they liked the butter or did not like the butter.

Students list and sequence the butter making steps.

- Ask students to **say** what the first step is in making butter.
- Write the student response on a sentence strip, in a complete sentence.
- Continue to ask students to **name** the steps involved in making butter, and write each on a sentence strip.
- Remind students of steps they do not list. Lead students in **reading** each direction step, in order.
- Mix up the steps. Lead students in **reading** each sentence and **selecting** which step comes first, second, etc.
- Sequence the steps by putting them on the board in sequential order as the students **identify** the steps.

Students write a response to the butter making experience.

- Each student **selects** a photo from the butter making experience and **glues** it on the top of a sheet of white paper.
- Underneath the photo, students **write** one sentence telling about what is happening in the photo.
- Put the photo sheets, and sequenced direction sentence strips, on a bulletin board display with the title, "Making Butter!"

Teacher Script

"Is everybody ready to make butter?"
"Who would like to open the whipping cream?"
"Can somebody please open the jar?"
"Now will somebody please pour the whipping cream into the jar?"
"Let's put the lid on real tight."
"It's time to shake it up/roll it! Everybody will have a turn!"
"Shake it up, and when the timer goes off, pass it on."
"Now we'll pour it all into the bowl."
"We made butter! I'll use the spoon to scoop out the butter and we'll add a sprinkle of salt."
"We can pour the buttermilk back in the jar and use it later to make pancakes!"

Teacher Note:

- **This process could take five to twenty-five minutes. While the students are shaking the jar, keep them engaged with one of the following activities:**
  -Lead students in a discussion about different uses for butter.
  -Ask students questions about the butter making process.
  -Show and read to students a book about the process of making butter.
- **If students are not able to shake a container, have them roll the container back and forth to each other.**

MATERIALS:

- **Butter Making Materials Picture Cards R#95**
- **clear jar with tight lid** *(baby food jar recommended)*
- **one pint heavy whipping cream**
- **salt**
- **large bowl and spoon**
- **timer**
- **butter**
- **bread** *(crackers may be used)*
- **plastic knife** *(one per student)*
- **small paper plates** *(one per student)*
- **glue**
- **white paper** *(8 1/2" x 11")*
- **writing tools**
- **sentence strips** *(4-8)*
- **digital camera**

R#95

MATERIALS:

- Store Picture Cards R#96
- poster board *(seven large sheets)*
- black marker
- gallon size resealable plastic bags *(six)*
- stapler
- note cards *(3" x 5")*
- Velcro®
- yarn or metal rings
- a tray or clear container on which to display items
- at least three to five items from each of these categories

R#96

food - raisins, tuna, rice, small can of mushrooms
clothes - socks, t-shirt, shorts, belt, etc.
office - envelope, pencils, markers, stapler, etc.
tool - pliers, screwdriver, nails, wrench, etc.
toy - game, puzzle, Legos, action figures, etc.
book - magazine, newspaper, children's book, etc.

NOTE: All items need to be able to fit in a gallon size bag.

PREPARATION:

- On one sheet of poster board, write the words, "Let's Go to the Store."
- On six sheets of poster board, staple the resealable bag at the bottom of the poster board and write both sentences. *(see sample)*
- Hole punch the side of all seven sheets of poster board. Put yarn, or metal rings, through the holes to make a book.
- Cut out the Store Picture Cards and put a piece of rough Velcro® on the back of each.
- Write the name of each item on a note card. Put a small piece of rough Velcro® on the back of each. Place the card near the item.
- When each Store Picture Card is selected, put the corresponding items on the tray or in the clear container.
- Cut six note cards in half, creating twelve small cards. On half the cards write the letter "a" and on the other half write the word "an." Put a small piece of rough Velcro® on the back of each card.

Students make a class big book entitled, "Let's Go to the Store!"

Students learn about the different kinds of stores.

- Show students each of the Store Picture Cards and lead students in **reading** the card.
- As each picture card is shown, ask students to **select** items, from those on display, that you could buy at that store.

book page

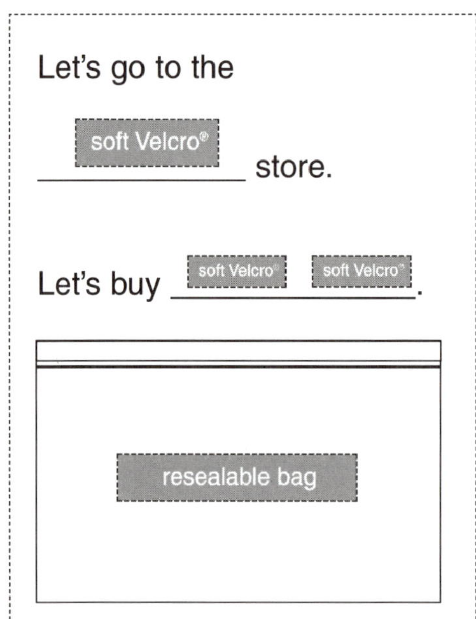

Students work together to make a class big book entitled, "Let's Go to the Store!"

- Show students the title page of the big book and lead them in **reading** the title.
- Lead students in **reading** the first book page.
- One student **selects** a Store Picture Card and places it on the first blank line. Students **read** the sentence.
- Another student **selects** an item from that store *(from those on display)* that they should buy there.
- The student places the word card on the blank line, and places the item in the plastic bag.
- The teacher directs the student to place the "a" or "an" card in front of the word card.
- This process continues for each of the Store Picture Cards.
- When each page has been completed, go back to the title page and lead students in **reading** each page of the book, as students take turns **turning the pages** of the book.
- As each page is read, allow students to take the object out of the bag to touch and more closely examine it.

LESSON #4

Students write rules to the game, "Crazy Rules."

Students write the rules to the game, "Crazy Rules."

- Show students the game board, game markers, and die or spinner. Explain to students that in this game, each time a certain number is rolled or spun, the person who got that number is going to have to follow a special rule, such as quacking like a duck!
- Students take turns **selecting** one of the "Crazy Rules" rule cards.

  NOTE: If more than six students are participating, divide your class into two groups and make two sets of rule cards.
- Direct students to **cut** out each of the pictures/symbols and place them face up in front of them.
- Name each picture/symbol, and ask students to **identify** it. Read the related rule. *(See bottom of R#99.)*
- Tell students that they will **write** their own rule on their rule card. They can make up their own rule, **write** it in, and **draw** a picture of it in the box. Or they can **choose** one of the pictures/symbols, **glue** that in the box, and then **write** the related rule on the lines.

Students play the game, "Crazy Rules."

- Mount the six rule cards on a piece of 11" x 17" construction paper and put it in an area highly visible to all students.
- Students **select** a game marker and put it on the START game space.
- Students take turns rolling or **spinning** for a number. The student **reads** the rule that matches the number they rolled or spun. The student follows that rule instruction.
- The student then moves his/her marker forward that number of spaces.
- The first student to the FINISH line wins the game.

LESSON 4

MATERIALS:

- **"Crazy Rules" rule cards R#97, R#98**
- **"Crazy Rules" pictures/symbols R#99** *(one per student)*
- **writing tools**
- **glue**
- **scissors**
- **construction paper** *(11"x17")*
- **poster board** *(one large sheet)*
- **paper squares** *(2" x 2")*
- **game markers** *(such as colored blocks)* *(one per student)*
- **die or All-Turn-It® spinner**

PREPARATION:

- **Make a basic game board. Glue the paper squares in a path on the poster board from one end to the other. Write the words START and FINISH at the beginning and end of the path.**
- **Cut out the rule cards.**

R#97–R#99

LESSON #5

Students make a book entitled "Where Do You Live?"

MATERIALS:

- **"Where Do You Live?" Book Teacher Directions R#100**
- **"Where Do You Live?" Animal Book Page R#101**
- **"Where Do You Live?" Student Book Page R#102**
- **chart paper and black marker**
- **writing tools**
- **white construction paper or card stock**
- **construction paper in assorted colors**
- **scissors**
- **liquid glue**
- **sponge brushes or paintbrushes**
- **shallow containers**
- **crayons**
- **blue paint or finger paint**
- **dirt, potting soil**
- **craft sticks**
- **sugar or salt**
- **student pictures**
- **stapler**

LESSON 5

PREPARATION:

- **Copy onto card stock/white construction paper the "Where Do You Live?" Animal Book Page** *(four per student)* **and Student Book Page** *(one per student)*.
- **Copy the bottom half of R#100, one copy per student.**
- **Write the words "Where Do You Live?" on the board.**
- **Put the glue, sugar or salt, potting soil, and craft sticks in shallow containers. Put a spoon in the dirt and salt/sugar. Put sponge brushes or paintbrushes in the glue.**
- **On the top of the chart paper, write the words "Places Where Animals Live."**

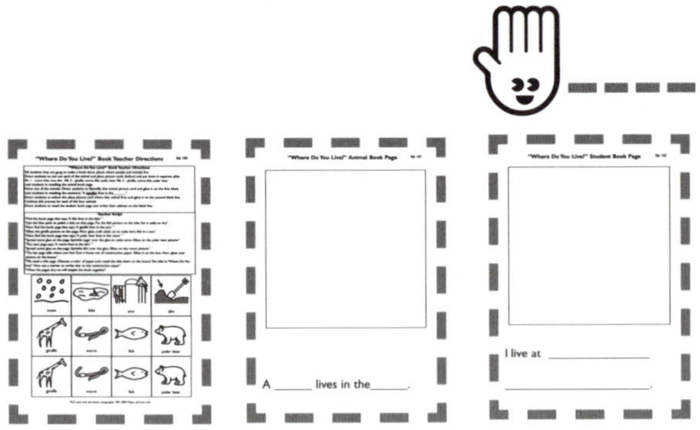

R#100 R#101 R#102

Students discuss places where people and animals live.

- Lead students in **naming** different places where people live.
- Ask students to **name** places where animals live. Write each response on the chart paper.
- Students **read** the list of places where animals live.
- Ask students to **say** if they would like to live in any of the places where animals live, and why.

Students make their own "Where Do You Live?" book.

- Explain to students that they are going to make a book about different places that animals and people live.
- Students follow Book Teacher Directions (R#100) to make their own book.
- After the books have dried and been stapled together, students **read** their books to each other.

WRITING LESSONS

EXTENSION ACTIVITIES part two

EAT:
WRITE A SUPER SUNDAE RECIPE

Students **write** their own recipe for a super sundae! Students **select** the kind of ice cream, sauce, fruit, and toppings. Students **write** down the ingredients for their sundae and the directions for making this sundae. Students **read** their recipes to each other. At a special celebration or party, bring in sundae ingredients and let students follow their recipes to create their own Super Sundaes!

WORK:
WRITE A BOOK, "HOW TO DO HOUSEHOLD CHORES."

Name a household chore and ask students to **say** how to do this chore. Write down all responses. Repeat this process for different chores. Give one page to each student and have that student **draw** or **color** an illustration of the chore. **Staple** the pages together in a book. For a fun parent gift, make copies of this and send it home.

GO:
WRITE DIRECTIONS TO YOUR CLASSROOM

Bring students to the front door of the school. Explain that they are going to write down the directions for how to get to their classroom. Select a student to **say** where they need to go first. Write this direction down in sentence format, "Go to the office. Turn right." Continue this process until students are at their classroom. Bring students back to the front door. Students take turns **reading** each direction, and all students follow those directions. Students find out if their directions lead them back to their room, or if they need to rewrite a direction!

PLAY:
WRITE AN INVITATION

Students **vote** on a team game they would like to play with another class, such as T-ball. Students **select** a class that they would like to invite. Each student **writes** and delivers an invitation to a student from that class, inviting them to come and play a fun game with their class!

LIVE:
LEARN AND WRITE ABOUT A PLACE WHERE OTHER PEOPLE LIVE

Check out books from the library on two or three different places where other people live. Show students each of the books. Students **vote** on which of the two or three places they would like to learn about. Read that book to the students. Students, as a whole class, **write** things about that place where people live.

EARLY LITERACY AND COMMUNICATION PROGRAM

Part three

Living With My Family

ablenet™

unit 2

my family

MEville to WEville

part three

Living With My Family

In the **Living With My Family** part, students will be able to communicate personal information, family routines and/or solutions for problem solving within a family.

Character Education

Each lesson in this section addresses aspects of character education. Look for the ☺ to identify where this occurs.

Content Learning Objectives

1. Student will be able to identify and say their city, address, and phone number.
2. Student will be able to state one thing they can do if they are upset with a family member.
3. Student will be able to name at least one thing that their family does during a particular time of the day.

Overview and Resources

Literature Book to Be Read:
"Families" by Ann Morris

Additional Book Recommendations:

"The Mitten Tree"
by Candace Christiansen
and Elaine Greenstein
(about a child helping others)
"Ordinary Mary's Extraordinary Deed"
by Emily Pearson and Fumi Kosaka
(about giving)
"The Giving Book"
by Ellen Sabin
"Share and Take Turns"
by Cheri J. Meiners and Meredith Johnson
"It's Mine!"
by Leo Lionni
(about sharing)
"No Laughing, No Smiling, No Giggling"
by James Stevenson
"Kids Around the World Celebrate
by Lynda Jones

Books to Be Created and Read by Students:
A Day in the Life of My Family
Important Information About Me!
My Helping Hands

Song Recommendations:
"Celebrate Good Times"
by Kool & The Gang
"I Just Want to Celebrate"
by Glenn Hughes

Class Projects and Art Projects:
Make Pudding Parfaits
Make a Smiley Jar
Make a Puppet Family
Make a Family Sharing Bag
Tambourines Using the Sharing Bag
Make and Give Away Greeting Cards
Celebration of Learning
Joke Survey Using Laughometer
Poster Collage of People Helping People
Make a Family Celebration Mobile
Make a Celebration Day Poster
Make and Break Personal Piñata

Games:
The Helping Hand
Who Gave the Gift?
Concentration Game About Celebrating
The Word Collect Game
The Scrambled Sentence Game
Find a Solution

Home/School Activities:
Family Creature
Use the Celebration Day Poster

unit 2
my family

Learning New Words	Vocabulary Activities	Word Wall Lessons	Literacy Lessons	Writing Lessons
Lesson #1 Pg. 78 Students learn about the word **"help."**	**Activity #1 Pg. 84** Students read and respond to scenarios in which they ask for help.	**Lesson #1 Pg. 90** Students practice saying and writing the word wall words.	**Lesson #1 Pg. 94** Students identify pictures of people helping each other.	**Lesson #1 Pg. 100** Students write a letter to a family member.
Lesson #2 Pg. 79 Students learn about the word **"share."**	**Activity #2 Pg. 85** Students make sharing bags and use them while doing a collaborative project.	**Lesson #2 Pg. 90** Students participate in a Sentence Completion Activity.	**Lesson #2 Pg. 95** Students make a Family Celebration Mobile.	**Lesson #2 Pg. 101** Students make a book entitled, **"A Day in the Life of My Family."**
Lesson #3 Pg. 80 Students learn about the word **"give."**	**Activity #3 Pg. 86** Students make greeting cards and give them away.	**Lesson #3 Pg. 90** Students participate in the Mind Reader activity.	**Lesson #3 Pg. 96** Students play the **"Find a Solution"** game.	**Lesson #3 Pg. 102** Students make a book entitled, **"Important Information About ME!"**
Lesson #4 Pg. 81 Students learn about the word **"laugh."**	**Activity #4 Pg. 87** Students participate in a Celebration of Learning.	**Lesson #4 Pg. 91** Students participate in The Word Collect Game.	**Lesson #4 Pg. 97** Students make a Celebration Day Poster.	**Lesson #4 Pg. 103** Students make a book entitled, **"My Helping Hands."**
Lesson #5 Pg. 82 Students learn about the word **"celebrate."**	**Activity #5 Pg. 88** Students tell jokes and record the responses using the Laughometer.	**Lesson #5 Pg. 91** Students participate in The Scrambled Sentence Game.	**Lesson #5 Pg. 98** Students share with their family about their day.	**Lesson #5 Pg. 104** Students follow written directions to make and break **Personal Piñatas.**
Extension Activities Pg. 82	**Extension Activities Pg. 88**	**Home Activity Pg. 92**	**Extension Activities Pg. 98**	**Extension Activities Pg. 104**

unit 2 my family LESSON Planner

* Select lessons/activities from each curriculum area to present every day. We recommend starting with the Learning New Words curriculum area (*e.g. Students learn about the word "help"*) and continue with other lessons related to that vocabulary word (look across the grid for related lessons, all with the same #) before moving on to lessons focused on a new vocabulary word.

Create Your Own...

Create your own daily plans by filling in each day with lessons/activities across the literacy areas. Check each literacy area that you select a lesson/activity from, and write the specific name on the line to the right of that literacy area.

Daily LESSON Planner

Monday	__ **Learning New Words** ____ __ **Vocabulary Activities** ____ __ **Word Wall Lessons** ____ __ **Literacy Lessons** ____ __ **Writing Lessons** ____
Tuesday	__ **Learning New Words** ____ __ **Vocabulary Activities** ____ __ **Word Wall Lessons** ____ __ **Literacy Lessons** ____ __ **Writing Lessons** ____
Wednesday	__ **Learning New Words** ____ __ **Vocabulary Activities** ____ __ **Word Wall Lessons** ____ __ **Literacy Lessons** ____ __ **Writing Lessons** ____
Thursday	__ **Learning New Words** ____ __ **Vocabulary Activities** ____ __ **Word Wall Lessons** ____ __ **Literacy Lessons** ____ __ **Writing Lessons** ____
Friday	__ **Learning New Words** ____ __ **Vocabulary Activities** ____ __ **Word Wall Lessons** ____ __ **Literacy Lessons** ____ __ **Writing Lessons** ____

unit 2

my family

part three

Throughout these **Learning New Words** lessons, students will be learning about their family and growing in their understanding of what it means to live with their family. Students will participate in activities in which they problem solve family situations, celebrate with their families, and learn about ways they are able to help their family.

This "character and community" icon will signal a lesson activity through which this sense of "Who I Am" can be reinforced.

LEARNING NEW WORDS

3

Students learn about the word "help."

MATERIALS:

- vocabulary cards Set Three R#103, R#104
- chart paper and black marker
- All-Turn-It® spinner *(optional)*
- picture/name cards
- pudding parfait ingredients
  - one box vanilla wafers or graham crackers
  - one pkg. (4 oz.) instant pudding
  - two cups cold milk
  - one 8 oz. container frozen whipped topping (thawed)
  - three bananas
  - chocolate syrup
  - additional toppings such as sprinkles (optional)
- pudding making supplies
  - small bowls or paper cups (one per student)
  - spoons (one per student)
  - large spoons
  - dull plastic knives
  - spatula
  - mixer or whisk
  - resealable bags
  - large bowl
  - measuring cups

PREPARATION:

- Put the student picture/name cards facedown in a stack, or on the large overlay of the All-Turn-It® spinner.

OPTION: To make this recipe more low-cost and less time consuming, omit whipped topping, bananas, and chocolate and simply mix up the pudding, crush the wafers, and layer the two ingredients.

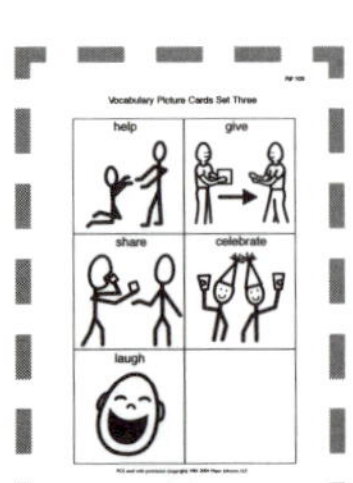

R#103

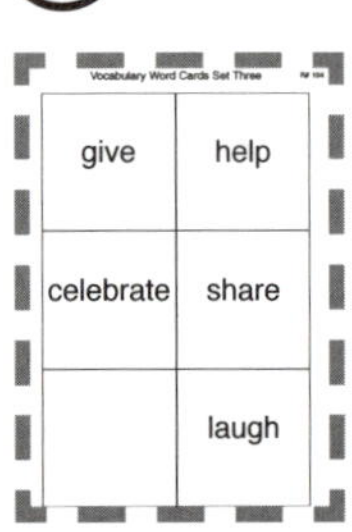

R#104

Students are introduced to the word "help."

- Show students the "help" vocabulary card. Lead students in **saying** the word multiple times.
- Use the word "help" in multiple sentences while asking students for help.
  "(Jamie), will you please help me and open the door?"
  "(Brad), will you help me move these books to my desk?"
- Students provide requested help by following teacher requests.
- Ask students to think about and **say** ways they can help out at home. *(To help students generate ideas, list out categories, such as mealtime, pet care, with a little brother or sister, in their bedroom, in the garden.)* Write each idea on the chart paper and lead students in **reading** it.

Students help the teacher make pudding parfaits.

- Explain to the students that you want to make a special treat for them, but it's too much work to do by yourself and you need their help.
- Tell students that you will need everybody to help, and that they will take turns helping make the recipe.
- Lead students through the process of making the recipe. When finished, students may eat their pudding parfaits.

Teacher Script

"Thanks for helping me make this special treat!"

"First, we need to crush the vanilla wafers. Who will help me put them in these two bags?"

"Great. Now, who will help me crush the wafers? Squish the bag with your hands!"

"Thanks. Now I need somebody to help me pour two cups of milk into the bowl."

"Thank you. Will somebody help me **cut** open the pudding and dump it in the bowl?"

"Great! I need more help! Who will help **mix** up the pudding?" (Use mixer or whisk.)

"Looking good! Who will help me add the whipped topping? We need to fold it in with a spatula."

"We're almost done! I need some people to cut the bananas into slices. Who will help me cut bananas?"

"Great! We're ready to put the parfaits together! Who wants to help?"

"First we need to spoon some wafer crumbs into the bottom of each cup/bowl. Who will help?"

"Now I need people to help spoon some pudding into each cup/bowl."

"We need people to help put two banana slices in each cup/bowl."

"The last step is the chocolate sauce! Everybody can help put that on the pudding parfaits!"

"We'll put them in the refrigerator. Then they'll be ready to eat. I wonder if anybody will help me eat them?"

OPTION: When crushing wafers, use a double bag, seal it tightly, then allow students in wheelchairs to roll over the bag to crush the wafers! Or, have students step on the bags.

Students learn about the word "share."

Part 1

Students play a game of The Helping Hand to review the word "help."

- Show students the "help" vocabulary card. Lead students in **reading** the word multiple times.
- Tell students that they are going to play a game called The Helping Hand and practice helping each other.
- Explain the rules to students. *(See Teacher Script.)*
- Students follow teacher directions to play The Helping Hand game.
- When the game is over, students **discuss** how it felt to be frozen and need help, and how it felt to receive help.

Part 2

Students learn about the word "share."

- Show students the container of treats. Tell them this is a special treat you are going to pass out.
- Give the entire container of treats to one student or adult and tell him/her that they get all of the treats.
- Ask the other students to **say** if they think you did a good job of passing out your treats.
- Ask students to **say** how they feel about not getting any treats while one student gets all of the treats.
- Ask the students if there is another way of passing out the treats. Help students come to the conclusion that you can share the treats and each person can have one treat.
- Ask the student/adult with the treats if he/she will share, and pass out one treat to each person.
- Encourage students to **say** "thank you" to the person giving out the treats.

Students practice sharing with others.

- Explain to students that there are ways of sharing things other than giving something to somebody.
- Show students a book and a music CD and ask them if they know how they could share these things.
- Model for students how to share a book by reading it to the class, a CD/tape by turning on the CD or tape player, and a stuffed animal by passing it around.
- Students take turns **selecting** a bag. Students take out the item and share it with the class in the following ways:

  Book - **read** to the class

  CD/tape - **turn on** the music for the class

  Crayons and large roll of paper - put out on table and let everyone gather around and **color** on the paper

  Stuffed animal - pass around

  Legos - give some to everybody and work to build something together *(students may **select** a Lego to use)*

  JoKe - **read** the joke to the class

NOTE: When each item is shared, set a timer for 5 to 10 minutes in which students can share the activity.

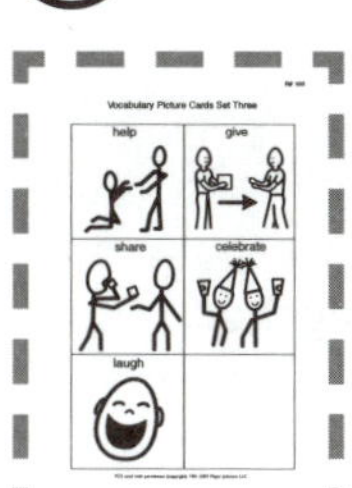

R#103

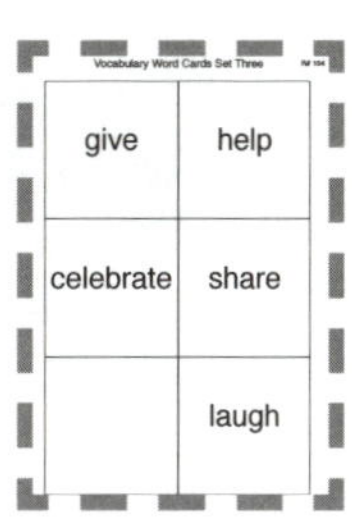

R#104

MATERIALS:

- **vocabulary cards Set Three R#103, R#104**
- **easy to wear glove or mitten**
- **special hat** *(bandanna, sticker, etc. may be substituted)*
- **treats - enough for whole class** *(stickers, candy, etc.)* **in a container**
- **timer**
- **paper bags** *(six or more)*
- **activity materials for sharing: box of crayons, Legos, children's book, written joke, music with CD or tape player, stuffed animal**
- **large roll of paper**

PREPARATION:

- **Put each of the activity materials in a paper bag and staple or tie it.**

Teacher Script

"The Helping Hand is played like freeze tag."
"One student will wear a special glove/mitten, and this turns their hand into The Helping Hand!"
"One other student will be the tagger and will wear this special hat."
"When the tagger touches you, you have to freeze. You can't move. You need help!"
"The student with The Helping Hand will be moving around. When you see The Helping Hand, ask for help."
"The student with The Helping Hand will say to you, 'I will help you' and will shake your hand with the special Helping Hand. You are now free again!"
"When you hear the teacher say, 'Everybody freeze,' everybody should freeze and we'll get a new tagger and a new student to wear The Helping Hand."

LESSON #3

Students learn about the word "give."

MATERIALS:

- **vocabulary cards Set Three R#103, R#104**
- **Smiley Jar Materials:**
  - card stock
  - scissors
  - small clean jar with lid (one per student)
  - fabric paint with brushes
  - large colored pom-poms (or cotton balls)
  - wiggle eyes
  - yarn in assorted colors
  - glue
- **Smiley Jar Tag R#105**
- **picture/name cards**
- **All-Turn-It® spinner** *(optional)*
- **shallow containers**

PREPARATION:

- **Put the picture/name cards in a stack or facedown on the large overlay of the All-Turn-It® spinner.**
- **Designate a particular chair as being the Sharing Chair. Only the person sharing is able to sit on the Sharing Chair.**
- **Put the various Smiley Jar materials in shallow containers, easily accessible to all students.**
- **Copy The Smiley Jar Tag onto different colors of card stock, at least one per student.**
- **Make a sample Smiley, Smiley Jar, and Smiley Jar Tag.**

R#103

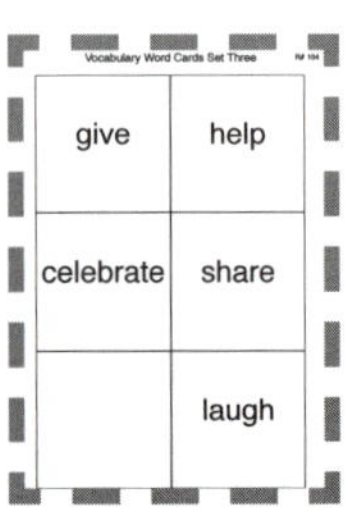

R#104

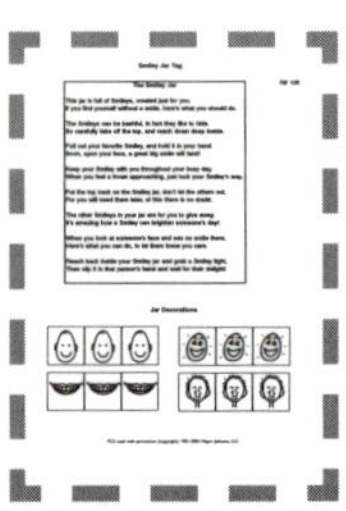

R#105

Part 1
Students review the word "share."

- Ask students to **name** things that they are able to share with others.
- Explain to students that something else we can share with others is information, or stories, about ourselves.
- Tell students that they are going to take turns sharing something special about themselves.
- Students take turns drawing or **spinning** for the picture/name card of the next student to come and share.
- On their turn, the student goes to the Sharing Chair and **tells** the class one special thing or story about himself/herself.

Part 2
Students learn about the word "give."

- Show students the "give" vocabulary card. Lead the students in **reading** the word three to five times.
- Ask students to **name** gifts that people have given them.
- Explain to students that there are things other than gifts to give.
- Students follow teacher directions to give things to each other. Model each for the students as the request is given.

Teacher Script

"Give a high five to a boy."
"Give a handshake to the teacher."
"Give a book to another student."
"Give a smile to a girl."

Part 3
Students follow directions to make a Smiley Jar.

- Show students a sample of the Smiley Jar and tell them they are going to make one and give it to somebody special.
- Students take a Smiley out of the jar, look at it and touch it.
- Students **select** or **name** the person for whom they want to make a Smiley Jar.
- Students follow teacher directions to make a Smiley Jar.

Smiley Jar Direction Script

"First, we're going to decorate the outside of our Smiley Jars. **Cut** out any Smiley faces you like. **Glue** them on the jar."
"**Choose** a color paint. Pick up the brush and **paint** smiley faces, and anything else, on the outside of the jar."
"Now we're going to make Smileys to put in the jar. **Choose** a color pom-pom you like."
"Take two eyes and **glue** them on the Smiley."
"Your Smiley needs a mouth. **Choose** a color yarn you like. **Cut** off a a small piece and **glue** it as a mouth under the eyes."
"**Choose** another color, then keep making Smileys until your jar is full of Smileys."
"Now we're going to make a special gift tag to attach to the Smiley Jar."
"Get out your Smiley Jar Tag and let's **read** it together."
"Now **cut** out the Smiley Jar Tag. We'll punch a hole in it, and tie yarn through."
"When the jar **dries**, we'll put the Smileys in the jar and tie the Smiley Jar Tag to the jar."
"Then your Smiley Jar is ready to give away!"

Students learn about the word "laugh."

Part 1
Students review the word "give."

Students play the game, "Who Gave the Gift?"

- Students take turns being the special student to receive a gift.
- On their turn, the student comes up front and sits with their back to the class.
- One student from the class takes a gift bag, sneaks up to the chair, and puts the bag under the chair.
- When the student returns to their original chair, all of the students **read**/chant the words on the poster board, substituting the student's name in the blanks.
- The student in the chair turns around and **selects** or **names** the student they think gave them the gift. The student continues to make guesses until the correct student is identified.
- When the game is over, all students may open their gift bags and **look** at what's inside.

Part 2
Students learn about the word "laugh."

- Show students the "laugh" vocabulary card. Lead the students in **saying** the word at least three to five times.
- Do several silly things to make the students laugh and use the tape player to record them laughing. The silly things might include: dancing, jumping up and down, wearing your shoes on your hands, singing a silly song, etc.
- Play back the tape.
- Ask students to **say** why people laugh.

Students do things to make people laugh.

- Explain to students that each student is going to do something to make everyone else laugh.
- Students take turns drawing or **spinning** for a Laugh Card.
- The student follows the direction on the card. *(See Teacher Note.)*
- When all students have had a turn, students **vote** on which Laugh Activity they thought was the most funny, or got the most laughs.

Teacher Note:

Consider these adaptations for students who need additional support:

- Pair each student with a student peer or a staff.
- Record the joke, song, pig oink, book, and puppet words on a voice output device.
- For dancing and blowing things about, plug the tape player and hair dryer into a PowerLink®3 control unit.
- For the bubbles and picture taking, use the switch adapted bubble machine and digital camera.

R#103–R#104

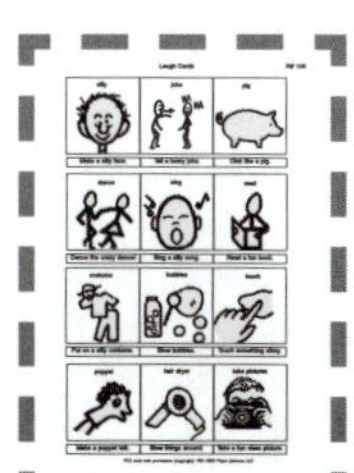

R#106

MATERIALS:

- **vocabulary cards Set Three R#103, R#104**
- **Laugh Cards R#106**
- **poster board** *(one large sheet)*
- **black marker**
- **small gifts such as stickers, wrapped candy, pencils, etc.**
- **lunch size paper bags**
- **ribbon**
- **student picture/name cards**
- **tape recorder with blank tape**
- **All-Turn-It® spinner** *(optional)*
- **Laugh Activity materials**
  - **white paper and black marker**
  - **CD or tape player with music**
  - **several silly books**
  - **something slimy**
  - **bubbles**
  - **costume, mask, or fun headband**
  - **puppet**
  - **hair dryer**
  - **digital camera**
  - **song sheets and joke sheets** *(see preparation)*

PREPARATION:

- **Write these words on a large sheet of poster board: ______, ______, there's a gift under your chair! Turn around and look at us, and guess who put it there!**
- **Put one small gift in each bag. Tie it with a ribbon.**
- **Cut out the Laugh Cards. Put them facedown in a stack or on the large overlay of the All-Turn-It® spinner.**
- **Make joke sheets and song sheets. On white paper write out at least three different jokes and two different silly songs** *(such as "On Top of Spaghetti")*.
- **Put all Laugh Activity materials in a student accessible area.**

LESSON #5

Students learn about the word "celebrate."

MATERIALS:

- **funny book**
- **vocabulary cards Set Three R#103, R#104**
- **Celebrate Picture Cards R#107**
- **card stock in two different colors**
- **What We Use to Celebrate props**
  - written speech
  - small present
  - cd/cassette tape
  - party streamers
  - cake mix
  - juice box
  - party hat

PREPARATION:

- **Copy the What We Use to Celebrate cards and the What We Do to Celebrate cards onto two different colors of card stock.**
- **Put the What We Use to Celebrate props in a student accessible area.**

R#103

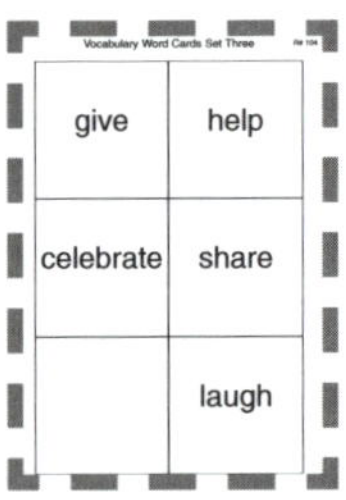

R#104

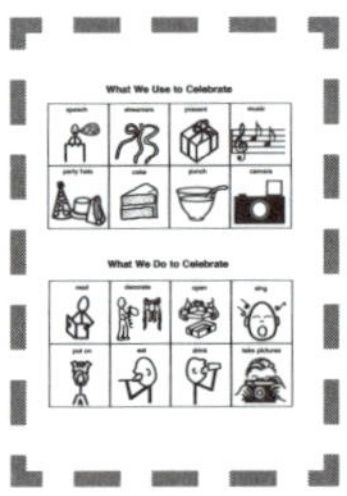

R#107

Part 1
Students review the word "laugh."

- The teacher, or student, **reads** the funny book to the class.
- Students take turns **telling** the class what parts made them laugh.
- Students take turns **showing** the class the pictures they think are funny.

Part 2
Students learn about the word "celebrate."

- Show students the word "celebrate" and lead them in **saying** the word at least three to five times.
- Students take turns **selecting** a What We Use to Celebrate prop from the selection of props.
- As each prop is selected, students **say** what people do with that prop - what it is used for.
- Students **tell** the class about times they have celebrated using that What We Use to Celebrate item.

Students play a concentration game to learn about celebrating.

- Place the What We Use to Celebrate and the What We Do to Celebrate cards facedown, in two separate areas, on a table or in a playing area.
- Students take turns **selecting** two cards, one of each color.
- The teacher directs the student to **look** at the What We Do to Celebrate card first and **name** the picture/symbol.
- The teacher then asks the student to **say** what they would use to celebrate in that way.
- The teacher directs the student to **look** at the What We Use to Celebrate card and **say** if that is what they would use to celebrate in the way named on the What We Do to Celebrate card.
- If that is a match, the student keeps the pair of cards. If not, the student places them facedown.
- The student with the most matches wins the game. The other students **clap** for the winner.

EXTENSION ACTIVITIES

LEARNING NEW WORDS

HELP:
HELPFUL PEOPLE

Students **name** people in the community who help others, such as police officers. Students **discuss** how each of these people help others. The teacher arranges for an interview with a person that fills one of those roles. Students interview one of those people and **ask** him/her to tell them about the ways they help other people and why they like helping people.

GIVE:
THE GIFT OF TIME

Students **ask** classroom teachers and staff if there are things their class could do for them to give them the gift of their time. This gift of time might be reading to younger students, stuffing envelopes for a secretary, or watering plants in the school.

SHARE:
SHARING DILEMMA

Bring an entire cake or loaf of bread into the class. Tell students that the treat is for them, but they must share it equally with each other. Ask students to **name** some ways that they could share the treat among themselves. Students **vote** on the way they think is the best. Students then share the treat in that way.

LAUGH:
WHAT'S SO FUNNY?

Students go for a walk around the school, preferably at lunch time or during recess time when other students and staff are not in class. Students look for other students or staff who are laughing. When they **identify** people who are laughing, they **ask** that person to please tell them what made them laugh. Students **write** down the response. When they return to the class, students **read** each of the responses. Students **count** up the number of different reasons they recorded for a person laughing.

CELEBRATE:
CELEBRATIONS IN DIFFERENT COUNTRIES

Students gather information from books and the Internet about ways that people around the world celebrate different holidays. Students compare the celebration customs of the United States and different countries. Students **identify** the celebration customs that are the same, and the celebration customs that are different. Students **say** if they think they would like to celebrate that holiday in that country.

MEville to WEville

part three

Throughout these **Vocabulary Activities** students have opportunities to develop meaningful relationships and a sense of belonging as they interact with others in many large group activities.

This "character and community" icon will signal a lesson activity through which this sense of belonging can be reinforced.

unit 2
my family

In lesson #4, students will participate in a Celebration of Learning. During this Celebration of Learning they will each have an opportunity to show one piece of class work they have done. Over the next few days, be looking for great student work that can be used during this activity. A student created book from Writing Lesson #2, #3, or #4 would be a great piece of work to show.

ACTIVITY #1

MATERIALS:

- vocabulary cards Set Three R#103, R#104
- Help Scenario Cards R#108
- small paper lunch bags *(one per student)*
- construction paper
- crayons/markers
- yarn
- scissors
- glue
- card stock
- tape or stapler
- All-Turn-It® spinner *(optional)*

R#103

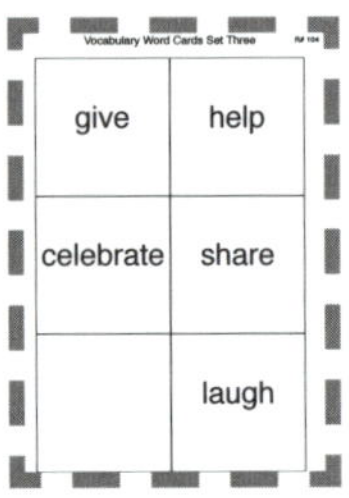

give	help
celebrate	share
	laugh

R#104

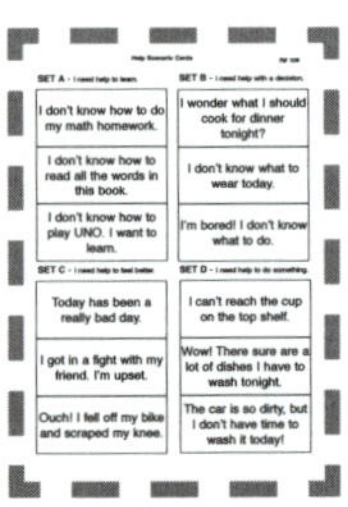

Help Scenario Cards

SET A - I need help to learn.	SET B - I need help with a decision.
I don't know how to do my math homework.	I wonder what I should cook for dinner tonight?
I don't know how to read all the words in this book.	I don't know what to wear today.
I don't know how to play UNO. I want to learn.	I'm bored! I don't know what to do.

SET C - I need help to feel better.	SET D - I need help to do something.
Today has been a really bad day.	I can't reach the cup on the top shelf.
I got in a fight with my friend. I'm upset.	Wow! There sure are a lot of dishes I have to wash tonight.
Ouch! I fell off my bike and scraped my knee.	The car is so dirty, but I don't have time to wash it today!

R#108

PREPARATION:

- Copy the Help Scenario Cards onto card stock. Cut out each card, keeping each set separate and labeled. Put Set A in a stack or on the large overlay of the All-Turn-It® spinner.

- Make a sample puppet.

"It is one of the beautiful compensations of this life that no one can sincerely try to help another without helping himself."

CHARLES DUDLEY

Students read and respond to scenarios in which they ask for help.

As a class, students make a puppet family.

- Show students the sample puppet. Tell students that their class is going to make a puppet family, and each student is going to make their own puppet that will be part of the puppet family.
- Students turn the bag upside down with the flap facing them, like a puppet.
- Students **select** a color they want for their puppet eyes. Students **cut** two eye shapes out of construction paper and **glue** them on the paper bag.
- Students continue to **select** colors for the nose, mouth, and ears. Students **cut** out those shapes and **glue** them on the puppet.

  OPTION: Pre-cut shapes in different colors to use as the eyes, nose, mouth and ears. Students then **select** the shape and color they want, and **glue** those shapes on the puppet.
- Students **select** a color yarn they want for hair and **cut** strips of that color yarn in the lengths they want. Students **glue** the yarn on the paper bag for hair.
- Students use crayons or markers to **color** and **draw** clothes and other designs/decorations on the puppet.

Students read and respond to scenarios in which a family member needs help.

- Show students the "help" vocabulary word. Lead students in **saying** the word multiple times.
- Explain to students that there are different things that people in our families may need help with, and different ways that we can help them.
- Explain to students that sometimes people in our families need help learning to do something *(Set A)*.
- Ask students to **say** ways in which we can help someone learn how to do something. Lead students to answers.

  SET A - **Help to Learn:**
  Show them how to do it. Tell them how to do it. Do it together with them. Practice with them.
- Students take turns drawing or **spinning** for a Help Scenario Set A Card. The student puts on their puppet and **reads** the card, in a fun puppet voice if they want.
- The other students put on their puppets and take turns **telling** the puppet with the problem how they will help him/her, or by actually **saying** or doing something to help the puppet with the problem. EX: "I'll read the book with you and help you practice the words you don't know."
- This process continues for each additional set of Help Scenario Cards *(Sets B, C, D)*. For each set, ask students to **say** ways in which we can help someone who needs that particular type of help, and lead them to appropriate answers.

  SET B - **Help With a Decision:**
  Help them list out choices. Ask questions about what they like or what they prefer. Offer suggestions.

  SET C - **Help to Feel Better:**
  Listen. Talk to them. Give them a hug. Spend time with them. Make a card or picture for them.

  SET D - **Help to Do Something:**
  Do the task/job for the person. Do the task/job with the person. Do part of the task/job for the person.
- Encourage the puppet with the problem to **say** "thank you" to the puppet family for their help.

Students make sharing bags and use them while doing a collaborative project.

Students practice sharing materials while making tambourines.

- Divide students into groups and give each group a Sharing Bag.
- Students follow teacher directions to share the materials in the Sharing Bag with others and make tambourines.
- Lead students in **discussing** if it was hard to share or easy to share with each other, and why.
- Students share music with each other by taking turns **turning on** the music and shaking their tambourines.

Students make their own Family Sharing Bag and use it with their family.

- Show students a Family Sharing Bag. Explain to students that they will make their own Family Sharing Bag to bring home.
- Put all Home Project Materials in a central location. Name and show each item. Direct students to **identify** it and put one in their bag.
- Tell students they will use these things to make a Family Creature. Show the sample Family Creature.
- Students **select** a color of construction paper, **write** the words, "Family Sharing Bag" on the paper, and **glue** it on the bag.
- Students fold the bag and **staple** it shut. They **staple** the Family Creature Parent Note on the bag.
- Students bring home their Family Sharing Bag.
- When the Family Creatures are returned, students take turns **showing** them to each other.

Teacher Script

"Today we're going to make tambourines and share music!" (Show sample.)

"First you'll decorate the back of each paper plate." (Show materials in the Sharing Bag.)

"These things are in the Sharing Bag. That means you will need to share everything that's in the bag with each other."

"After the plates are decorated, put one plate on the table, right side up. Pour beans into it."

"Put the second plate, upside down, on top of the first plate and staple the two plates together."

"Now pick them up and shake them! Let's make some music!"

MATERIALS:

- **vocabulary cards Set Three R#103, R#104**
- **Classroom Project Materials**
  - **brown grocery bags** *(four to six bags)*
  - **CD/tape player with music**
  - **crayons** *(in boxes - four to six boxes)*
  - **assorted decorations** *(glitter, etc.)*
  - **scissors** *(four to six pairs)*
  - **glue** *(four to six glue bottles or glue sticks)*
  - **construction paper** *(in assorted colors)*
  - **dinner size paper plates**
  - **dry beans or noodles**
  - **stapler**
- **Home Project Materials**
  - **Family Creature Parent Note R#109** *(one per student)*
  - **brown grocery bags** *(one per student)*
  - **assorted containers** *(one per student)* *(coffee cans with lids, shoe boxes, etc.)*
  - **crayons** *(in boxes - one box per student)*
  - **glue stick** *(one per student)*
  - **colored construction paper**
  - **assorted decorations**

PREPARATION:

- **Make a Sharing Bag for each group of students. Include one box of crayons, one glue stick, a few sheets of construction paper, and a handful of miscellaneous decorations. Write the words "Sharing Bag" on the front of each bag.**
- **Make a sample tambourine, Family Sharing Bag and Family Creature.**
- **Write the words, "Family Sharing Bag" on the board.**

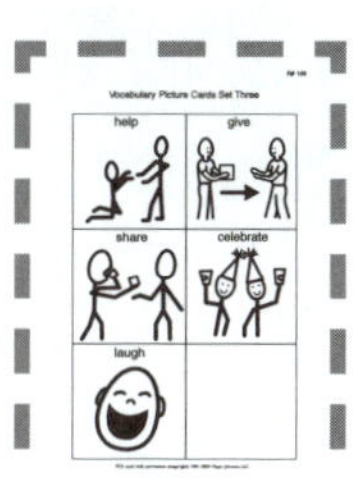

R#103

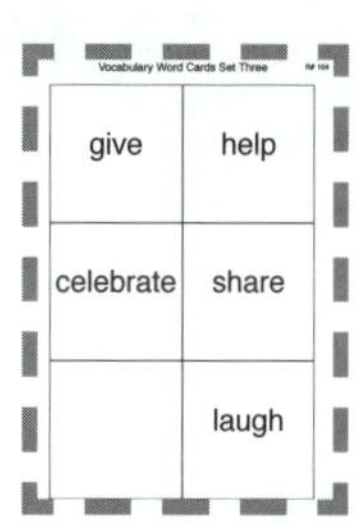

R#104

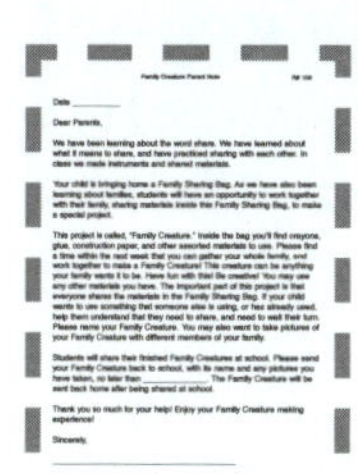
R#109

ACTIVITY #3

MATERIALS:

R#103

give	help
celebrate	share
	laugh

R#104

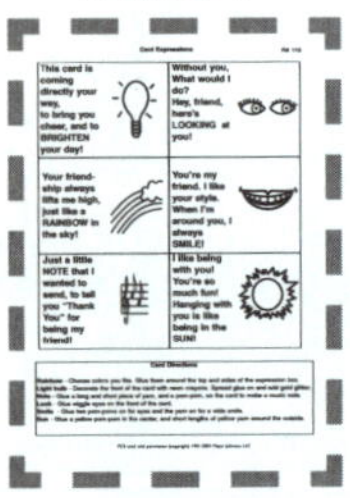

R#110

- **vocabulary cards Set Three R#103, R#104**
- **Card Expressions R#110** *(several copies)*
- **various commercial and/or homemade greeting cards**
- **note cards** *(3" x 5")*
- **construction paper** *(in assorted colors)*
- **writing tools**
- **scissors**
- **glue**
- **crayons/markers**
- **glitter**
- **craft eyes**
- **pom-poms**
- **yarn**
- **chart paper**
- **black marker**

PREPARATION:

- **Cut apart the individual boxes on the Card Expressions R#110. Keep the expression boxes in like sets.**
- **Make a sample of each different kind of card. Put each card in a different area, with the matching expression box.**
- **Pre-fold the construction paper to make cards. Fold it in half from top to bottom, then fold in half again from side to side to make small cards. Make enough for several per student.**
- **At each card area, place pre-folded cards in a variety of colors. Put glue, scissors, note cards, and writing tools at each center. See the Card Making Materials box for additional materials to put at each center.**

Students make greeting cards and give them away.

Students examine different kinds of greeting cards that people give to other people.

- Show students the "give" vocabulary card. Lead the students in **saying** the word multiple times.
- Show students several different types of greeting cards. Students take turns **reading** a card.
- As each card is read, ask students to **say** what they think that card means and why somebody might give that card to another person.
- Students **say** reasons why people might give each other cards. The teacher writes the ideas on the chart paper.

Students make cards to give away to others.

- Show students each of the different kinds of cards they will be able to make and give away.
- Lead students in **reading** each card.
- Direct students to **glue** the expression box on the front of the card, near the bottom.
- Show students the design on the card. Tell students how they will add the design to the card. *(See Card Directions on the bottom of R#110.)*
- Students follow the teacher directions to make the appropriate design on the front of the card.
- When finished with the front of the card, students open up the inside and **glue** a white note card on the right side.
- Students **write** their name on the note card, and decorate it however they like with crayons and markers.

Students select people to give cards to, and give them to those people.

- Students **look** at each card and **say** a name of a person they want to give the card to. Encourage students to think of friends, or adults, in the school they want to give cards to. Students **write** the name of the person on the outside of the card.
- Students take their cards and bring them to the people they selected.
- When students return from giving their cards away, they **discuss** how they felt when giving the cards away.

NOTE: Consider having students make an additional set of cards to bring home.

Card Making Materials

Rainbow - construction paper *(pre-cut in small shapes)*
Lightbulb - glitter, neon crayons
Smile - pom poms, yarn *(1 1/2 inch strips)*
Look - craft eyes
Note - pom-poms, yarn *(1 inch and 1/4 inch strips)*
Sun - yellow pom-poms, yellow yarn *(1/2 inch strips)*

Students participate in a Celebration of Learning.

Students learn about the Celebration of Learning.

- Show students the "celebrate" vocabulary card. Lead the students in **saying** the word several times.
- Ask students to **name** different reasons why you would celebrate.
- Tell students that learning new things is also something to celebrate.
- Ask students to **name** some of the things they have learned that they can celebrate. Write each thing on chart paper.
- Explain to students that they are going to celebrate all of the great things they have learned so far this year!

Students prepare for the Celebration of Learning.

NOTE: As students participate in each celebration preparation activity, show the appropriate Celebrate Picture Card and use the words, "Let's get ready to celebrate by ...."

- Decorate with streamers: Students **select** a color streamer, **cut** it into strips, and tape them up around the room.
- Prepare speech: Students complete the sentence, "This year I have learned ________" by **writing** in the blank one thing they have learned.
- Make party hats: Students **select** a color construction paper and **cut** along the black line. Students **look** at the board and **write** the word "celebrate" on the hat. Students **color** and **glue** on decorations. Students fold the paper to make a cone shape, and **glue** or tape the two sides together.
- Prepare cake: Students prepare the cake by spreading frosting or by **cutting** open the wrappers of snack cakes.
- Make punch: Students make punch by pouring one or more different kinds of juice/beverage into the punch bowl. Students may **turn on** the mixer or blender to mix the punch. Students pour the punch into individual cups.

Students participate in the Celebration of Learning.

NOTE: As students participate in each celebration activity, show the appropriate Celebrate Picture Card and use the words, "Let's celebrate by ...."

- Read speech: Students take turns **reading** their sentence about what they have learned and **show** their student work.
- Put on party hats: Students put on the party hats they made.
- Play music: Students take turns **selecting** music they would like to play and **turn on** the music. Students may celebrate by **singing** and dancing to the music.
- Open presents: Students are each given a present. Students rip or **cut** the wrapping paper.
- Eat cake: Students give each other a piece of cake.
- Drink punch: Students give each other a cup of punch.
- Take pictures: Students **take pictures** of each other participating in the Celebration of Learning.

R#103-R#104

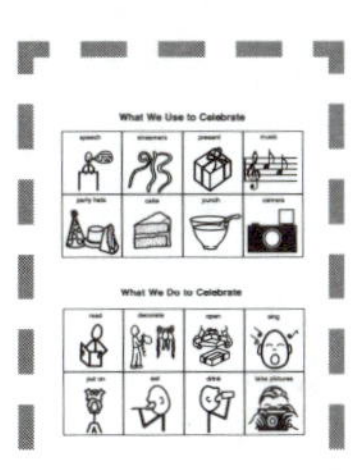

R#107

MATERIALS:

- **vocabulary cards Set Three R#103, R#104**
- **Celebrate Picture Cards R#107**
- **crepe paper** *(streamers)*
- **chart paper and black markers**
- **scissors**
- **tape**
- **sentence strips** *(one per student)*
- **writing tools**
- **one special piece of work that each student has done**
- **music CD or tape player with music** *(several choices)*
- **construction paper in assorted colors**
- **stapler**
- **crayons, markers**
- **assorted hat decorations** *(buttons, pom-poms, sequins, etc.)*
- **glue**
- **cake and frosting or individually packaged snack cakes**
- **beverage/juice, punch bowl, and cups**
- **small gifts, such as a treat or a sticker** *(one per student)*
- **wrapping paper, tissue paper, or decorated lunch sacks**
- **digital camera**

PREPARATION:

- **Wrap and label one small present per student.**
- **Use a thick black marker to draw a black line forming a half circle that takes up as much paper as possible, horizontally on assorted colors of construction paper.**
- **On each sentence strip, write the sentence "This year I have learned ____________."**
- **Write the word "celebrate" on the board.**

ACTIVITY #5

Students tell jokes and record the responses using the Laughometer.

R#103-R#104

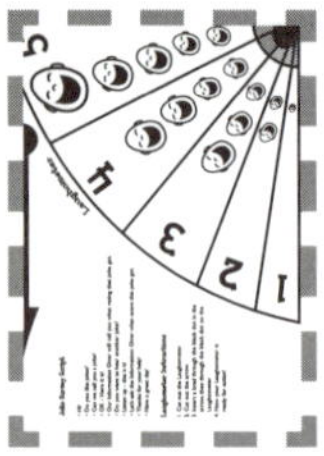

R#111

MATERIALS:

- vocabulary cards Set Three R#103, R#104
- Laughometer R#111
- white paper • card stock
- construction paper
- black marker • adult scissors
- metal brads/fasteners
- adhesive Velcro®
- clipboards *(one per group)*
- writing tools

PREPARATION

- Copy the Laughometer onto card stock. Follow the directions to assemble it.
- Select two jokes that students will tell.
- Write each joke on a sheet of white paper.
- With the construction paper horizontal, write the title Joke Survey across the top. Under the title write the title of one joke on one side and the title of the other joke on the other side. Leave room underneath to record the Laughometer scores.
- Put a joke survey on each clipboard and use Velcro® attach a writing tool.

Students learn about the Laughometer.

- The teacher shows and explains the purpose of the Laughometer.
- The teacher leads students in **reading** each level number as he/she points it out on the Laughometer, and explains that the higher the number, the harder the person/group is laughing.
- The teacher demonstrates the Laughometer by telling a joke or doing something funny and having a staff or student helper laugh really loud and heartily, then laugh just a little. The teacher holds the Laughometer and moves the dial to show the level of laughter that the person achieved.

Student teams do a joke survey of people in their school.

- Students take turns being assigned to and fulfilling the following roles as they do a joke survey:

  Survey Reader - **Reads** the Joke Survey Script (R#111) to the survey participants.

  Joke Reader - **Reads** the joke to the class.

  Laughter Evaluator - **Selects** the number showing how strong the laugh was. Moves the dial to that number.

  Information Giver - **Tells** the survey participants the Laughometer ratings for each joke.

  Recorder - **Writes** the number of the rating on the joke survey, under the appropriate joke.
- When the joke survey is completed, students add up the ratings for each joke and **identify** the winning joke.

VOCABULARY EXTENSION ACTIVITIES

HELP: CLASSROOM HELPERS

Students go into another class and help younger students with an art project or other project that they need help with. Before students go into the room, make a list of ways they will help. Lead students in **reading** the list. Lead students in practicing **asking** the younger students, "Do you need help?" When students return to their classroom, they **discuss** different ways that they were able to help.

GIVE: GUESS THE MYSTERY GIFT

Put a gift, or a picture or name of a gift, inside a gift wrapped box or bag. Give students clues about the gift, such as how it sounds, what it looks like, who you would give it to, where you would buy it, etc. Students **ask** questions to get more information. Students make guesses and **say** what they think the gift is. When a student correctly **identifies** the item, that student may take a turn at describing and giving clues to the class about the next mystery gift.

SHARE: SHARE YOUR SPACE!

Students invite another class to come and join them for a lesson or activity, and share their room and everything in it. Each student in the class is assigned a buddy from the visiting class. The students **tell** the visiting students the rules of the classroom and any other information the visitors need to know. The students share their supplies and classroom materials with the visitors. After the visitors leave, the students **discuss** how they felt when they were able to share their personal space and materials with others.

LAUGH: IT'S A LAUGH OFF!

Students challenge another class, or a group of staff members, to a Laugh Off! The object is for the contestants to not laugh, or even smile, during the course of the game. The students hosting the game will **say** funny things, do funny things, **ask** funny questions, **sing** silly songs, and **tell** funny jokes to the contestants to try to get them to laugh. When a contestant laughs, one student, who is the referee, will **tell** that contestant that he/she is out of the game. The last remaining contestant wins the game!

CELEBRATE: CLASSROOM CELEBRATION DAY POSTER

For one week, put up the Celebration Day Poster from Literacy Lesson #4. On each day of the week, put up a different Celebration Day Card showing what is being celebrated. Use the Celebration Day Cards from the lesson, or create your own fun things to celebrate. You could celebrate the color purple and all the day's lessons could somehow incorporate the color purple. Students follow teacher directions to join in on the celebration activities.

part three

Throughout **The Word Wall Lessons**, students will have active roles as they read the word wall words, lead activities, and provide directions to other students. As students engage in these roles of reader, leader, and teacher, look for opportunities to communicate to them the importance of what they are doing.

This "character and community" icon will signal a lesson activity through which students can have a valued role and learn to understand the importance of their role.

unit 2

my family

In these Word Wall Lessons, students will have opportunities to practice identifying, reading, spelling and writing the words.

LESSON #1, #2, #3

LESSON 1

R#112

Students practice saying and writing the word wall words.

MATERIALS:

- **Word Wall Words Set Three R#112**
- **writing tools**
- **letter/word pointer**
- **chalk or dry erase markers**

- The teacher writes a word wall word on the board in large, bold letters.
- A student comes to the board and uses the pointer to point out each letter of the word and lead the students in chanting out, or loudly **saying**, each letter.
- Each student takes a turn leading the class in chanting the words. Include words from Part 1 *(we, have, the)*, Part 2 *(see, do, are)*, and Part 3 *(help, work, is)*.
- The students **write** each word wall word several times using one or more writing tools.

LESSON 2

R#112

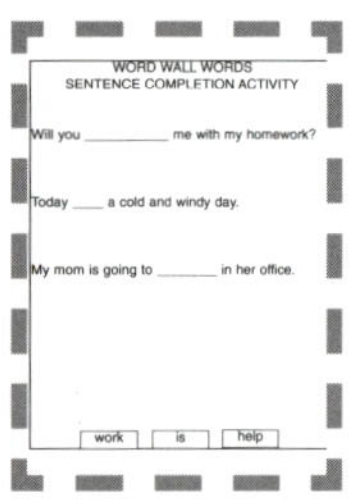

R#113

Students participate in a Sentence Completion Activity.

MATERIALS:

- **Word Wall Words Set Three R#112**
- **Sentence Completion Activity R#113** *(one per student)*
- **writing tools**

- The teacher shows each word wall word and leads students in **clap/chanting** it multiple times.
- As each word is clap/chanted, students **identify** that word on the bottom of their Sentence Completion Activity.
- The teacher leads students in **reading** each sentence on the Sentence Completion Activity.
- Students **identify** the word on the Sentence Completion Activity that fits in that sentence.
- Students **write** the correct word in the blank.

OPTION: Students may **cut** out that small word box and **glue** it on the blank line.

LESSON 3

R#112

R#114

Students participate in the Mind Reader activity.

MATERIALS:

- **Word Wall Words Set Three R#112**
- **Mind Reader Script R#114**
- **writing tools**
- **note cards** *(3″ x 5″)*
- **craft sticks**
- **glue or tape**

- The teacher shows, and leads students in **clap/chanting**, each of the three word wall words.
- Students **write** each of the three word wall words on a separate note card.
- Students tape or **glue** a craft stick to the back of each note card.
- As the teacher calls out one of the words, students **identify** that word card and wave that word card sign.
- A student, or the teacher, **reads** the clues from the Mind Reader Script to the class.
- Students **select** the word wall word which they think is being described and wave that word card sign.
- The teacher affirms or re-directs each student's choice.
- Students **say** the word together as a class.

LESSON #4

Students participate in The Word Collect Game.

Students prepare for The Word Collect Game.

- The teacher shows students each of the word wall words, and leads students in **saying** each word multiple times.
- The teacher divides the class into two different teams.
- The teams take turns rolling or **spinning** for a number.
- The team **counts** out that many word cards, and together **reads** each word. The team keeps those cards.
- When all words have been used, the teams **count** their cards. The team with the most cards wins the game.

PREPARATION:

- **Cover the die by wrapping masking tape around all sides of it, or by placing a dot sticker on each side. On each side, in black marker, write the number one, two, or three** *(two of each number)*. **If using the All-Turn-It® spinner, create nine different number cards with the numbers one, two, and three** *(each on three cards)* **and place them faceup on the large overlay of the All-Turn-It® spinner.**

LESSON 4

MATERIALS:

- **Word Wall Words Set One R#25, Set Two R#78, and Set Three R#112**
- **note cards** *(3" x 5")*
- **die or All-Turn-It® spinner**
- **dot stickers or masking tape**
- **Unit 1 Word Wall Words - use word cards from Unit 1 or create word cards by writing each of the following words on a note card:** me, who, and, I, it, you, like, to, what.

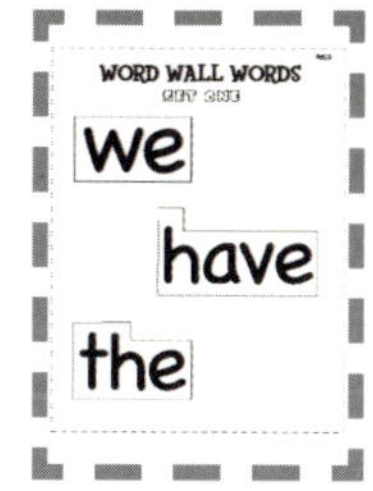

R#25

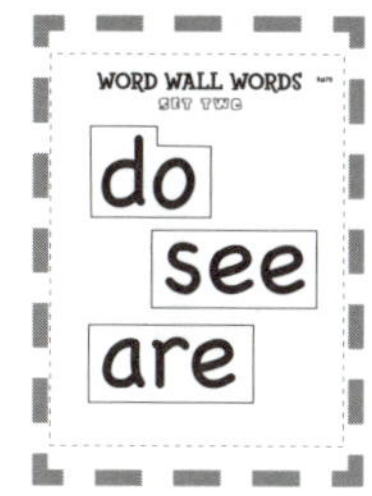

R#78

R#112

LESSON #5

Students participate in The Scrambled Sentence Game.

Students participate in The Scrambled Sentence Game.

- The teacher shows students each of the word wall words and leads students in **saying** each word multiple times.
- The teacher shows and leads students in **reading** each sentence.
- The teacher directs the student to take the words out of a bag/envelope, **read** each word, then put them in a different order to try and make a sentence out of the words.
- When students have created a sentence and have **read** it to the teacher, they **write** the sentence number *(written on the envelope)* and the sentence on paper.
- Students trade envelopes and unscramble additional sentences.

Sentences:

1. I like to work.
2. I like to help.
3. I like you.
4. We work.
5. What do you like?
6. Do you see me?
7. We help you work.
8. You and I like to help.
9. I see you work.
10. What do you have?
11. Do you have it?
12. We see you.

LESSON 5

MATERIALS:

- **Word Wall Words Set One R#25, Set Two R#78, and Set Three R#112**
- **note cards** *(4"x 6")*
- **writing tools and paper**
- **envelope or resealable bag**
- **Unit 1 Word Wall Words** me, who, and, I, it, you, like, to, what

PREPARATION:

- **Create Scrambled Sentence bags. For each sentence, write each word and punctuation mark that is part of the sentence on a separate note card. Put them in an envelope or resealable bag.**
- **Write the sentence number on the envelope/bag.**
- **Write each sentence on the board.**

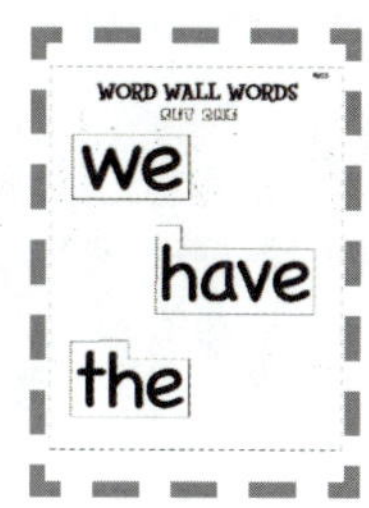

R#25

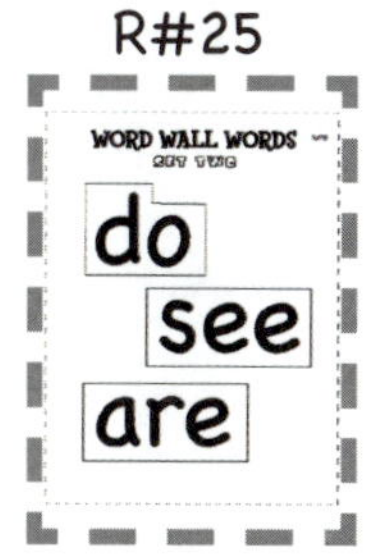

R#78

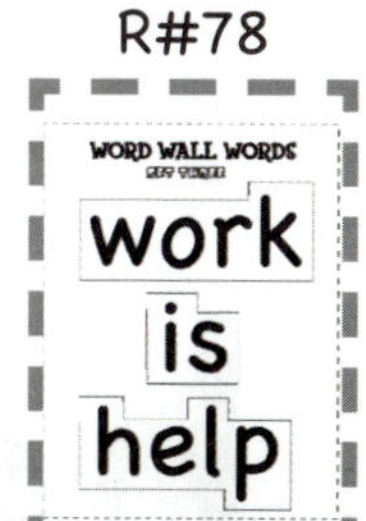

R#112

Dear Parents,

Your child is currently working on the following words: **work, is, help.**

Whenever possible, please take the time to reinforce these words with your child by having him/her write the words, say the words, and spell the words. Below is an activity to do with your child to help him/her learn each of the three word wall words.

Sincerely,

____

Word Making

Directions:

Cut out each of the word cards and letter cards below. Place the letter cards face up on a work surface. To make the cards easier for students to pick up, place each card at the edge of the work surface, with one side hanging off.

You may either put all of the letters out at once, or put out just the letters for one word at a time. Show your child one of the word cards and read the word with your child. Then ask your child to make the word by finding the correct letters and putting them together, side by side, to create the word.

If your child is non-verbal, record the word on a voice output device so he/she can read the word.

If your child is not able to physically manipulate the letter cards, show your child the word card, and explain that he/she is going to spell the word by telling you what letters to put down. Show your child two or more letter cards (one being the correct letter) and ask him/her to find the letter that comes first. Your child may grasp, point to, or eye gaze at the letter of their choice. Then repeat the process, asking your child to find the letter that comes next. Continue this process for each letter of the word. As your child identifies each letter, place the letters in a place visible to your child.

Word cards
work
is
help

w		o
e	r	s
i		h
p	l	k

unit 2

my family

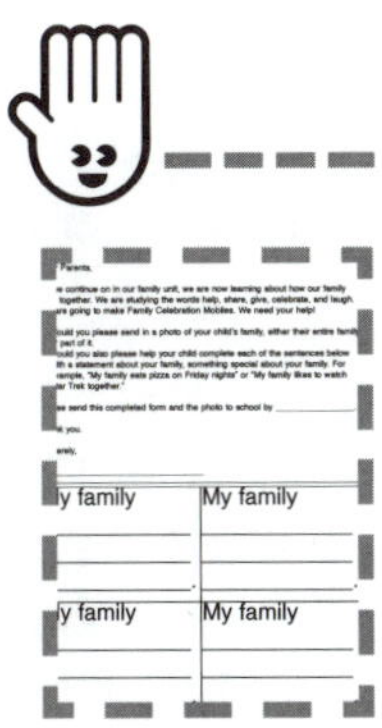
R#115

Teacher Note: **Prior to teaching lesson #2, send home** **Parent Note R#115.**

part three

Throughout these **Literacy Lessons**, students and teachers will have frequent opportunities to acknowledge the contributions and accomplishments of others. When student responses are given, acknowledge the person who contributed it and acknowledge the value of that response.

This "character and community" icon will signal a lesson activity that provides an opportunity for students and teachers to acknowledge each other.

LESSON #1

MATERIALS:

- ***"Families"* by Ann Morris**
- **vocabulary cards Set Three R#103, R#104**
- **white paper** *(8 1/2" x 11")*
- **note cards** *(4" x 6")*
- **writing tools**
- **poster board** *(one large sheet)*
- **magazines**
- **glue**
- **scissors**
- **black marker**
- **digital camera** *(optional)*

PREPARATION:

- **Use the black marker to write the title, "People Help Each Other" at the top of the poster board.**

R#103

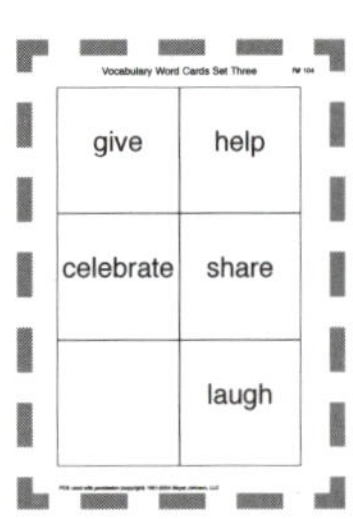

R#104

Students identify pictures of people helping each other.

Students identify pictures of people helping each other.

- Show students the "help" vocabulary card. Lead students in **saying** the word multiple times.
- Students take turns **turning the pages** in the book "Families." As each page is turned, the teacher asks the students, "Is somebody in this family helping someone else?"
- Students answer by **saying** "yes" or "no." Affirm student's answer or direct the student to the appropriate response and explain the reason for that answer.
- Show students pages in the book "Families" that show the family members helping each other.
- Ask a student to **select** a book picture of a family helping each other and place the "help" vocabulary card on the picture.
- Ask students to **say** how the family is helping each other.

Examples:

pg. 9 - The mom is wiping the girl's tears.
pg. 11 - The parents are helping the boys learn how to play the violin.
pg. 12 - The girl is helping her dad with the fishing net.
pg. 16 - The girl is helping her mother make dough.
pg. 19 - The children are helping their family make masks.
pg. 23 - The boy is helping his dad make fishing lures.
pg. 25 - The mom is helping the boy read a book.
pg. 28 - The boy is helping his mom push his dad on the swing.

- Write each student response on a separate sheet of white paper in sentence form in large, bold letters to create sentence papers.
- Lead students in **reading** each sentence.

Students identify specific pictures of people helping each other.

- Put the sentence papers in a stack. Students take turns drawing a sentence paper and **reading** it.
- Students take turns **turning the pages** of the book and **looking** for that picture. When the student sees the picture, he/she **identifies** it.

  NOTE: Direct students to focus on particular pages by marking a page for them to start at, immediately before, or on, the page which has the picture they need.
- Continue until each student has had at least one turn at **reading** a sentence and **identifying** the picture.

Students make a poster collage of people helping each other.

- Students **look** through magazines and **identify** pictures of people helping other people.
- Students **cut** out the pictures.

  OPTION: Students go through the school and **take pictures** of people who are helping each other.
- Students **glue** each picture on a note card.
- On each note card, the student **writes** one sentence telling how the person is helping.
- Students take turns **reading** each note card to the class.
- Students **glue** their note cards on the poster board.
- The teacher puts the poster on display in the classroom or hallway.

Students make a Family Celebration Mobile.

Teacher Note: Send home Parent Letter R#115 several days prior to teaching this lesson.

Student learn about the Family Celebration Mobile project.

- Students **look** at the sample Family Celebration Mobile.
- The teacher leads the students in **reading** the sentence, "I Celebrate My Family" and **reading** each of the family sentence boxes stapled on the streamers.
- Explain to students that our families are very important, and that students are going to make a mobile like this to celebrate their family.

Students make their own Family Celebration Mobile.

- Students follow teacher directions to make their own Family Celebration Mobile.

Students share their Family Celebration Mobiles with each other.

- Students take turns **showing** their Family Celebration Mobile to the class.
- On their turn, each student **reads** the sentence "I Celebrate My Family" on the front of their plate.
- The student also **reads** the sentence inside each family sentence box stapled on the streamers.

Teacher Script

"Is everybody ready to make a Family Celebration Mobile?"
"Take one paper plate."
"**Choose** a color paint and **paint** the front of the plate."
"**Dry** the plate."
"**Glue** your family photo in the center of the plate."
"Now **look** at the board and we'll **read** the words, 'I Celebrate My Family.' "
"Use a marker or crayon to **write** that sentence on the paper plate."
"**Write** your name on the front of the plate."
"Now we need streamers! **Choose** the color crepe paper you want."
"**Cut** strips of the crepe paper to make streamers."
"**Staple** each streamer on the bottom of the paper plate."
"Now **cut** out each of the family sentence boxes."
"**Staple** each sentence box somewhere on a streamer."

MATERIALS:

- **vocabulary cards Set Three R#103, R#104**
- **Family Celebration Mobile Parent Letter R#115** *(completed)*
- **large paper plate** *(one per student)*
- **tempera paint in various colors**
- **sponge brushes or large paintbrushes**
- **crepe paper in assorted colors**
- **scissors**
- **stapler**
- **family photos** *(sent in from home)*
- **glue**
- **writing tools**
- **black markers, crayons**

PREPARATION:

- **Make a sample Family Celebration Mobile.**
- **Cut crepe paper into long strips. Sort them into piles according to colors.**
- **Write the words, "I Celebrate My Family" on the board.**

R#103

R#104

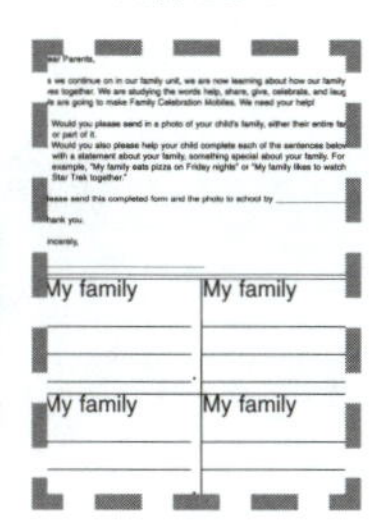

R#115

Students play the "Find a Solution" game.

MATERIALS:

R#103

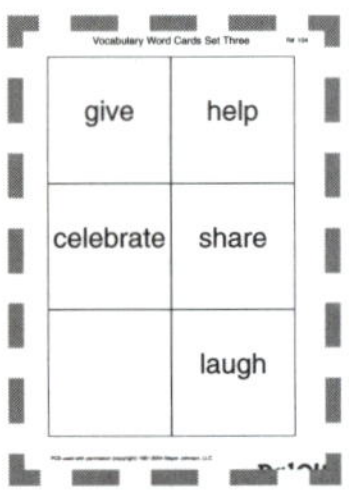

R#104

R#116

- vocabulary cards Set Three R#103, R#104
- "Find a Solution" Game Cards R#116
- card stock *(two sheets - different colors)*
- adult scissors
- All-Turn-It® spinner *(optional)*
- display tool

PREPARATION:

- Copy the Situation Cards R#116 and the Solution Cards R#116 onto two different colors of card stock. Cut the cards out, and keep them separate.
- Place the Situation Cards in a stack or on the large overlay of the All-Turn-It® spinner.
- As each student has a turn, place three to four Solution Cards (including the correct card) on the display tool.

Students participate in the "Find a Solution" game.

- Show students each of the Solution Cards and lead them in **reading** each card.
- Students take turns drawing or **spinning** for a Situation Card.
- The student **reads** the card to the class.
- The student **looks** at the Solution Cards and **selects** a solution for the problem.
- The student **tells** the class how they would solve the problem.

Students act out the situation in the "Find a Solution" game.

- Students take turns drawing or **spinning** for a Situation Card.
- The student **reads** the Situation Card.
- One or more students act out that situation on the card, playing the role of the person mentioned in the situation.
- The student who drew the card then must role play an appropriate solution to this problem.

"As long as you live,
keep learning how to live."

SENECA

Students make a Celebration Day poster.

Students learn about the Celebration Day poster.

- Show students the "celebrate" vocabulary card. Lead students in **saying** the word at least three to five times.
- Show students the sample Celebration Day poster.
- Lead students in **reading** the sentence, "Today We Celebrate" and **reading** the word on the card clipped on the poster.
- Ask students to **say** ways that they think the class could celebrate that. Read the three suggested ideas.
- Tell students that today is a Celebration Day and they will celebrate *(the card on the poster)* throughout the day.
- Explain to students that there are many other things they can celebrate.
- Students take turns drawing a card and **reading** it.
- Students then **say** different ways to celebrate that. The student or teacher **reads** the three suggested ideas *(R#117)*.
- Put several Celebration Day Cards on display and ask students to **select, show,** and **read** their favorite card from those on display.

Students follow directions to make their own Celebration Day poster.

- Explain to students that they will make their own Celebration Day posters to bring home. Then they can have Celebration Days with their family.
- Students **select** a color of paint.
- Students **paint** their card stock. Students may **select** additional colors as they paint.
- Students **dry** the painting.
- Students **cut** out the Celebration Day Sign and **glue** it on the card stock, at the top, creating a Celebration Day poster.
- Underneath the sign, students **glue** a clothespin, vertically, clip side up.
- Students **select** and **glue** on the card stock various decorations.
- Students **staple** the resealable plastic bag on the back of the Celebration Day poster.
- Lead students in **reading** the name of each of the Celebration Day Cards.
- Students **cut** out the Celebration Day Cards and put them in the resealable plastic bag.
- Attach a parent note to each Celebration Day poster.
- Students bring home their posters and share them with their family.

"Years may wrinkle the skin, but to give up enthusiasm wrinkles the soul."

SAMUEL ULLMAN

MATERIALS:

- **vocabulary cards Set Three R#103, R#104**
- **Celebration Day Cards R#117** *(one per student plus one extra)*
- **Celebration Day Sign R#118** *(one per student)*
- **white card stock** *(one sheet per student)*
- **tempera paint in assorted colors**
- **sponge brushes or paintbrushes**
- **glue**
- **scissors**
- **assorted decorations** *(buttons, sequins, etc.)*
- **wooden clip clothespins** *(one per student)*
- **quart size resealable plastic bag** *(one per student)*
- **stapler**

R#103-R#104

R#117

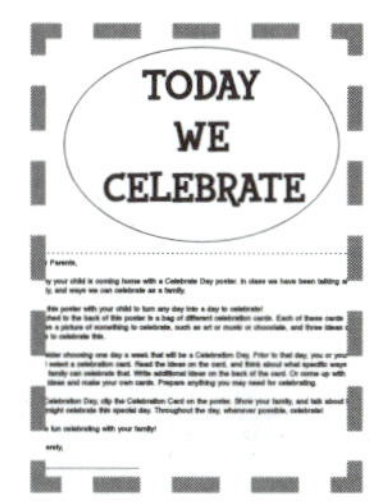

R#118

PREPARATION:

- **Make a sample Celebration Day poster. Clip on a Celebration Day Card.**
- **Select a Celebration Day Card representing something your class can celebrate that day. Clip it on the Celebration Day poster.**
- **Cut each Celebration Day Sign R#118 on the black line. The parent note will be sent home with each poster.**
- **Copy one set of the Celebration Day Cards onto card stock. Cut them out. Put them facedown in a stack.**

Example:

LESSON #5

Students share with their family about their day.

MATERIALS:

- vocabulary cards Set Three R#103, R#104
- Family Information Sharing R#119
- writing tools
- note cards 4" x 6"

PREPARATION:

- Write each of the following questions on a note card to create Sharing Cards:
  - What did you eat for breakfast today?
  - Did you ride the bus to school today?
  - What's the name of a book you like?
  - What kind of music do you like to listen to?
  - How many people are in your family?
  - Do you have a cat or a dog?
  - Did you watch anything cool on TV last night?
  - Do you have plans for this weekend?
  - What do you and your friends like to do together?

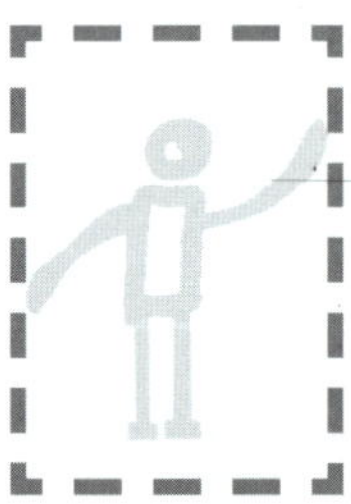

R#103–R#104

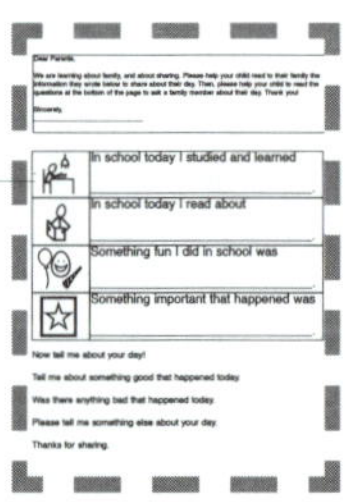

R#119

Students practice sharing information about themselves by asking and answering questions.

- Show students the "share" vocabulary card. Lead them in **reading** the word multiple times.
- Lead the class in **reading** each of the Sharing Cards.
- Explain to students that they are going to break into groups and practice asking each other these questions. Students will be able to share more about themselves by answering the questions.
- Divide students into three groups. Give each group three Sharing Cards.
- Students take turns drawing a Sharing Card.
- That student **asks** the students in his/her group that question.
- The students in the group take turns **answering** the question.
- When students have gone through their stack of cards, they may exchange Sharing Cards with another group of students and **ask** new questions.

Students write information about their day to share with their family.

- Lead students in **reading** the sentence, "In school today I studied and learned ____________."
- Direct students to **write** information on the blank to complete the sentence.
- Continue this process for each of the sentences in the boxes.
- Direct students to **read** each of the sentences below the boxes to practice **asking** their family about their day.
- Tell students to bring home their papers and use them to share information about their day, and to find out about the day of a family member.

EXTENSION ACTIVITIES LITERACY LESSONS

HELP: COUPON BOOK

Make a template for a coupon that says: This Coupon Good For ______ Minutes of Help with __________. Students **say** ways they can help around the house and **write** the number of minutes they will help for and the type of help they will give, on the blank lines. Students bring their coupon books home to their family so that their family can redeem them for help from the student.

SHARE: SILLY SKIT

Write a short, silly skit about a family who is very selfish and never shares anything with anybody. Assign a role to each student. Students practice **reading** their lines and act out the skit for another class or other group of people. Have somebody videotape the skit. Students watch the skit and **discuss** the problems the family has because they won't share. Students **identify** different ways that the family in the skit could share with each other, and the difference that might make in their family.

GIVE: RAISE MONEY TO GIVE TO CHARITY

Students learn about different charities. Students **vote** on a charity they want to earn money for. Students follow directions to make a popular craft, such as seasonal refrigerator magnets, decorated gift bags, greeting cards, or bookmarks. Students **tell** staff and students about the crafts and how much they cost. Students **write** the charity name, craft name, description, and price on posters. Students hang posters up to advertise their fund raiser.

CELEBRATE: PLAN A CELEBRATION

Students **vote** on a celebration that takes place in another country that they would like to celebrate in their class. Students **write** a list of things they will do to celebrate this particular holiday as people in this other country do. Students prepare and participate in the celebration.

LAUGH: WHAT'S YOUR STORY?

Send a note home with students asking their family to work together to **write** down a true, funny story about something that happened in their family. The stories are sent to school, and students take turns **reading** their stories to each other. Students **vote** on the story they think is the most funny! Use the Laughometer.

MEville to WEville

Teacher Note: **Prior to teaching Writing Lesson #4, send home the Parent Note R#124 with three blank note cards (3"x 5").**

unit 2

my family

R#124

part three

Throughout these **Writing Lessons**, students will be making choices as to what elements they want on the pages of the books they are creating. Give all students opportunities to let their own voice be heard as they communicate individual selections and read their completed books to the class.

This "character and community" icon will signal a lesson activity in which students will have an opportunity to express their preferences and let their own voice be heard.

Students write a letter to a family member.

MATERIALS:

- **Letter Writing R#120** *(one per student)*
- **Optional Family Member vocabulary cards R#4, R#5**
- **sample letters**
- **assorted real stamps**
- **chart paper**
- **black marker**
- **writing tools**
- **writing paper**
- **scissors**
- **glue**
- **envelopes** *(letter size)* *(one per student)*

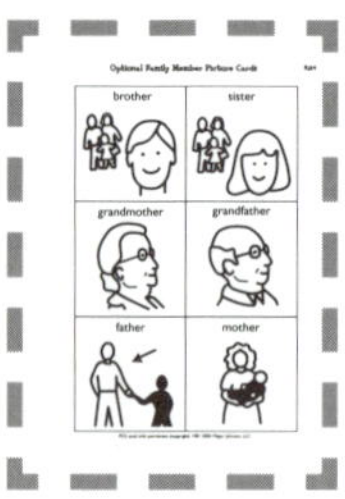

R#4

R#5

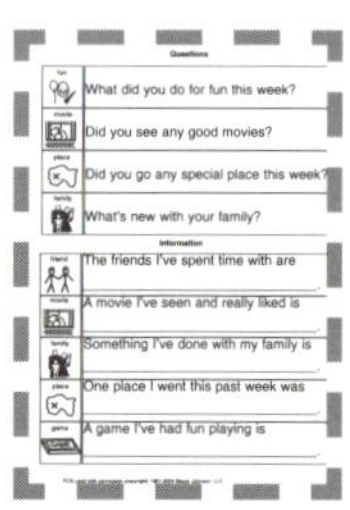

R#120

Students learn about the letter writing project.

- Students **look** at sample letters.
- Explain to students that writing and sending letters in the mail is one way of sharing information with people, including people in our family who do not live with us, such as a grandparent, aunt or uncle.
- Select one or two sample letters and read them to the students.
- Ask students to **say** some of the questions that were asked in the letter, and some of the information that was written.
- Students **discuss** the type of information to include in a letter to a friend or family member who they don't see often.

As a class, students write a letter to another class or to a person they all know.

- Ask students to **say** how to begin the letter. Write the salutation, such as Dear (Sam), on the first line of the chart paper.
- Ask students to **say** what they should ask and tell the person in the letter.
- Write student responses in complete sentences on chart paper.
- Ask students to **say** how to end the letter. Write the closing, such as, From (Mrs. Smith's Class) at the end of the letter.
- Lead students in **reading** the letter.
- On the envelope, write the address of the person, and put on a stamp. Write the class and school address in the upper left hand corner of the envelope. Explain to students that all these things are needed in order to send a letter in the mail.

Students write a personal letter to a family member.

- Students **select** a family member *(from vocabulary cards R#4, R#5)* to whom they would like to write a letter, preferably someone not living with them.
- Write the word "Dear"on the board and direct students to **write** that word on their paper, then **write** the name of the person the letter is being sent to.
- Write the sentence, "Hi. How are you?" on the board. Explain to students that this is a polite way to begin a letter.
- Direct students to **write** that sentence on the first line on their paper.
- Lead students in **reading** each of the questions on Letter Writing R#120.
- Direct students to **select** and **cut** out the questions they want to ask the person, and **glue** them under the first sentence they wrote.
- Lead students in **reading** each of the information sentences on Letter Writing page R#120.
- Direct students to **select** and **cut** out the information sentences they would like to include in their letter.
- Direct the students to **write** the completion of each sentence on the blank line.
- Direct students to **glue** those sentences on their paper, and to **write** any additional sentences they want.
- Direct students to **write** their name at the bottom of the letter.
- Direct students to fold the letter, put it in an envelope, and **write** the name of the person on the envelope.

NOTE: You may want to attach a sticky note to the envelope asking a parent to please see that this letter gets sent to the indicated person.

Students make a book entitled "A Day in the Life of My Family."

Students learn about the bookmaking activity.

- Show students the sample book. Lead students in **reading** the title of the book.
- Explain to students that this is a book about some of the things that people in your family do throughout the day.
- Students take turns **turning the pages** of the book.
- On each page, lead students in **reading** each sentence on the page.
- Explain to students that they are each going to make their own book about things that their family does during a day.

Students each make their own book entitled, "A Day in the Life of My Family."

- Students follow teacher directions to create the cover and book pages.
- Students put their pages together in the order of morning, day, evening.
- Students put their pages inside the cover and **staple** the book.
- Students **write** their name on the book cover.
- Students take turns **showing** and **reading** their books to their class.

Teacher Script

"First, **choose** a color of construction paper. Fold it in half like this (demonstrate) to make a book cover."

"Now look at the board and **read** the words. **Write** these words on your book cover, in big letters."

"Now **cut** out the three pictures on the very top of your paper - morning, day, and evening."

"The first part of the day is morning. **Identify** the picture of 'morning' and **glue** it on the very top box."

"Get out another book page. After morning comes day time. **Identify** the picture of 'day' and glue it on the very top box."

"Now let's do page three. The last part of the day is evening. **Identify** the picture of 'evening' and glue it on the top box."

"Now we will do some writing on each page."

"Find page one, with the picture of morning on it."

"**Write** the word 'morning' on the blank line."

"Now let's **read** the sentence."

"What do the people in your family do in the morning?"

"**Select** those pictures and **cut** them out. **Glue** each picture on a box on the page."

"Now, next to each picture, complete the sentence 'My family ________' by **writing** words about the picture to say what your family does. For example, next to breakfast, you could write the words 'eats breakfast' and the sentence would read, 'My family eats breakfast.' "

NOTE: Repeat this sequence of direction steps for the "day" and "evening" pages.

MATERIALS:

- **Book Pictures R#121**
  (one per student)
- **Book Page R#122**
  (three per student)
- **writing tools**
- **markers, crayons**
- **glue**
- **scissors**
- **construction paper**
  (11" x 17")
- **stapler**
- **black marker**

PREPARATIONS:

- **Make a sample "A Day in the Life of My Family" book.**
- **Write the words "A Day in the Life of My Family" on the board.**

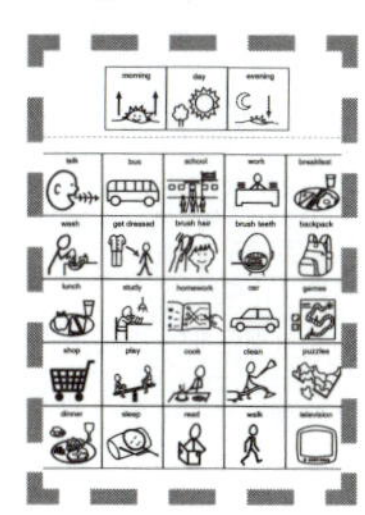

R#121

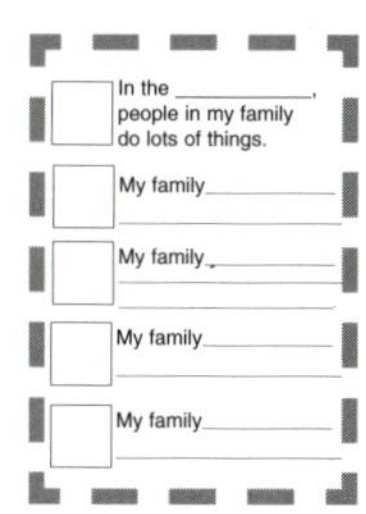

R#122

Students make a book entitled "Important Information About ME!"

MATERIALS:

- "Important Information About ME!" R#123 *(one per student)*
- students school pictures *(small wallet size)*
- black marker
- writing tools
- note cards *(3" x 5")*
- phone *(working or non-working)*
- state map
- stapler

PREPARATION:

- Create a set of number cards for each student by writing numbers zero through nine on note cards, one number per card.
- Create a personal information page for each student. Write each student's name, address, and phone number on a sheet of paper.
- Make a sample "Important Information About ME!" book.

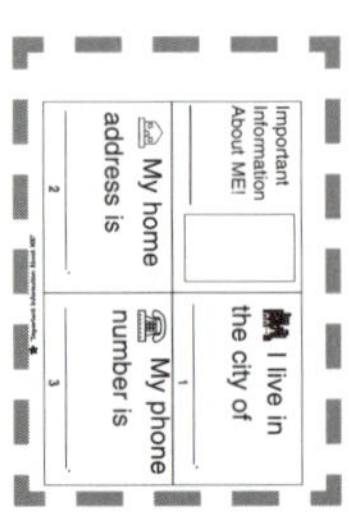

R#123

Students learn and practice address and telephone information.

- Ask students to **tell** you what city they live in.
- Write the name of the city on the board. Lead students in **reading** the city name several times.
- Show students the map and point out the city, or cities, in which the students live. Students take turns coming to the map and **identifying** the city in which they live.
- Explain to students that an address is a special number assigned to a home.
- Give students their personal information page. Help each student **identify** and **read** their address to each other.
- Give students a set of number cards and direct them to **identify** the numbers that make up their address and put them in the correct order.
- Direct students to **identify** their phone number on their personal information page and **read** it to another student.
- Students take turns coming to the phone and practicing dialing their home phone number.

Students make their own book entitled, "Important Information About ME!"

- Show students the sample book and lead them in **reading** the title.
- Explain to students that they will make their own book with information about their city, address, and phone number.
- Direct students to **cut** out the four mini book pages (R#123) by cutting on the black lines.
- Direct students to **identify** the title page that has only writing.
- Students **read** the title page.
- Direct students to **write** their name on the line on the title page.
- Direct students to **glue** their picture on the box.
- Direct students to turn the page over so it is front side down.
- Direct students to **identify** page one, with the picture of the city.
- Students **read** page one.
- Direct students to **say** and **write** on the line the name of the city in which they live.
- Direct students to turn the page over and put it on the title page.
- Direct students to **identify** page two, with the picture of the house on it.
- Students **read** page two.
- Direct students to **say** and **write** on the line their home address.
- Direct students to turn the page over and put it on page one.
- Direct students to **identify** page three, with the picture of the telephone on it.
- Students **read** page three.
- Direct students to **say** and **write** on the line their phone number.
- Direct students to turn the page over and put it on page two.
- Direct students to flip the stack of pages over and **staple** the pages together.
- Students take turns **reading** their books to each other.

NOTE: Provide as many opportunities as possible for students to read their books and practice their information.

Students make a book entitled "My Helping Hands."

Students learn about the "My Helping Hands" book.

- Show students the front of the sample "My Helping Hands" book.
- Ask students to show you their hands and wiggle their hands, or wave their hands.

  NOTE: For students who do not have use of their hands, consider asking those students to activate a switch using whatever body part they consistently use. Explain to that student how that body part acts as their hands.
- Explain to students that there are many different ways they can help people in their family.
- Explain that they use their hands to help in many of those ways.
- Students take turns **turning the pages** of the sample "My Helping Hands" book and **reading** each page.

Students make their own "My Helping Hands" book.

- Students **select** a color of construction paper and **count** out five sheets.
- On the first sheet, students **look** at the board and use a black crayon or marker to **write** the words "My Helping Hands" on the paper. The paper should be horizontal as students write the words.
- Students take this paper, and one other sheet of the construction paper, and set it aside.
- Students begin with each of the other sheets horizontally.
- Students take turns **reading** each of the sentences on their "My Helping Hands" Parent Note R#124.
- Students **cut** out each of the sentence boxes.
- Students **glue** one sentence box on each of the three sheets of construction paper, on the bottom.
- Students **read** each sentence again, then **look** at the three pictures they have drawn and **select** the picture that matches the sentence. Students **glue** that picture on the right side of the page, above the sentence.
- When all three pages have a sentence box and a picture card on them, tell students that when people help, we often say that we are using "helping hands" to help out.
- Explain to students that we are going to make a "helping hand" on each of these pages.
- Show students how to dip their hand in the white finger paint, then put their hand on the left side of the book page, above the sentence to make a handprint. Students make a handprint on each of the three pages. Students get out the title page and put both handprints on that.
- Students may sprinkle glitter on the wet white paint, or wait until the paint dries and then **paint** or **glue** decorations on each hand.
- When all pages have been completed, students put the three book pages in between the title page and the plain back page and **staple** the pages together.

Students read their "My Helping Hands" books to each other.

- Students draw or **spin** for the student who will share their book.
- When it is his/her turn, the student comes to the Sharing Chair and **reads** their book.
- The student **shows** each page to the class.

Teacher Note: **Send the "My Helping Hands" Parent Note R#124, with three note cards, home several days before teaching this lesson.**

MATERIALS:

- **"My Helping Hands" Parent Note R#124** *(returned from home)*
- **construction paper** *(8 1/2" x 11")*
- **black crayon or marker**
- **note cards** *(3" x 5") (three per student)*
- **scissors**
- **glue**
- **white finger paint**
- **paper plates or shallow containers**
- **miscellaneous decorations** *(buttons, glitter, etc.)*
- **tempera paint in assorted colors and small paintbrushes** *(optional)*
- **stapler**
- **writing tools**
- **student picture/name cards**
- **All-Turn-It® spinner** *(optional)*

PREPARATION:

- **Make a sample "My Helping Hands" book.**
- **Write the words, "My Helping Hands" on the board.**
- **Designate and/or decorate a chair to be the Sharing Chair.**

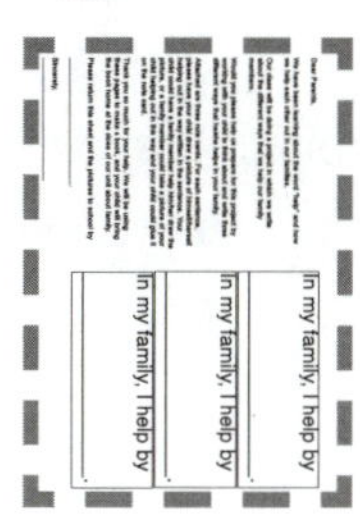

R#124

LESSON #5

Students follow written directions to make and break Personal Piñatas.

MATERIALS:

- "Personal Piñata" Directions R#125
- full size piñata for show *(optional)*
- brown paper lunch sacks
- old newspapers *(in single sheets)*
- prizes *(enough for a handful per student)*
- paint stirring sticks *(one per student)*
- crepe paper *(streamers)* in long strips
- large, shallow container
- crayons/markers
- yarn *(long strips)* • stapler
- hole punch • scissors • glue

PREPARATION:

- Make a Personal Piñata sample.
- Decide how many prizes you would like in each piñata. Write that number in the blank on sentence number one of the Personal Piñata Making Directions.

Students learn about piñatas.

- Show students the piñata. Ask students to describe it by **saying** how it looks.
- Explain to students what a piñata is, how it is used, and when it is used.

Students follow directions to make their own Personal Piñata.

- Explain to students that they are going to make their own Personal Piñata.
- Students **read** and follow each step of the Personal Piñata Making Directions.
- Students **show** the class their piñatas.
- Students **color** or **draw** decorations on a prize bag *(paper lunch sack)*.

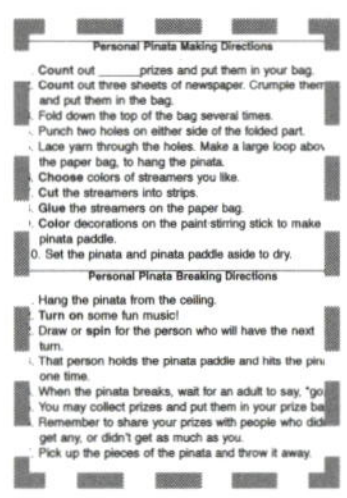
Personal Pinata Making Directions
Count out ______ prizes and put them in your bag.
Count out three sheets of newspaper. Crumple them and put them in the bag.
Fold down the top of the bag several times.
Punch two holes on either side of the folded part.
Lace yarn through the holes. Make a large loop above the paper bag, to hang the pinata.
Choose colors of streamers you like.
Cut the streamers into strips.
Glue the streamers on the paper bag.
Color decorations on the paint stirring stick to make pinata paddle.
10. Set the pinata and pinata paddle aside to dry.
Personal Pinata Breaking Directions
Hang the pinata from the ceiling.
Turn on some fun music!
Draw or spin for the person who will have the next turn.
That person holds the pinata paddle and hits the pin… one time.
When the pinata breaks, wait for an adult to say, "go…
You may collect prizes and put them in your prize ba…
Remember to share your prizes with people who did… get any, or didn't get as much as you.
Pick up the pieces of the pinata and throw it away.

R#125

Students follow directions to break one or more of the Personal Piñatas.

- Hang one of the sample personal piñatas from the ceiling.
- Students **read** and follow the Personal Piñata Breaking Directions.
- Students bring home their personal piñatas and Personal Piñata Directions.

Students write directions for making and breaking a piñata.

- Ask students to **name** the materials used in making a piñata.
- Students **say** the first step in making a piñata.
- Students continue to **say** each step of the piñata making and breaking process.
- Students take turns **writing** each step on chart paper.
- Students **read** the completed direction sheet.

EXTENSION ACTIVITIES

WRITING LESSONS

HELP: THANK YOU NOTES

Direct students to think about somebody who has helped them recently. Ask students to **name** that person, and to **say** how that person helped them. Direct students to **write** a note to that person saying "Thank You" for their help. Students may decorate the note or turn it into a card. Students send the thank you note to the person.

SHARE: SHARE SOMETHING NICE!

Students each draw one or two names of students. Each student thinks of one nice thing about that student and **writes** it down on the piece of paper with the student's name. The name papers are put in a large hat. Students take turns pulling out, or **spinning** for, a name paper and **reading** the student name and the nice thing that is written about that student.

GIVE: THE GIFT OF ENCOURAGEMENT

Explain to students that encouragement is one thing that we are able to give to each other. Ask students to think of different types of encouragement that they could say to others. Students take turns **writing** each of those words, sentences, or phrases on chart paper. Students **identify** times or situations in which it would be appropriate to give the gift of encouragement to somebody.
Role play, or use a puppet to act out situations in which you or the puppet are discouraged and could use encouragement.
Help the student to appropriately respond by **saying** a word of encouragement, and/or by doing something encouraging such as giving a hug.

CELEBRATE: WRITE AN INVITATION

Students **write** an invitation to a mini celebration, such as Donut Day or Movie Day. Students **select** who they want to invite and **write** the information about the event on the invitation. Students then prepare and carry out the celebration.

LAUGH: WHY DO PEOPLE LAUGH?

Students brainstorm a list of things that make people laugh. Students take turns **writing** each thing on chart paper. Students **look** at the list and each student **names** those things on the list that would make them laugh, and those things that would not make them laugh.

EARLY LITERACY AND COMMUNICATION PROGRAM

Part four

ASSISTIVE TECHNOLOGY
Quick Set Up Guide

and the ACTION DICTIONARY

ablenet™

unit 2

my family

MEville to WEville

ASSISTIVE TECHNOLOGY
Quick Set Up Guide

MEville to WEville

This section includes photos of specific assistive technology tools, quick set up instructions, recording instructions and information regarding the special features of the recommended tools for students with severe disabilities to actively participate in the MEville to WEville lessons.

TIP: Make sure your devices have batteries and are turned ON before starting your activities.

Communication Tools

PAGE 108

- BIGmack® communicator
  (can substitute LITTLEmack™ communicator)
- LITTLE Step-by-Step communicator
  (can substitute BIG Step-by-Step communicator)
- Step-by-Step communicator with levels
- iTalk2™
  (can substitute two LITTLEmack™ communicators)
- TalkTrac™ Plus wearable communicator
- TalkTrac™ Plus wearable communicator with levels
- SuperTalker™ progressive communicator

Access Tools

PAGE 112

- Switches:
  -Big Red® switch
  -Jelly Bean® switch
  -Specs® switch
- Battery Device Adapter and Notching File
- Single Switch Latch and Timer (SLAT)
- PowerLink®3 control unit

Participation Tools

PAGE 114

- Battery-operated fan
- Battery-operated scissors
- Digital camera
- Stapler
- Paint 'N' Swirl™
- Talking Photo Album
- Talking Symbols™ notepad

Learning Tools

PAGE 116

- All-Turn-It® spinner
- BookWorm™ literacy tool

Mounting Tools

PAGE 117

- UltraStik™ adhesive
- Universal Switch Mounting System with friction knob
- Slim Armstrong Mounting System
- Sensitrac™ Mounting System adjustable arm

Communication Tools

Communication tools provides opportunities for individuals who are non-verbal and/or working on beginning communication skills to express themselves. These tools are commonly called voice output communication aids (VOCA).

BIGmack® communicator

Delivers a single message up to 75 seconds.

Recording Instructions

1. Turn ON.
2. Press and hold both the RECORD button and the switch top at the same time.
3. Record message, then release both RECORD button and switch top.
4. Press the switch top to play the message.

LITTLE Step-by-Step communicator

Delivers sequential messages up to 75 seconds.

Recording Instructions

1. Turn ON.
2. Press and hold the RECORD button on back of device until the red light appears.
3. Press and hold the switch top.
4. Record message, then release the switch top.
5. Repeat steps 3-4 until all messages are recorded.
6. Press, then release the RECORD button (red light goes off).
7. Press the switch top repeatedly to play the message.

Step-by-Step communicator with levels

Delivers sequential messages up to 75 seconds. Ability to store messages on up to three levels.

Recording Instructions

1. Turn ON.
2. Move slide switch to level1.
3. Press and hold the RECORD button on back of device until the red light appears.
4. Press and hold the switch top.
5. Record message, then release the switch top.
6. Repeat steps 4-5 until all messages are recorded into this level.
7. Move slide switch to level 2.
8. Repeat steps 4-6 until all messages are recorded into level 2.
9. Move slide switch to level 3.
10. Repeat steps 4-6 until all messages are recorded into level 3.
11. Press, then release the RECORD button once. The red light will turn off.
12. Move slide switch to desired level and press switch top repeatedly to play messages.

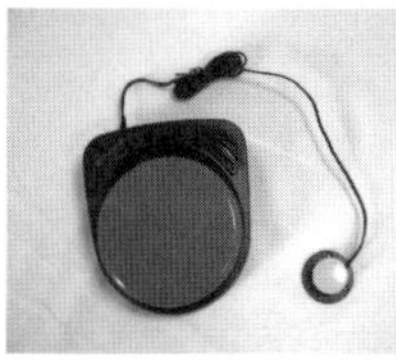

BIGmack® communicator with switch

LITTLE Step-by-Step communicator with switch

Step-by-Step communicator with levels with a switch

Outcome

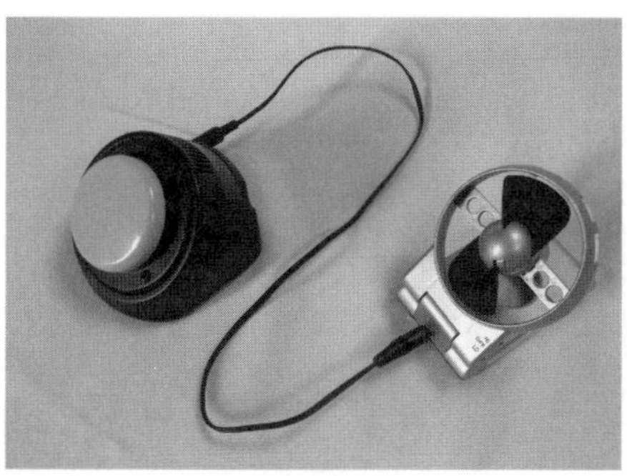

Outcome

Advanced Features:

1. **External Switch Operation**
   Allows operation of the BIGmack communicator, LITTLE Step-by-Step or Step-by-Step communicator with levels through an external switch (such as a Specs switch) that best meets the individual's unique needs.

   Quick Set Up Instructions
   1. Plug the external switch into the jack labeled SWITCH on the back of the device.
   2. Record a message.
   3. Press the external switch top to play the message(s).

2. **Toy/Appliance Operation**
   Allows a student to activate a battery-operated toy/appliance for the length of the recorded message. See Battery Systems on page 112 for adapting toys/appliances with a Battery Device Adapter.

   Quick Set Up Instructions for BIGmack® communicator
   1. Turn ON.
   2. Record message into BIGmack communicator.
   3. Plug the toy/appliance cable into the toy/appliance jack on the BIGmack communicator.
   4. Plug other end of the toy/appliance cable into the pre-adapted battery-operated toy or appliance.
   5. Press the switch top to activate the toy and play the message.

   Quick Set Up Instructions for LITTLE Step-by-Step communicator and Step-by-Step communicator with levels
   1. Turn ON.
   2. While recording a message sequence into LITTLE Step-by-Step communicator or Step-by-Step communicator with levels, decide which message you want to pair with the activation of the toy/appliance and press the RECORD button once during the recording of that message.
   3. Continue to record the remaining sequence of message(s).
   4. Plug the toy/appliance cable into the toy/appliance jack on the device.
   5. Plug other end of the toy/appliance cable into the pre-adapted, battery-operated toy or appliance.
   6. Press the switch top to activate toy and play messages.

3. **Repeat Feature**
   This feature is included in the LITTLE Step-by-Step communicator and the Step-by-Step communicator with levels. It allows any message in the sequence to be repeated.

   Quick Set Up Instructions
   1. Turn ON.
   2. Record the entire message sequence into device.
   3. Play a message to be repeated.
   4. Press the RECORD button once, after the message has ended.
   5. The same message will repeat each time the switch is pressed.
   6. To continue to the next message, press RECORD button once.

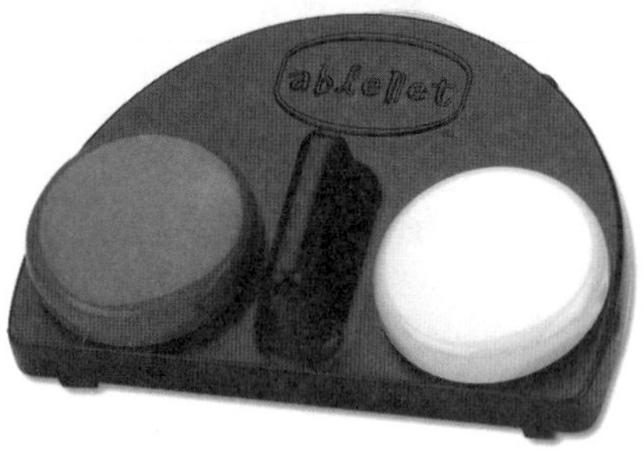

iTalk2™ communicator

iTalk2™ communicator

Delivers a single message up to 8.5 seconds per activation area.

Quick Set Up Instructions

1. Turn ON.
2. Press and hold the RECORD switch and desired switch top.
3. Record message, then release both the RECORD button and switch top.
4. Repeat steps 2-3 for recording the other location.
5. Press the desired switch top to play the message.

Outcome

Advanced Features:

Toy/Appliance Operation

Allows students to activate a battery-operated toy/appliance for the length of the recorded message. See Battery Systems on page 112 for adapting toy/appliances with a Battery Device Adapter.

Quick Set Up Instructions for iTalk2™

1. Turn ON.
2. Record message into a message location.
3. Plug the toy/appliance cable into the corresponding toy/appliance jack on the iTalk2™.
4. Plug other end of the toy/appliance cable into the pre-adapted battery-operated toy or appliance.
5. Press the desired switch top to activate the toy and play the message.

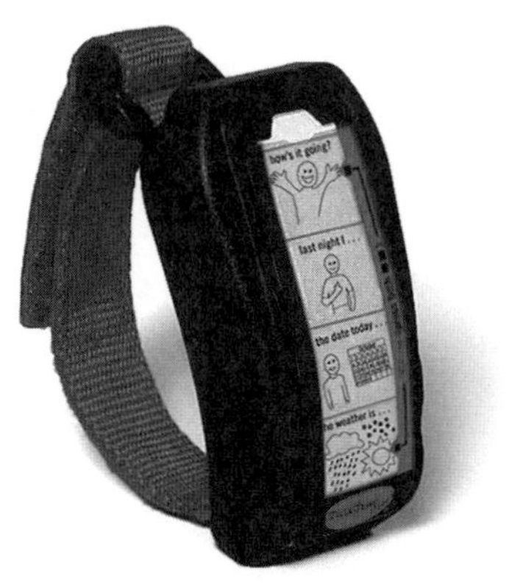

TalkTrac™ Plus wearable communicator

TalkTrac™ Plus wearable communicator

Delivers a single message up to 15 seconds per first three locations and 25 seconds on the last location.

Quick Set Up Instructions for TalkTrac Plus

1. Press, hold and then release the RECORD button. *(red light appears)*
2. Press and hold a message location.
3. Record the message(s) and then release that location.
4. Repeat steps 2-3 for all other message locations.
5. Press and release the RECORD button. *(red light turns off)*
6. Press the desired location to play the message.

**Volume is adjusted by pressing on the two blue arrows at the same time.*

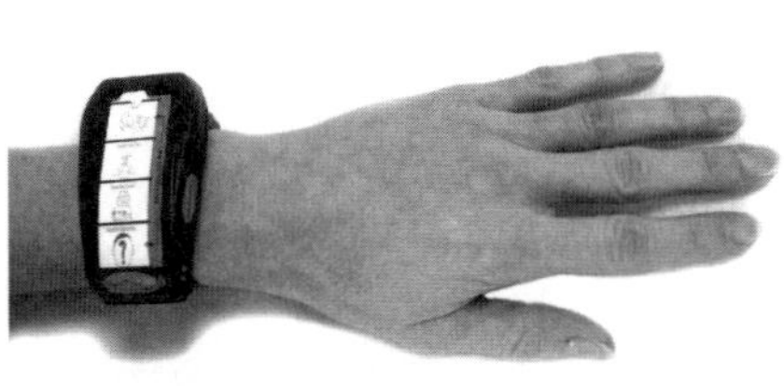

Outcome

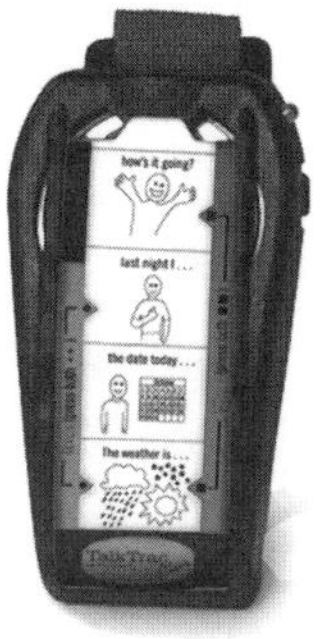

TalkTrac™ Plus wearable communicator with levels

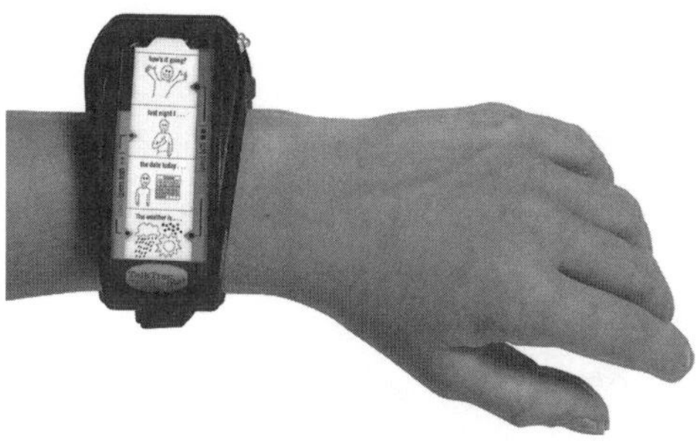

Outcome

TalkTrac™ Plus wearable communicator with levels

Delivers a single message up to 15 seconds per first three locations and 25 seconds on the last location.

Quick Set Up Instructions

1. Press, hold and then release the RECORD button. *(red light appears)*
2. Press and hold a message location.
3. Record the message and then release that location.
4. Repeat steps 2-3 for all other message locations.
5. Record the second level: Press the two green arrows at the same time.
6. Press and hold a message location.
7. Record the message and then release that location.
8. Repeat steps 6-7 for all other message locations.
9. Press and release the RECORD button. *(red light turns off)*
10. Press the desired location to play the message.

** To move between levels, press the two green arrows at the same time and then release.*

** Volume is adjusted by pressing on the two blue arrows at the same time.*

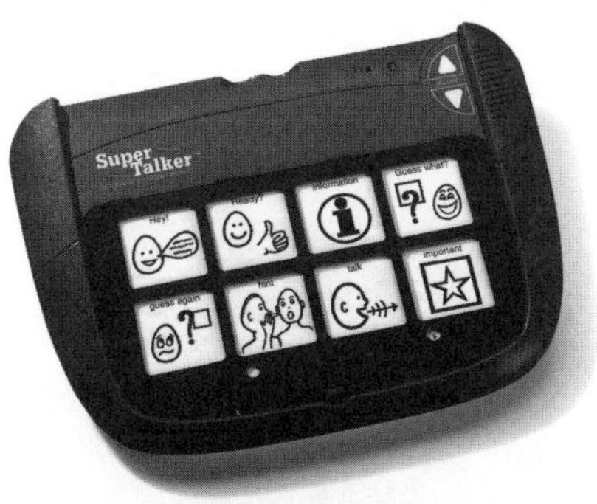

SuperTalker™ progressive communicator

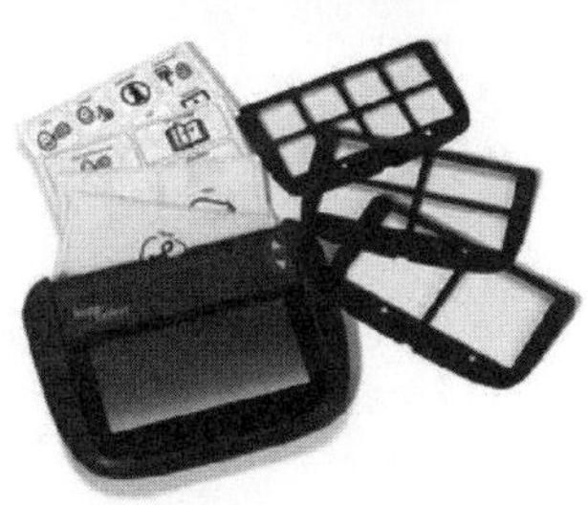

SuperTalker™ progressive communicator

Delivers multiple messages up to 16 minutes within the 8 communication levels. Includes four keyguards to support students' growing communication needs.

Record a Level

1. Turn power ON.
2. Place a communication overlay on the SuperTalker.
3. Attach the corresponding keyguard.
4. Select the LEVEL number and GRID number on the control panel.
5. Press and hold the RECORD button until the red light appears.
6. Press and hold the desired message location.
7. Record the message and then release that location.
8. Repeat steps 6-7 for all other message locations.
9. Press RECORD button to exit record mode. (red light turns off)
10. Press the desired message location to play the message.

Multiple Level Recording

1. Must select a new LEVEL.
2. Select a new GRID, if changing number of messages.
3. Follow steps 2-9 above to record an additional level.

Keyguard Storage

The keyguard storage area is under the instruction panel on the back of the SuperTalker. It allows for the storage of three keyguards.

The SuperTalker contains the following advanced features:

- Toy/appliance Jack that allows for activation of toys or appliances.
- Step Ahead Jack that allows messages to be played in a sequence using an external jack.
- Volume control with a Lock Out feature to maintain a constant volume level, if desired.

Access Tools are the student's means to accessing the activity. The three areas included in this section are Switches, Battery Systems and Electrical Systems. These empower students to turn ON/OFF most battery or electrical toy/appliances, providing them with opportunities to participate in a range of instructional activities.

AbleNet Switches

AbleNet switches are available in five colors and three sizes to meet the unique and varied needs of your students.

Big Red® switch
5 inch switch top
Activation pressure = 5-6oz.

Jelly Bean® switch
2 1/2 inch switch top
Activation pressure = 2-3oz.

Specs® switch
1 3/8 inch switch top
Activation pressure = 3-4oz.

Battery Systems

Battery systems allow most battery-operated toy/appliances to be turned ON with a switch.

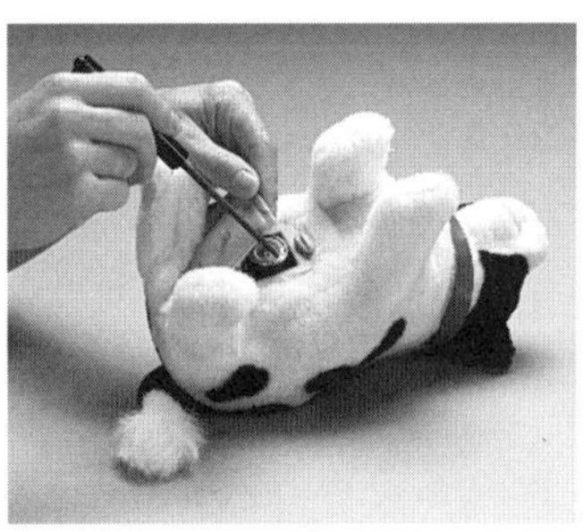

(figure A)

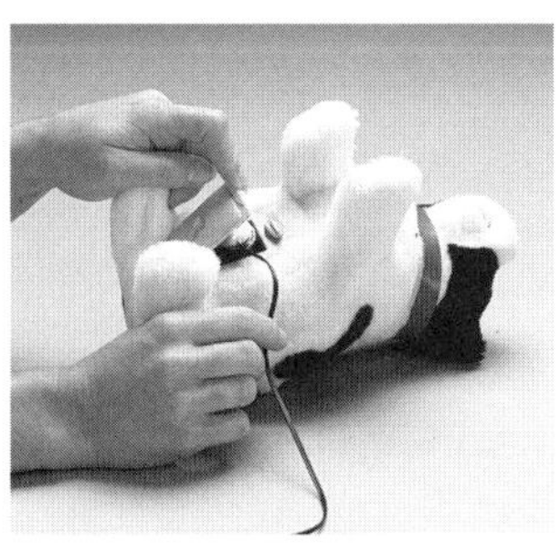

(figure B)

Quick Set Up Instructions

1. Open the battery compartment and notch the cover with a notching file. *(see figure A)*
2. Place the Battery Device Adapter between the battery and the connection. *(see figure B)*
3. Replace the battery cover, positioning the cord through the notch.
4. Plug a switch into the Battery Device Adapter.
5. Be sure your device is in the ON position and press the switch.

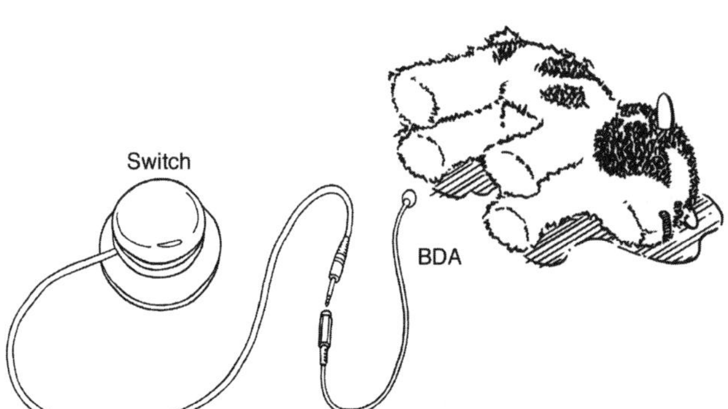

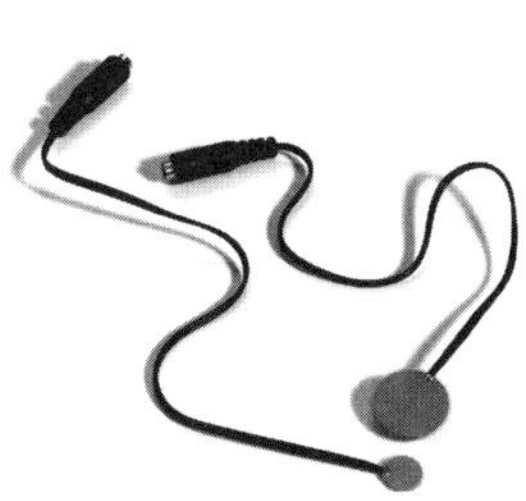

Battery Device Adapter
Available in sizes AA/AAA and C/D.

Notching File

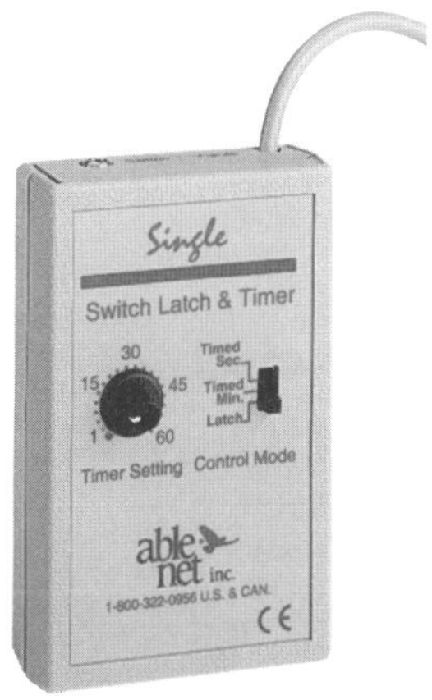

Single Switch Latch and Timer

Outcome

Battery Systems

Single Switch Latch and Timer (SLAT)

Add the Single Switch Latch and Timer to gain the three modes of control for the battery system. This ensures student success by allowing them to control the amount of time required for the activity.

Quick Set Up Instructions

1. Plug the gray SLAT cable into the Battery Device Adapter of the previously adapted toy/appliance.
2. Plug the switch into the jack labeled SWITCH.
3. Select desired mode of control.
4. Be sure your device is in the ON position and press the switch.

Modes of Control for the Single Switch Latch and Timer

Timed Seconds: Runs appliance from 1 to 60 seconds with each switch activation.
Timed Minutes: Runs appliance from 1 to 60 minutes with each switch activation.
Latch: First switch activation turns appliance ON; second activation turns it OFF.

PowerLink®3 control unit

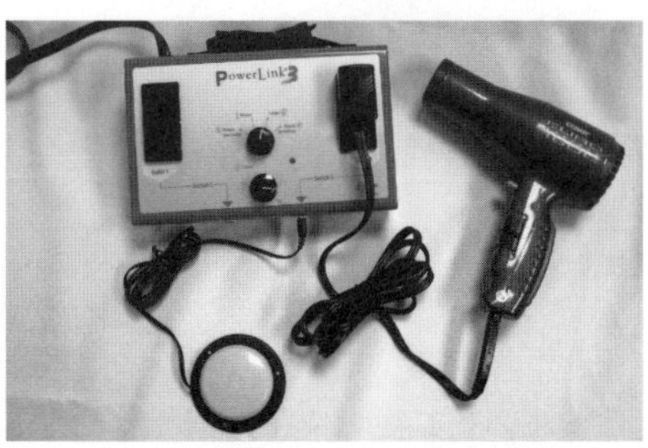

Outcome

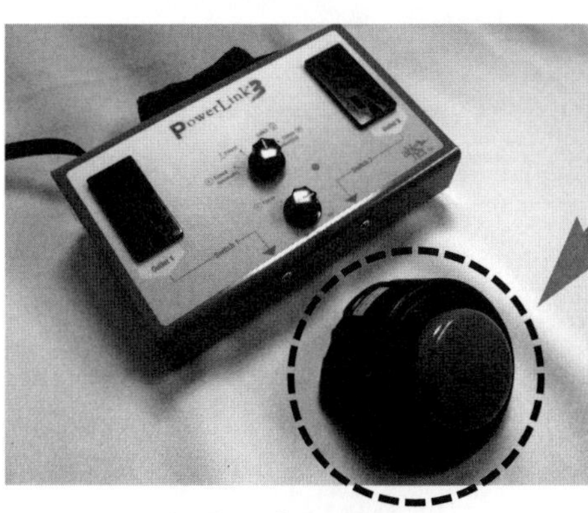

Airlink® Cordless

Electrical Systems

Electrical systems allow most electrically operated toys/appliances to be turned ON with a switch. Four modes of control described below are included on the PowerLink®3 control unit.

Quick Set Up Instructions

1. Plug PowerLink®3 into a wall outlet.
2. Plug electrical device into the PowerLink®3.
3. Plug a switch into corresponding jack.
4. Select mode of control, using the dial.
5. Be sure your device is in the ON position and press the switch.

Modes of Control for the PowerLink®3 control unit

Direct: Keeps appliances ON as long as the switch is activated.
Timed Seconds: Runs appliance from 1 to 60 seconds with each switch activation.
Timed Minutes: Runs appliance from 1 to 60 minutes with each switch activation.
Latch: First switch activation turns appliance ON; second activation turns it OFF.

Note: Gain cordless access by using AirLink™ Cordless switch

Participation Tools

Participation tools are the battery or electrically operated devices that support the student to participate in the activity. The student is responsible for activating a switch or manually turning on the device to participate in the activity. This section includes AbleNet tools that have been pre-adapted and those that require adaptation with a Battery Device Adapter.

Pre-adapted Devices

The devices below have a built-in switch jack, which eliminates the need for a Battery Device Adapter.

Battery-operated fan

Quick Set Up Instructions

1. Plug a switch into the built-in switch jack.
2. Be sure the fan is in the ON position and press the switch.

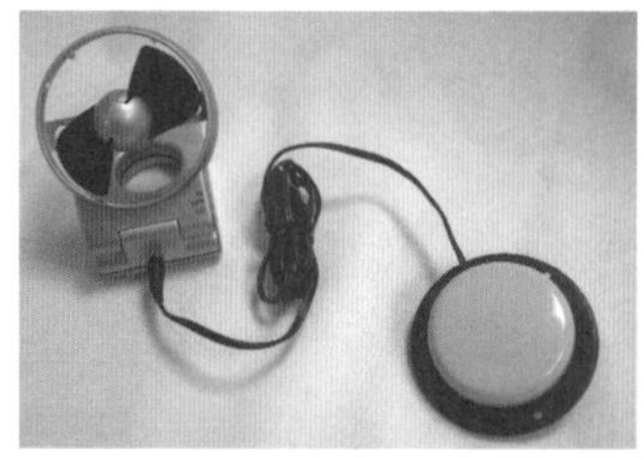

Outcome

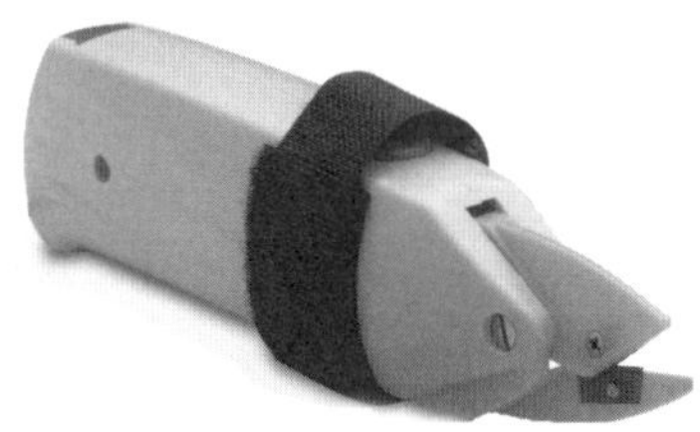

Battery-operated scissors

Quick Set Up Instructions

1. Plug a switch into the built-in switch jack.
2. Be sure the scissors are in the ON position and press the switch.

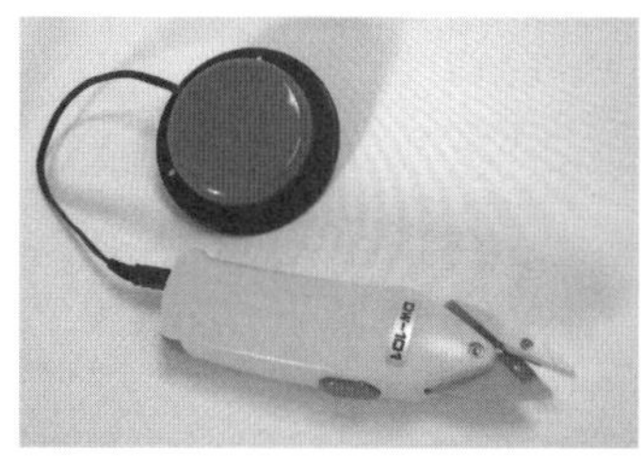

Outcome

Digital Camera

Quick Set Up Instructions

1. Plug a switch into the built-in switch jack.
2. Be sure your camera is turned ON and press the switch.

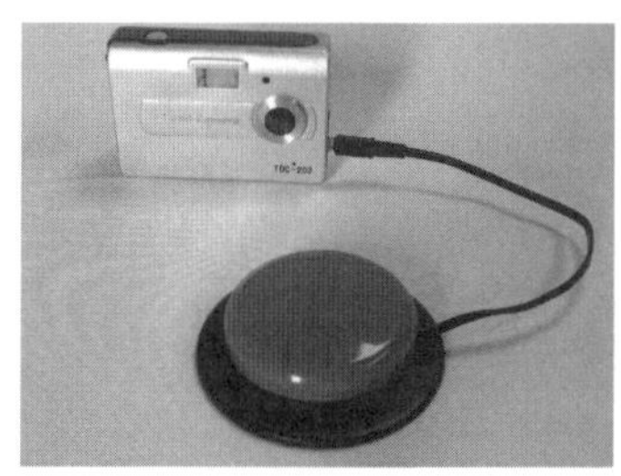

Outcome

Battery Device Adaptation Required for Device.

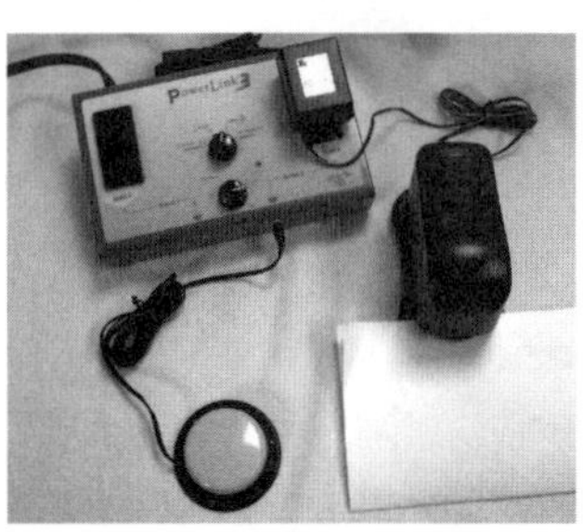

May also use electrically with the PowerLink®3 control unit and a switch.

Stapler battery/electrically operated

Quick Set Up Instructions

1. Open the battery compartment and notch the cover with a notching file.
2. Place the AA/AAA (size) Battery Device Adapter between the battery and the connection.
3. Replace the battery cover, positioning the cord through the notch.
4. Plug a switch into the Battery Device Adapter.
5. Be sure the stapler is in the ON position and press the switch.

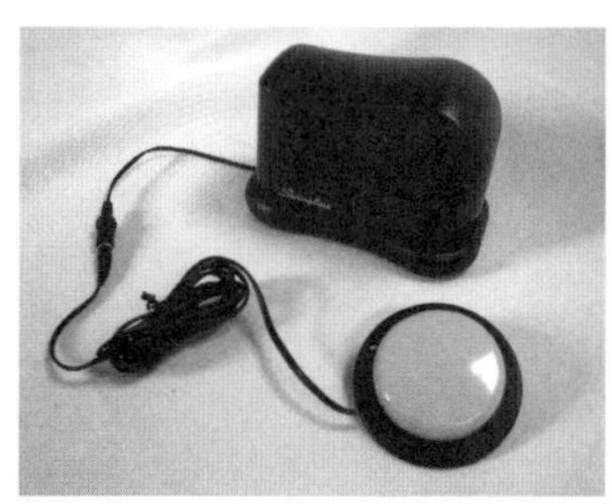

Outcome

Paint 'N' Swirl™

Paint 'N' Swirl™

Quick Set Up Instructions

1. Open the battery compartment and notch the cover with a notching file.
2. Place the C/D Battery Device Adapter between the battery and the connection.
3. Replace the battery cover, positioning the cord through the notch.
4. Plug a switch into the Battery Device Adapter.
5. Be sure the Paint 'N' Swirl™ is in the ON position and press the switch.

Outcome

Talking Photo Album

Talking Photo Album

Delivers a single message up to 10 seconds per each page.

Quick Set Up Instructions

1. Hold down the RECORD button and press the play button ▲.
   (red light appears)
2. Record the message into the microphone.
3. Release the RECORD button.
   (red light disappears)
4. Repeat steps 1-3 to record all messages.
5. Press the play button ▲ to play message.

Outcome

Talking Symbols™ notepad

Talking Symbols™ notepad

Delivers a single message up to 10 seconds per each page.

Quick Set Up Instructions

1. Pull the tab out of the battery compartment door.
2. Press the RECORD button and the play button at the same time and record the message into the speaker grill and then release.
3. Play the message by pressing the play button.
4. Insert a symbol into the clear pocket on top of the play button.
5. Press the play button to play message.

To mount: Use Velcro® or internal magnet

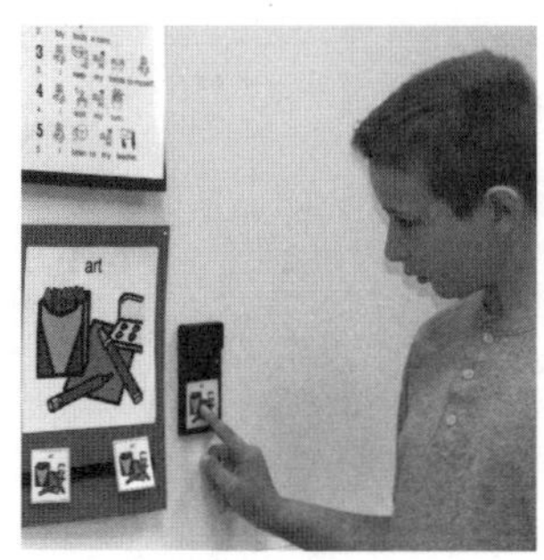

Outcome

Learning tools are devices and materials that support students to actively engage in a range of instructional activities that promote new learning experiences, increased knowledge and opportunities to socially interact with others.

All-Turn-It® spinner

All-Turn-It® spinner
Quick Set Up Instructions

1. Plug a switch into the built-in switch jack on the All-Turn-It spinner.
2. To activate: manually press the external switch, or press the small built-in switch on front of the device.

Outcome

BookWorm® literacy tool

BookWorm® literacy tool
Quick Set Up Instructions

1. Secure book on BookWorm. *(see figure 1)*
2. Attach removable stickers to correct location on each page. *(see figure 2)*
3. If book is over 8 page pairs: place a magnet on the left-hand bottom corner of the back of the eighth page pair.
4. Press red button on top of BookWorm until red light turns ON.
5. Record each page by pressing and holding the sticker or keypad location while reading the text on the page spread. *(see figure 3)*
6. Repeat step 5 for recording all pages.
7. Press red button on top until red light turns OFF.
8. To read: Plug a switch into the built-in switch jack on the BookWorm and press the switch or manually press the keypad location. *(see figure 4)*

Outcome

figure 1

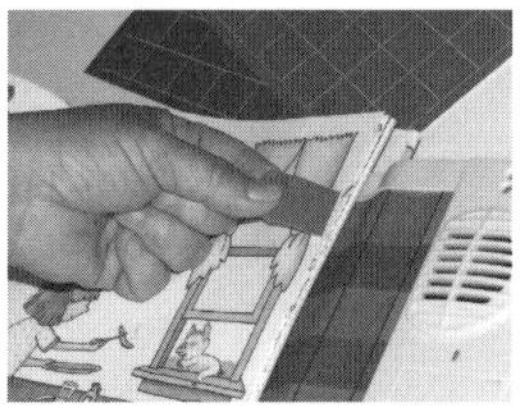

figure 2

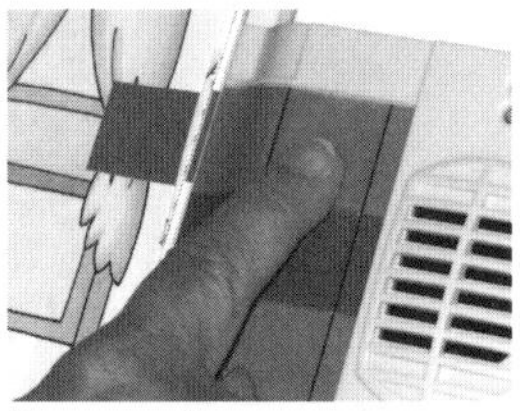

figure 3

figure 4

Mounting Tools

Mounting tools provide for secure switch placement, which is vitally important for student success when involved in communicating with others, reading, playing games or working on academic skills.

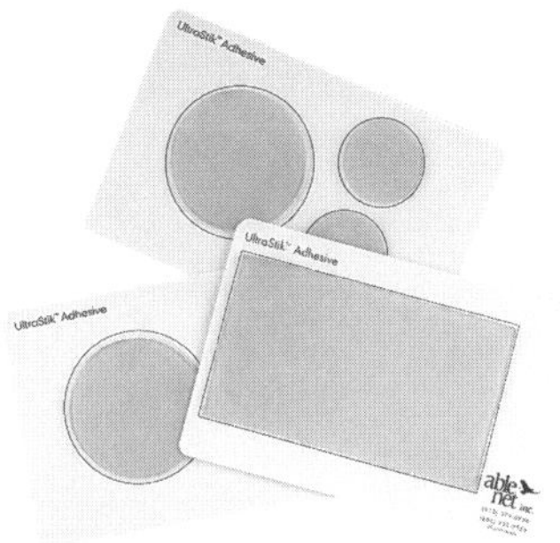

UltraStik® adhesive

UltraStik® adhesive

Quick Set Up Instructions

1. Place the UltraStik on a flat surface.
2. Lift up for quick and easy removal.

Outcome

Universal Switch Mounting System with friction Knob

Universal Switch Mounting System with friction Knob

Quick Set Up Instructions

1. Clamp onto anything flat or round, including wheelchairs.
2. Tighten the knob to lock all joints into position.
3. Attach a switch or VOCA using the screws and mounting plate provided.

Outcome

Slim Armstrong Mounting System

Slim Armstrong Mounting System

Quick Set Up Instructions

1. Clamp onto anything flat or round, including wheelchairs.
2. Tighten all the knobs to lock the flexor rod into position.
3. Attach a switch or VOCA using the screws and mounting plate provided.

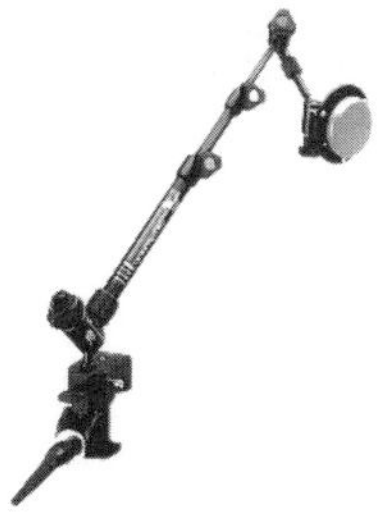

Outcome

Sensitrac® Mounting System with adjustable arm

Sensitrac® Mounting System with adjustable arm

Quick Set Up Instructions

1. Place Sensitrac on any clean, flat surface, such as a desk, tabletop or wheelchair tray.
2. Attach any switch or VOCA with Velcro®.
3. Adjust the position arm, and tighten knobs.
4. Remove by pulling up the tab.

Outcome

ACTION DICTIONARY

The **Action Dictionary** references every action verb that is used in the MEville to WEville supplemental curriculum. These action verbs are presented in bold throughout the manual. The **Action Dictionary** describes how student actions may be adapted or modified to enable active participation in the lesson activity.

The following verbs are provided in alphabetical order for quick and easy reference. Pictures/symbols are provided for each action verb to draw additional meaning and comprehension to the activity. Place pictures/symbols on communication devices and switches prior to beginning an activity.

answer

NOTE: Whenever possible, allow students to answer questions through the use of voice output devices. A voice output device gives students a real voice, and lets them respond and be heard just like other students.

Solution #1: The student uses the BIGmack® communicator to answer a single question.

BIGmack® communicator

Teacher: The teacher records a single answer on a BIGmack communicator.

Student: The student activates the BIGmack communicator one time to answer a single question.

Solution #2: The student uses the LITTLE Step-by-Step communicator to answer multiple questions.

LITTLE Step-by-Step communicator

Teacher: The teacher records a sequence of answers on a LITTLE Step-by-Step communicator.

Student: The student activates the LITTLE Step-by-Step communicator multiple times to answer a series of questions, such as when students are all giving answers to questions on a worksheet.

Solution #3: The student uses the SuperTalker™ to answer one or more questions.

SuperTalker™

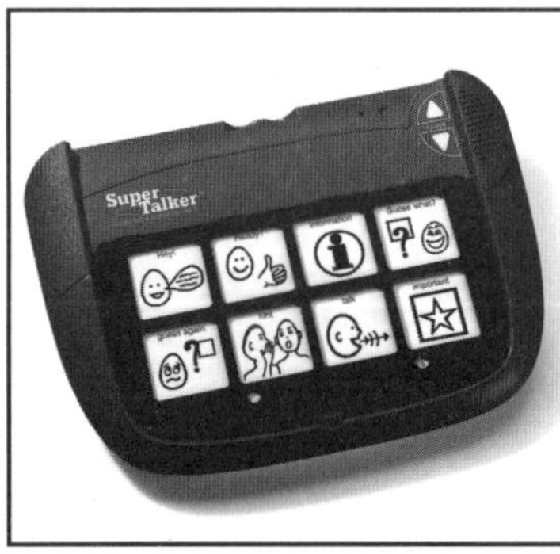

Teacher: The teacher places pictures/symbols representing answer choices on the SuperTalker overlay, and records an answer for each picture/symbol.

Student: The student selects and activates a message location to give their answer.

NOTE: SuperTalker includes keyguards for 1, 2, 4, and 8 messages.

Solution #4: The student makes a selection from a set of answer choices on display.

Display Tool

Teacher: The teacher creates pictures/symbols representing different answer choices. The teacher displays the pictures on a display tool, a felt board, or an eye gaze communication board.

Student: The student points to, grasps, or eye gazes at a picture/symbol representing their answer, from the selection of pictures/symbols on display.

NOTE: Use the underlined word(s) as a key word in an Internet search to find additional information.

TIPS:

1. Always allow enough "wait time" for students to activate a voice output device and give a vocal answer.
2. To the extent possible, try and match a male voice with a male student, a female voice with a female student, etc. It's great to have a regular education peer be the voice for the student.

NOTE: When an immediate answer is needed, write or draw two answer choices on Post-it® notes. Put each Post-it® note on a hand, and show both hands to students, allowing them to directly select an answer.

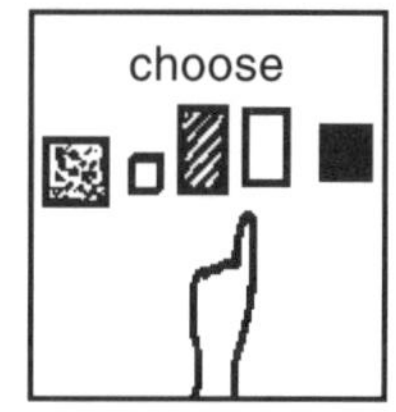

Solution #1: The student uses the All-Turn-It® spinner with a switch to make a random choice.

All-Turn-It® spinner and switch

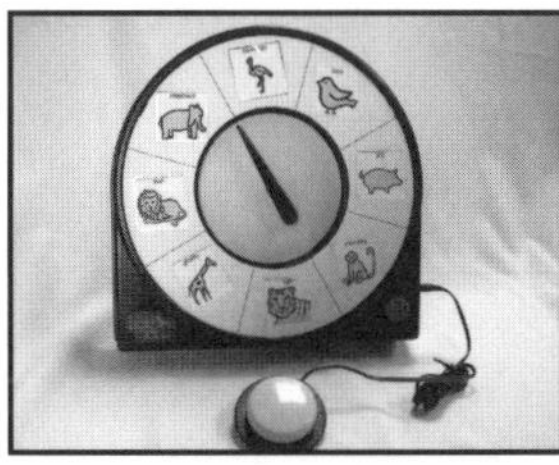

Teacher: The teacher places pictures/symbols or real items representing the various choices on the large overlay of the All-Turn-It spinner.

Student: The student activates the switch to operate the spinner and randomly selects a picture/symbol or item representing a choice.

Solution #2: The student uses the iTalk2™ communicator to choose from two options.

iTalk2™ communicator

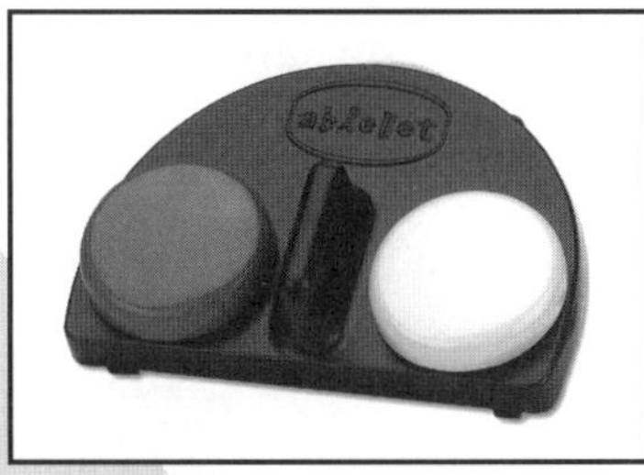

Teacher: The teacher places two pictures/symbols representative of two choices on the iTalk2 communicator.

Student: The student activates the iTalk2 communicator to verbally express their choice.

Solution #3: The student chooses from a display of items or pictures/symbols.

Display Tool

Teacher: The teacher clips pictures/symbols on a display tool. A display tool is created by gluing clothespins onto a strip of wooden trim. A selection of items or pictures/symbols to be selected from may also be held up in front of the student.

Student: The student points to or grasps an item or picture/symbol of their choice from the selection of items or pictures/symbols on display.

NOTE: Pictures/symbols, with Velcro® on the back, may also be displayed on a felt board.

Solution #4: The student uses an eye gaze communication board to make a choice.

Teacher: The teacher uses a piece of plexiglass to create an eye gaze communication board. The teacher puts pictures/symbols, representing various choices, on the eye gaze communication board. A selection of items or pictures/symbols to be selected from may also be held up in front of the student.

Student: The student eye gazes at the picture/symbol representing their choice.

NOTE: Use the underlined word(s) as a key word in an Internet search to find additional information.

TIPS:

1. When an immediate choice is required, write or draw two options on Post-it® notes. Put each Post-it note on one of your hands. Show both hands to students, allowing them to directly select their choice.

2. Direct a student's attention to each choice. "Look at the first choice right here. Now look at the second choice." Encourage the student to focus on the picture/symbol or item, even momentarily, so that you know he/she saw each choice.

3. Build choice-making into as many activities as possible during the school day. Some of these choices may include: white or chocolate milk, lunch food choice, color of game marker, where to sit for an activity, choice of people for partners, etc.

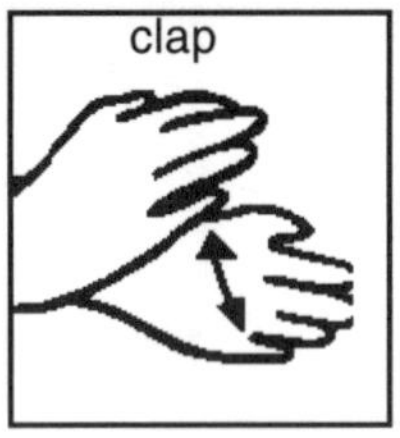

clap

Solution #1: Students use a BIGmack® communicator to clap at appropriate times.

BIGmack® communicator

Teacher: The teacher records a clapping sound on the BIGmack communicator.

Student: The student activates the BIGmack communicator to audibly make clapping sounds at times when it is appropriate to clap.

Solution #2: Students use an iTalk2™ communicator to clap and/or cheer.

iTalk2™ communicator

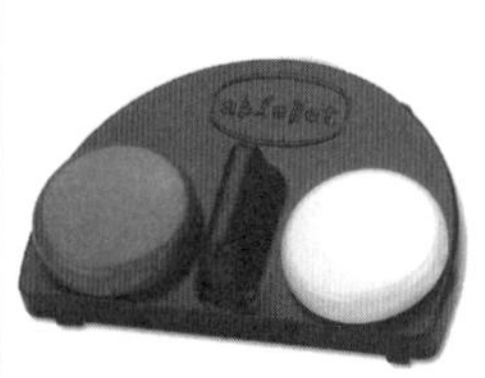

Teacher: The teacher places the CLAP picture/symbol and the CHEER picture/symbol on the iTalk2 communicator. The teacher records somebody clapping and somebody cheering.

Student: The student activates the iTalk2 communicator to either clap or cheer.

Solution #3: Students use small, plastic hand clappers to clap.

Teacher: The teacher gives the student a commercially purchased hand clapper and directs students to "clap."

Student: The student holds onto the plastic handle and shakes the hand clapper, causing the plastic hands to bang together and make a clapping sound. The handle can be widened by wrapping adhesive back, foam weatherstripping around it.

NOTE: Use the underlined word(s) as a key word in an Internet search to find additional information.

Solution #4: Students clap their hands on a table or wheelchair tray.

Teacher: The teacher places hand cutouts on the tabletop or wheelchair tray. The teacher directs the students to clap their hands on the paper hands.

Student: The student slaps his/her hands down on the paper hands on the wheelchair tray or table top, making a clapping sound.

TIPS:

1. Cue students as to the appropriate time to clap for a recognition situation or during a song or other activity where clapping is involved. A "clap" picture/symbol may be used to cue students as to the appropriate time to clap.
2. Have a leader up front, or a staff or student peer near a student, clapping directly with the student, modeling for that student when to clap.
3. For students who are tactile defensive, or to whom noise is strongly aversive, allow them to participate in clapping by holding up an "applause" or "clap" sign instead of forcing them to actually make a clapping sound.

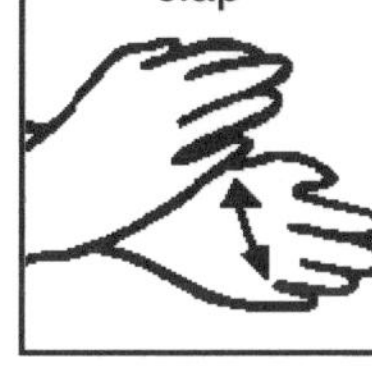

Solution #1: Students use a BIGmack® communicator to clap/chant letters, words, or phrases.

BIGmack® communicator

Teacher: The teacher records the series of letters, words, or phrases to be chanted on a BIGmack communicator, leaving pause between each. Each letter, word, or phrase may be paired with a clap sound as it is being recorded.

Student: The student activates the BIGmack communicator to clap/chant the series of letters, words, or phrases.

Solution #2: Students use a LITTLE Step-by-Step communicator to clap/chant a series of letters, words, or phrases.

LITTLE Step-by-Step communicator

Teacher: The teacher records a series of letters, words, or phrases in sequential order to complete a word, sentence(s), cheer or chant. Each letter, word, or phrase may be paired with a clap sound as it is being recorded.

Student: The student activates the LITTLE Step-by-Step communicator multiple times to sequentially clap/chant out a series of letters, words, or phrases.

Solution #3: Students use a hand clapper to clap.

Teacher: The teacher gives the student a commercially purchased hand clapper and directs students to "clap."

Student: The student holds onto the plastic handle and shakes the hand clapper each time that a letter, word, or phrase is chanted.

NOTE: Use the underlined word(s) as a key word in an Internet search to find additional information.

TIPS:

1. Have large, easy to see visuals of each letter, word, or phrase that the students are clap/chanting. One student may be assigned the responsibility of showing each visual as the other students chant.

2. To increase student interest, change the way in which the chant is done. For example, have students chant in a really loud voice, in a whisper voice, down low, way up high, etc.

3. Pair students up so that one student is clapping and the other student is chanting.

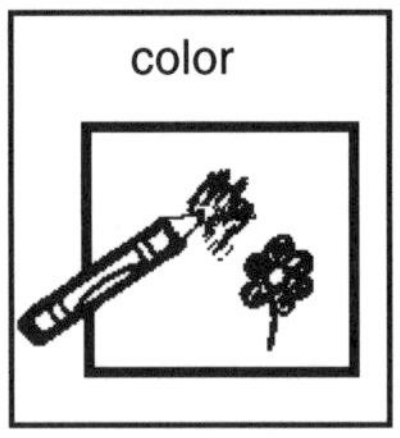

color

LITTLE Step-by-Step communicator

Solution #1: Students use the LITTLE Step-by-Step communicator to participate in coloring activities.

Example Student Script

"Do you want to color?"
"Let's use red first!"
"Now we'll switch to blue."
"How about green next?"

Teacher: The teacher records a sequence of coloring instructions on the LITTLE Step-by-Step communicator.

Student: The student activates the LITTLE Step-by-Step communicator multiple times to give a helper directions on coloring a picture with him/her.

iTalk2™ communicator

Solution #2: Students use an iTalk2™ communicator to participate in coloring activities.

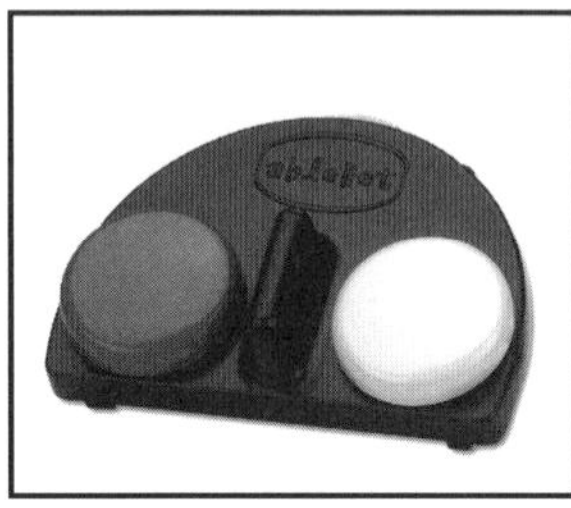

Teacher: The teacher places two color crayons/markers or two color pictures/symbols on the iTalk2 communicator.

Student: The student activates the iTalk2 communicator to ask to use one of two different colors. The colors can be changed throughout the coloring activity.

Solution #3: Students use adapted crayons/markers to participate in coloring activities.

Teacher: The teacher may extend the length of a crayon by putting it inside a piece of narrow PVC piping, or by taping two tongue depressors to either side of the crayon vertically and wrapping tape around them.

Student: The student grasps the adapted crayon/marker and uses it to color.

Teacher: The teacher may form a T-handle for a student by cutting a four to six inch long strip of foam piping insulation, making a slit in one side, and snugly inserting a marker or crayon into the slit.

Student: The student grasps the adapted crayon/marker and uses it to color.

Solution #4: Students color on a paper that is secured to a slanted work surface.

Teacher: The teacher clips or tapes paper on a slanted surface, such as a <u>writing slant board</u>, and brings it near the student.

Student: The student colors on the slanted surface. Students with limited range of motion may be more able to access a work surface that is on a slant or in a vertical position.

NOTE: Use the underlined word(s) as a key word in an Internet search to find additional information.

TIPS:

1. Tape the paper to the work surface so it does not move around. Or, place the paper on a magnetic board and place magnets on top of the paper to hold it down. Binder clips may also be used to attach the paper to a flat drawing surface.
2. For practice with coloring skills, laminate some coloring sheets that have large, simple outline shapes. Then outline the shapes in fabric paint or glue and let them dry. Students may use washable markers or crayons to color in between the lines. The surface can be wiped clean for multiple uses, and is more durable than paper.
3. Try out different kinds of coloring tools such as markers or chalk in different sizes to see what works best for individual students.

Solution #1: Students use the BIGmack® communicator to make a comment.

BIGmack® communicator

Teacher: The teacher records one general comment, such as "Cool!", into a BIGmack communicator.

Student: The student activates the BIGmack communicator to make a single comment.

Solution #2: Students use the LITTLE Step-by-Step communicator to make a series of comments.

LITTLE Step-by-Step communicator

Example Student Script

"I like your book!"
"The pictures are great!"
"Cool colors!"
"That's a fancy cover."
"You did a great job!"

Teacher: The teacher records a sequence of comments into a LITTLE Step-by-Step communicator.

Student: The student activates the LITTLE Step-by-Step communicator multiple times to make a series of comments.

Solution #3: The student selects a comment from a display of comment pictures/symbols.

SuperTalker™

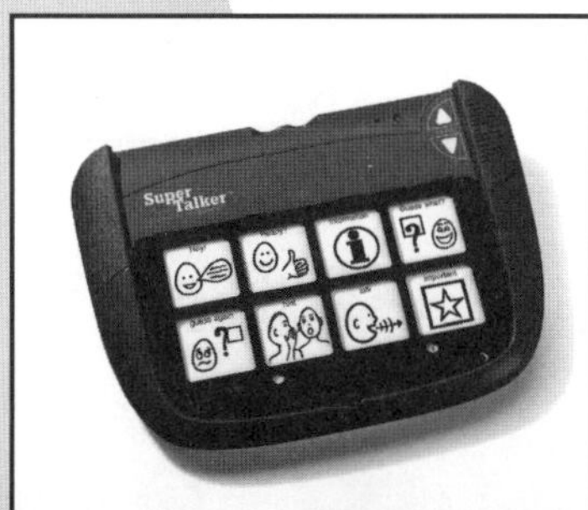

Display Tool

Teacher: The teacher creates pictures/symbols representing different generic comments students might make, such as "Right on!", "Oops!", "OK", "Later alligator!", "Wow!", "Yeah!", "Uh-Oh", and "Great!" The teacher may also create pictures/symbols representing comments that are specific to a certain situation, such as "That's soft!", "It's really bright!", "That would be fun to wear", "That's a cool shirt" if students are commenting about clothing. The teacher puts the pictures/symbols on the SuperTalker overlay and programs them into the device, or displays the pictures/symbols on a display tool, a felt board, or an eye gaze communication board.

Student: The student selects/activates a comment from the display.

NOTE: Use the underlined word(s) as a key word in an Internet search to find additional information.

NOTE: Super Talker™ includes keyguards for 1, 2, 4, and 8 messages.

TIPS:

1. Listen to the typical peers in your school. Listen for sayings/comments that you hear frequently by multiple students (Cool! Check it out! No Way! Awesome!). Make a list of the appropriate comments that you hear, and make a point to program these particular comments into voice output devices.

2. Keep one or more BIGmack and/or LITTLE Step-by-Step communicators with the "I have something to say" picture/symbol on them, readily available at all times. Encourage staff and student helpers to pick up the communicators and record appropriate comments on them during any activity.

3. When verbally guiding, directing, and encouraging students, use the language, "Tell us something about (the item/project)" rather than, "Hit the switch." This affirms that the student is using real communication when making a comment.

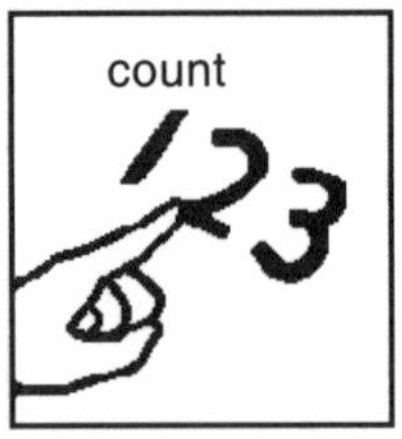

count

Solution #1: The student uses a BIGmack® communicator to participate in counting activities.

BIGmack® communicator

Teacher: The teacher records a sequence of numbers, from one to the final number, or number of objects being counted onto the BIGmack communicator. Leave a brief pause time between each number.

Student: The student activates the communicator one time to verbally count to a certain number, or to verbally count out a certain number of items.

Solution #2: The student uses a LITTLE Step-by-Step communicator to participate in counting activities.

LITTLE Step-by-Step communicator

Teacher: Starting with number one, the teacher records each number to be counted, in sequence, on the LITTLE Step-by-Step communicator, one number per step.

Student: The student activates the LITTLE Step-by-Step communicator one time per number, or per object that is being counted. When counting objects, the student is using one to one correspondence, and it is necessary for the student to stop activating the device as the last item is counted.

Solution #3: The student uses the SuperTalker® to count out a number set (1-8 objects).

SuperTalker™

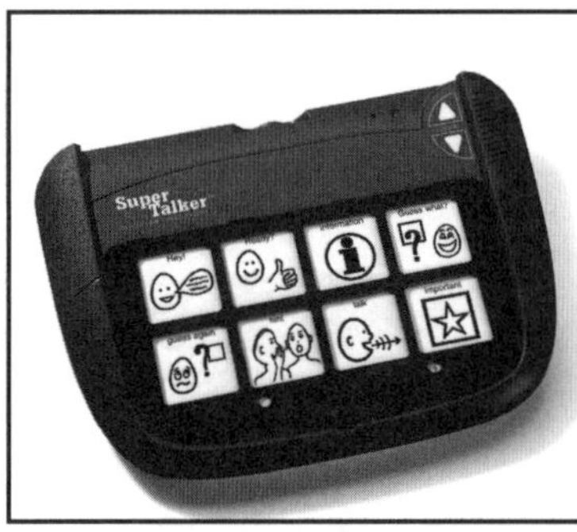

Teacher: The teacher places a number overlay on the SuperTalker and records each number into the device.

Student: Each time an object is shown, the student activates the next number in the sequence.

NOTE: SuperTalker® includes keyguards for 1, 2, 4, and 8 messages.

Solution #4: The student uses a counting grid or number line to participate in counting out object sets.

Teacher: The teacher makes a counting grid or number line, one number per box or space, each large enough to have an item placed on it.

Student: The student counts out an object set by putting one object on each numbered space, in sequential order. When all objects have been used up, the number that the last object is sitting on represents the final number of objects.

TIPS:

1. For students working on independently counting out object sets, clearly indicate a target area on which to put each object that will be counted.
2. Look for as many real counting opportunities throughout the day as possible, such as counting the number of school days, the number of books read, the number of words on a page, etc.

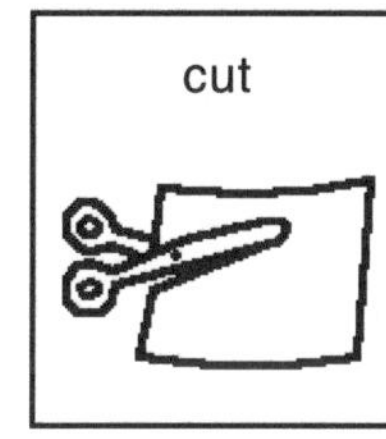

Solution #1: The student uses pre-adapted battery-operated scissors with a switch to participate in cutting activities.

Scissors and switch

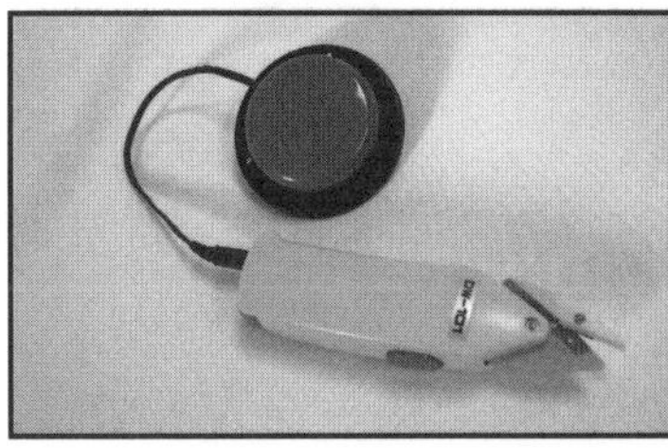

Teacher: The teacher attaches a switch to the battery-operated scissors.

Student: The student activates the switch and the helper manipulates the scissors to cut in the appropriate location.

Solution #2: The student uses pre-adapted battery-operated scissors with a LITTLE Step-by-Step communicator to participate in cutting activities.

LITTLE Step-by-Step communicator and scissors

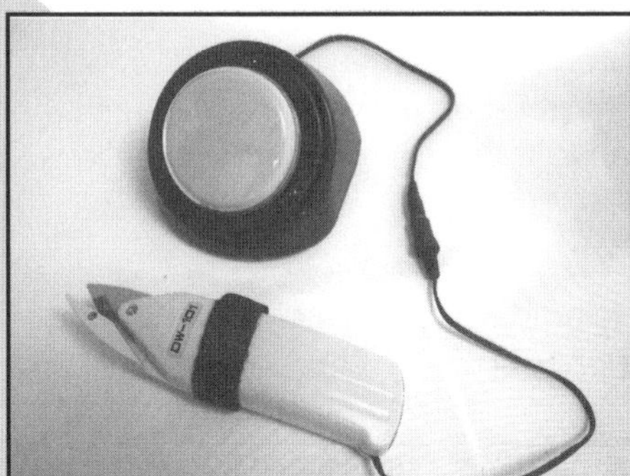

Example Student Script

"Hey, will you help me cut?"
"I'll turn on the scissors."
"You steer them."
"Are you ready?"
"Let's cut!"

Teacher: The teacher follows directions in the Quick Set Up Guide to record the script provided, or their own script, into the LITTLE Step-by-Step communicator, setting the communicator to activate the scissors on the "Let's cut!" message.

Student: The student activates the LITTLE Step-by-Step communicator multiple times to give a peer helper directions for the cutting activity, and to activate the scissors.

Solution #3: The student uses commercially available adapted or alternative scissors to participate in cutting activities.

Teacher: The teacher determines the most appropriate type of adapted scissors for a student. Some commercially available scissors include beginner scissors, self-opening scissors, scissors with double handles, and loop scissors.

Student: The student, who has some hand usage, uses the adapted scissors to participate in cutting activities.

NOTE: Use the underlined word(s) as a key word in an Internet search to find additional information.

TIPS:

1. Determine the position for each student that gives him/her maximal range of motion and arm/hand support.

2. Bold the lines to be cut on the paper with a bright highlighter, making it easier for students to identify the correct place to cut.

3. If using the pre-adapted battery-operated scissors, refer to the switch activation as cutting, ("John, turn on the scissors and finish cutting out your hat") rather than switch hitting ("John, hit the switch").

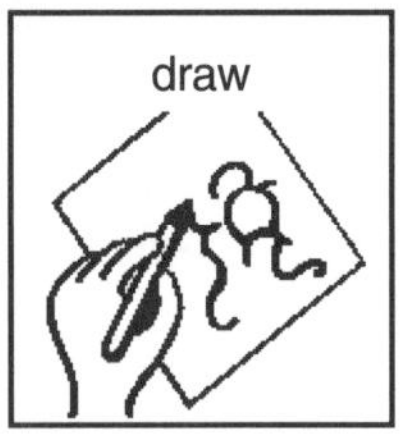

draw

Solution #1: The student uses a LITTLE Step-by-Step communicator to participate in drawing activities.

LITTLE Step-by-Step communicator

Example Student Script

"Let's draw a park!"
"We'll draw some grass."
"Now we need tall trees."
"Let's draw some squirrels!"
"How about a slide?"

Teacher: The teacher records a sequence of drawing instructions on the LITTLE Step-by-Step communicator.

Student: The student activates the LITTLE Step-by-Step communicator multiple times to direct somebody to draw a picture with them.

Solution #2: The student uses an iTalk2™ communicator to participate in drawing activities.

iTalk2™ communicator

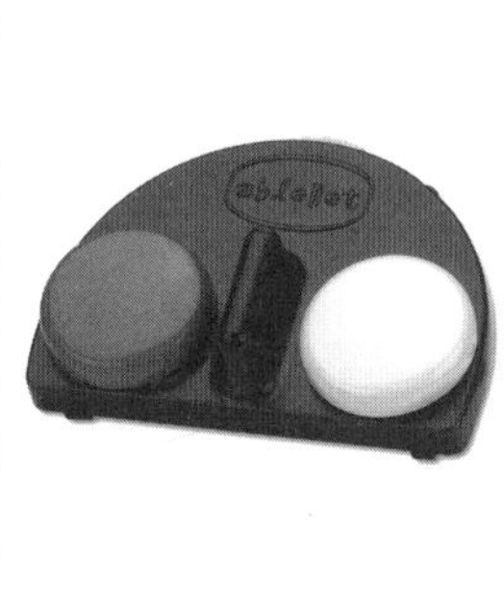

Teacher: The teacher places pictures/symbols of two different types of designs (such as a straight line, polka dots, a curvy line, a square, a circle) on the iTalk2 communicator. The teacher records the drawing directions related to those designs (such as, "Draw a curvy line" and "Draw a straight line") on the iTalk2 communicator.

Student: The student activates the iTalk2 communicator to direct somebody to help them make a particular type of design on their paper.

Solution #3: The student uses adapted writing tools to participate in drawing activities.

Teacher: The teacher broadens the width of a writing tool by wrapping adhesive back, foam weatherstripping or foam piping insulation around it.

Student: The student grasps the adapted writing tool and uses it to draw.

Teacher: The teacher uses a hand strap to attach a writing tool to the student's hand.

Student: The student moves their hand on the paper to draw with the attached writing tool.

Solution #4: The student uses drawing supports to participate in drawing activities.

Teacher: The teacher uses a highlighter to draw a design for the student.

Student: The student traces over the highlighted area with a pencil or other drawing tool.

Teacher: The teacher tapes a selected stencil on top of the paper.

Student: The student moves a pencil or other drawing tool inside the stencil lines.

TIPS:

1. Tape the paper to the work surface so it does not move around. Or, place the paper on a magnetic board and place magnets on top of the paper to hold it down. Binder clips may also be used to attach the paper to a flat drawing surface.
2. For children with visual impairments, place the drawing paper on a textured surface, such as sandpaper or corrugated paper, so that they can hear and more easily feel the drawing tool as it moves across the drawing surface.
3. Make easy, inexpensive stencils. Laminate a piece of card stock, or smaller square or rectangle shaped piece of card stock. Then use a die cutter to cut the shape out of the center of the card stock.

Solution #1: Students use a hair dryer with a PowerLink®3 control unit and a switch to participate in a drying activity.

PowerLink®3 control unit with hair dryer and switch

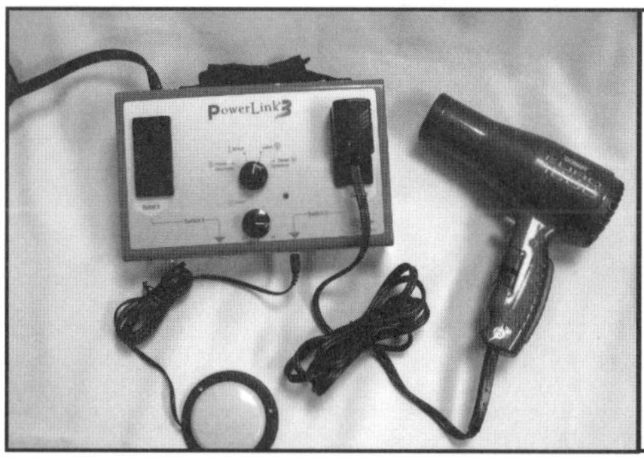

Teacher: The teacher assigns a staff or student helper to hold the hair dryer toward the item being dried.

Student: The student activates the switch to turn on the hair dryer and dry the item.

Solution #2: Students use a pre-adapted battery-operated fan to participate in a drying activity.

Fan and switch

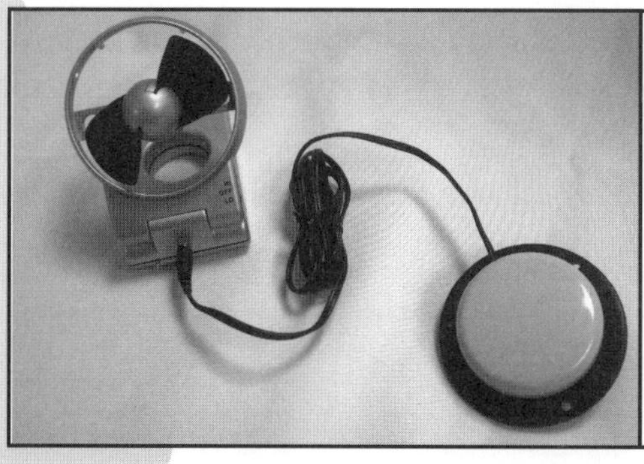

Teacher: The teacher places the fan in front of the item to be dried, or another student, peer helper, or staff person holds the fan near the item to be dried.

Student: The student activates the switch to turn on the fan and dry the item.

Solution #3: Students use a LITTLE Step-by-Step communicator and a battery-operated fan to participate in a drying activity.

LITTLE Step-by-Step communicator and fan

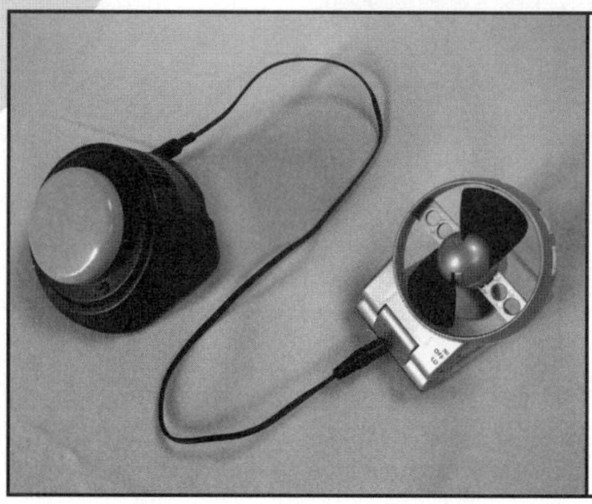

Example Student Script

"I need to dry my project."
"Let's turn on the fan."
"Aim the fan toward my project."
"Is it almost dry?"
"Thanks for your help."

Teacher: The teacher follows directions in the Quick Set Up guide to record the script on the LITTLE Step-by-Step communicator, one line per step, setting the LITTLE Step-by-Step communicator to activate the battery-operated fan on the "Let's turn on the fan" message.

Student: The student activates the LITTLE Step-by-Step communicator multiple times to give drying directions to a staff or student helper.

TIPS:

1. When using a battery-operated fan, set the fan on a piece of nonskid Dycem™ mat or UltraStik™ to prevent it from being moved out of position.

2. Place a BIGmack® or LITTLEmack communicator with the "please" picture/symbol near the fan or hair dryer. Record the sentence, "Please change the position of the fan/hair dryer." This allows the student to have a greater degree of control over the drying activity.

3. Craft time is a great time to use a hair dryer. Hair dryers work well for drying glue and paint, and often increase the interest level of students.

4. For students who are visually impaired, tie streamers to the fan for a visual effect.

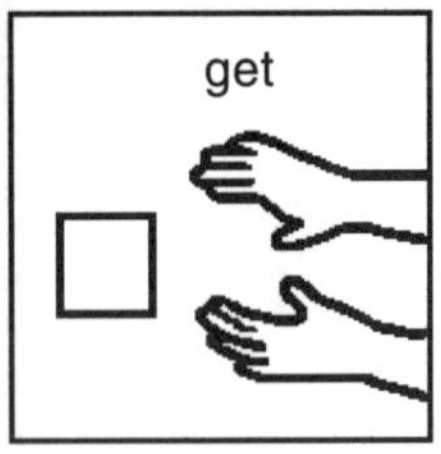

get

Solution #1: The student uses the LITTLE Step-by-Step communicator to participate in the process of getting something that they need or want.

LITTLE Step-by-Step communicator

Example Student Script

"Could you help me?"
"I need my backpack."
"Would you please get it for me?"
"It's right near the door."
"Thanks!"

Teacher: The teacher records on the LITTLE Step-by-Step communicator a sequence of directions for getting something for a student.

Student: The student activates the LITTLE Step-by-Step communicator multiple times to direct a staff person or student helper as to what they would like that person to get, or help them get, and where the helper needs to go to get the item.

Solution #2: The student uses the iTalk2™ communicator to participate in the process of getting something that they need or want.

iTalk2™ communicator

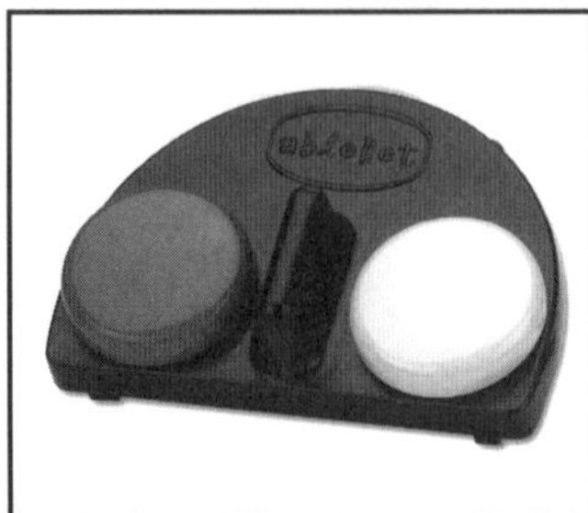

Teacher: The teacher records the names of two different things to get on the iTalk2 communicator, and places both representative symbols on the iTalk2 communicator.

Student: The student activates the iTalk2 communicator to ask a helper to get one of two particular items for him/her.

Solution #3: Students use assisted/adapted carrying devices or supports to help them get something.

Teacher: The teacher places a piece of Dycem™ or UltraStik™ on a wheelchair tray, or on a push cart.

Student: The student wheels himself/herself, or pushes a cart to the location of an item, puts the item on the tray or cart and moves it to the desired location.

Teacher: The teacher gives the student a hand held carrying basket, or places a carrying bag with a shoulder strap on the student's shoulder.

Student: The student carries the basket or bag, moves to the place to get the item, places the item in the bag (or somebody places it in the bag for him/her), and moves back to his/her desired location.

TIPS:

1. Have one of the classroom jobs be to get materials needed for activities. Two students may be assigned to this job, so that both could get the needed materials, or one student could direct and the other student could get the materials.

2. Evaluate the set-up of the materials in your classroom. Set up areas for supplies, books, free-time activities, etc. in such a way that the materials are accessible. Using wide, open, shallow bins that are at lower levels and in uncluttered areas help make materials more accessible and easier for students to get.

3. Gallon milk jugs with the top cut off work well as carrying containers. Run electrical tape or duct tape along the top edge to soften the sharp edge.

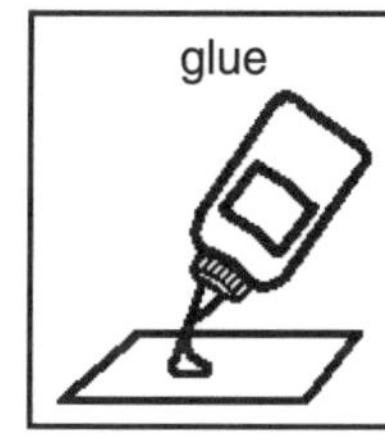

Solution #1: The student uses a BIGmack® communicator to participate in gluing activities.

BIGmack® communicator

Teacher: The teacher records the sentence, “Will you please help me put glue on this?” on the BIGmack communicator.

Student: The student activates the BIGmack communicator one time to ask a staff or student peer to help him/her administer glue. The student can be directed to activate the BIGmack communicator each time they would like to apply more glue.

Solution #2: The student uses a LITTLE Step-by-Step communicator to participate in gluing activities.

LITTLE Step-by-Step communicator

Example Student Script

“HI! Can you help me?”
“I need to put glue on this.”
“I need one drop of glue on that dot.”
“Thanks!”

Teacher: The teacher records the script into the LITTLE Step-by-Step communicator, making the script specific to the particular gluing activity.

Student: The student activates the LITTLE Step-by-Step communicator multiple times to give a peer or staff helper directions on how to assist the student with the gluing activity.

Solution #3: The student uses a sponge brush and liquid glue in a shallow container to participate in gluing activities.

Liquid glue and sponge brush in shallow container

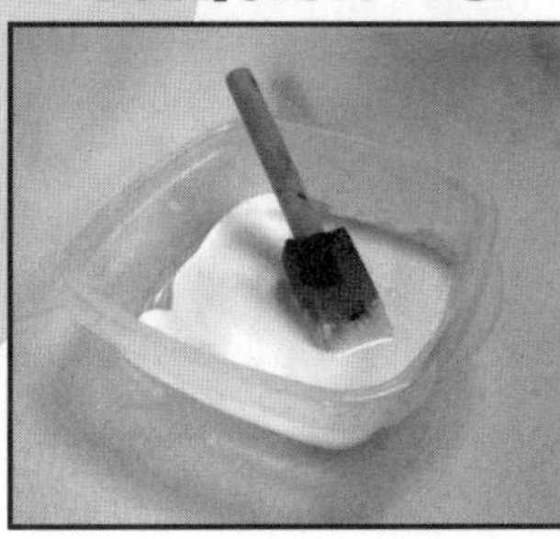

Teacher: The teacher secures a shallow container to the work surface with Velcro® or UltraStik™, pours liquid glue into the container, and puts a sponge brush in the container.

Student: The student grasps the sponge brush and uses it to apply glue to the appropriate area.

Solution #4: The student uses adapted glue tools to participate in gluing activities.

Teacher: The teacher adapts a liquid glue pen (one filled with clear glue), by poking a small hole in the covering of the tip to increase the ease with which glue is dispensed.

Student: The student grasps the glue tool and uses it to apply glue to the appropriate area.

Teacher: The teacher adapts a glue stick by wrapping adhesive back, foam weatherstripping around it to increase the width of it.

Student: The student grasps the glue tool and uses it to apply glue to the appropriate area.

TIPS:

1. Secure the paper or object to the table or work surface so that it does not move around when a student is applying glue to it.
2. Highlight the area on the paper or item where glue needs to be applied.
3. A student may work together with a peer helper. The student is responsible for holding the glue tool and bringing it to the paper, and the peer helper is responsible for positioning and moving the paper/item so that glue is applied to the correct area.

identify

identify

BIGmack® communicator

Solution #1: The student uses the BIGmack® communicator to identify something or someone.

Teacher: The teacher records on the BIGmack communicator the name of a picture/symbol, item or person the student has been asked to identify.

Student: The student activates the BIGmack communicator to say the name of a picture/symbol, item or person that he/she has been asked to identify.
Ex: "This shape is a rectangle."

iTalk2™ communicator

Solution #2: The student uses the iTalk2™ communicator to identify something or someone.

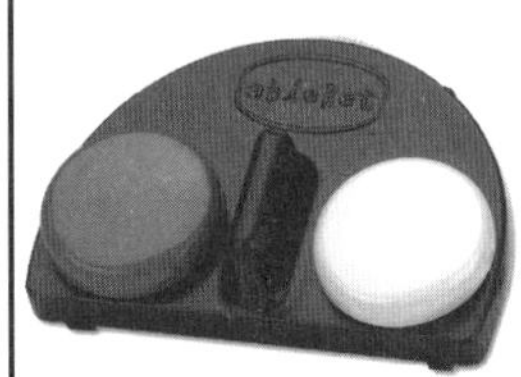

Teacher: The teacher records two different names of items, names of people, or descriptive words or phrases into the iTalk2 communicator. One should be the correct item/person/description that the student was asked to identify.

Student: The student activates the iTalk2 communicator to identify the requested item, person, or description.

NOTE: If the student selects an incorrect picture/symbol, direct the student to the correct picture/symbol, explaining to the student why that picture/symbol correctly identifies the requested item, person, or description.

Display Tool

Solution #3: The student uses a display tool to identify a picture/symbol of something or someone.

Teacher: The teacher clips a selection of pictures/symbols on a display tool. At least one picture/symbol should be the item/person/description that the student was asked to identify. A display tool is created by gluing clothespins onto a strip of wooden trim. The teacher may also hold up for the student several different items or pictures/symbols from which the student selects.

Student: The student points to or grasps the picture/symbol or item that identifies the requested item/person/description.

NOTE: Pictures/symbols, with Velcro® on the back, may also be displayed on a felt board.

Solution #4: The student uses an eye gaze communication board to identify something or someone.

Teacher: The teacher uses a piece of plexiglass to create an eye gaze communication board. The teacher puts a selection of pictures/symbols on the eye gaze communication board. One picture/symbol should be the item/person/description that the student was asked to identify.

Student: The student eye gazes at the identifying picture/symbol.

NOTE: Use the underlined word(s) as a key word in an Internet search to find additional information.

TIPS:

1. To make pictures/symbols easier to grasp and remove from a felt board, use a glue gun to attach them to squares of fun foam. Then put a square of rough Velcro® on the back of each square and attach them to the felt board.
2. Direct a student's attention to each choice. "Look at the first choice right here. Now look at the second choice." Encourage the student to focus on the picture/symbol, even momentarily, so that you know they saw each choice.
3. Build word/picture vocabulary identification activities into your reading time. Copy off different pages from the book and cut out pictures of items/characters/scenes that you want students to identify.

Solution #1: The student uses the Talking Symbols™ notepad to confirm a desired location and specific activity instructions. Talking Symbols can also be used for assignments, reminders, and motivational messages.

Talking Symbols™ notepad

Sample:
"cards" picture/symbol: "This is the cards center. Play a card game with one or more people."
"spelling" picture/symbol: "Write each spelling word on your paper."
"quiet" picture/symbol: "Remember to sit quietly at your desk and do your work."
"smile" picture/symbol: "You're doing great work! Keep smiling."

Teacher: The teacher selects a desired symbol, places it in the symbol holder and records an appropriate message. The teacher then places the Talking Symbol in the desired location.

Student: The student activates the message by pressing the picture/symbol.

Solution #2: The teacher uses pictures/symbols to label the environment. The student moves to/points to the indicated picture/symbol to name/confirm the activity/location.

Boardmaker Picture/Symbol

Teacher: The teacher selects a desired picture/symbol, and places it in the desired location in the classroom.

Student: The student moves to/points to the picture/symbol to name confirm the activity/location.

Solution #3: The student uses pictures/symbols to label locations, items, and pictures.

Boardmaker Picture/Symbol

Teacher: The teacher creates a picture/symbol for each location, item, or picture he/she would like students to label.

Student: The student labels locations, items, and pictures by selecting and attaching the appropriate picture/symbol.

TIPS:

1. Use Talking Symbols at activity centers. Students unable to read can independently activate the Talking Symbol to confirm/name and listen to the center instructions.

2. Use the Talking Symbol as a reminder to students of behavior expectations. Select a picture/symbol appropriate for the behavior (hands in lap), record a related message ("During morning meeting we keep our hands in our lap"), and place the Talking Symbol in a student accessible place within the environment where that behavior is expected.

3. Use the Talking Symbol as a reminder to students of task expectations. Select a picture/symbol appropriate for the task (count), record a related message ("Count six marbles into each bowl"), and place the Talking Symbol in a student accessible place within the environment where that task will be completed (work table, desk).

4. Use Talking Symbols as a way for students to indicate when they have completed a task. When the student completes the task, the student activates the Talking Symbol with the "all done" picture/symbol to say, "I'm all done."

look

look

Solution #1: The student uses the BIGmack® communicator to participate in an activity that requires students to look at one particular thing.

BIGmack® communicator

Teacher: The teacher records into the BIGmack communicator a sentence asking students to look at something in particular. For example, “Hey, everybody, look at this word up on the board.”

Student: The student activates the BIGmack communicator to ask the class to look at something in particular.

Solution #2: The student uses the LITTLE Step-by-Step communicator to direct the class to look at one or more specific items.

LITTLE Step-by-Step communicator

Example Student Script

“Look up here!”
“This is a picture of my pet lizard.”
“His name is Scooby.”
“Look at his tail! Isn’t it big?”

Teacher: The teacher records on the LITTLE Step-by-Step communicator a sequence of instructions that direct students to look at one or more particular thing(s).

Student: The student activates the LITTLE Step-by-Step communicator multiple times to instruct others to look at different parts, or different aspects of, something particular.

Solution #3: Visual supports are used to assist students in looking at something particular.

Teacher: The teacher copies off the page containing the item students have been asked to look at, increasing the size of the item so that it is easier for students to see.

Teacher: The teacher isolates the item to be looked at by putting it on a blank board or paper so it’s the only thing on which students need to focus.

TIPS:

1. Be sure to give students plenty of wait time to focus their attention on what they have been requested to look at.

2. The more motivating, interesting, colorful, and fun something is, the more likely a student is to look at it. Something simple, like shining a flashlight on an item or making picture/word cards on neon paper, may make it more appealing for the student.

3. For students with visual impairments, or students who need added tactile experience, let them “look” at the item with their eyes and/or their hands. Add texture to the item or picture and students may look at the item by examining it with their hands and/or eyes.

mark ✓

Solution #1:

The student uses the BIGmack® communicator to participate in the process of making a mark on a specific location on a worksheet, voting chart, or other paper.

BIGmack® communicator

Teacher: The teacher programs the BIGmack communicator to ask somebody to help the student mark their paper.

Student: The student activates the BIGmack communicator one time to ask somebody to help them mark a selected location.

Solution #2:

The student uses the iTalk2™ communicator to participate in the process of making a mark on a specific location on a worksheet, voting chart, or other paper.

iTalk2™ communicator

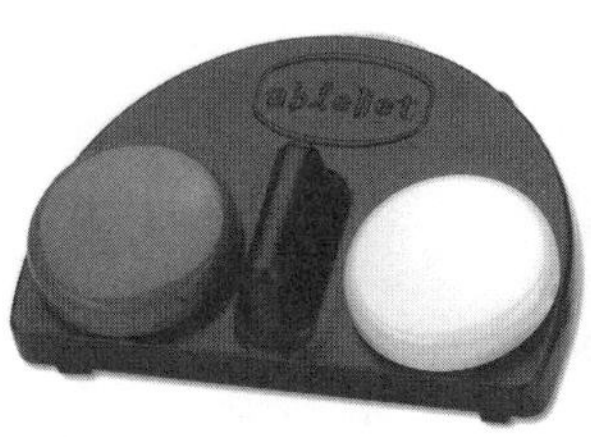

Teacher: The teacher places on the iTalk2 communicator pictures/symbols representing two different things (answer choices, BINGO spaces, vote preferences) that may be marked. The teacher records into the iTalk2 communicator two sentences asking somebody for help in making a mark on a location showing a specific thing.

Student: The student activates the iTalk2 communicator to select a picture/symbol that represents the specific thing they would like to mark, and ask for help in marking that on their paper.

Solution #3:

The student uses adapted writing tools to participate in the process of making a mark on a specific location on a worksheet, voting chart, or other paper.

Teacher: The teacher adapts a writing tool by wrapping adhesive back, foam weatherstripping around the handle of any writing tool.

Student: The student uses the adapted writing tool to mark their paper.

Teacher: The teacher adapts BINGO markers or Crayola® Mini-stampers as necessary by wrapping adhesive back, foam weatherstripping around the marker or stamper.

Student: The student grasps the marker or stamper and presses it straight down on the selected area, leaving a dot or a stamp.

TIPS:

1. Tape the worksheet/voting chart/paper to the work surface so it does not move around when a student is making a mark. Double-sided tape can be used so that there is not tape on the front of a student's paper.

2. Outline the area to be marked (corresponding to the answer the student selected) with a marker or highlighter. The student then makes a mark in that designated area.

3. Enlarge a worksheet on the copier to increase the size of the area that will be marked. If necessary, cut the worksheet in half or in sections and enlarge each section.

4. If students need answer choices displayed on a choice board so that they can select their answer before marking it, make an extra copy of the worksheet, cut out the answer choices, and have them ready to display.

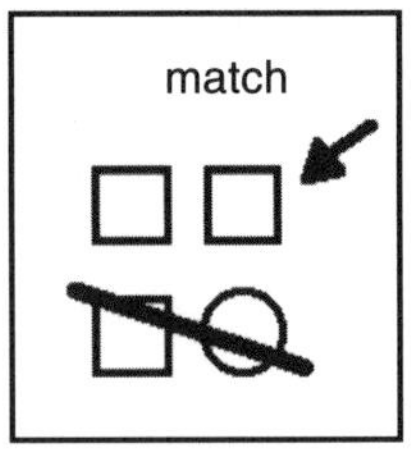

match

Solution #1: The student uses the All-Turn-It® spinner with a switch to participate in matching activities.

All-Turn-It® spinner and switch

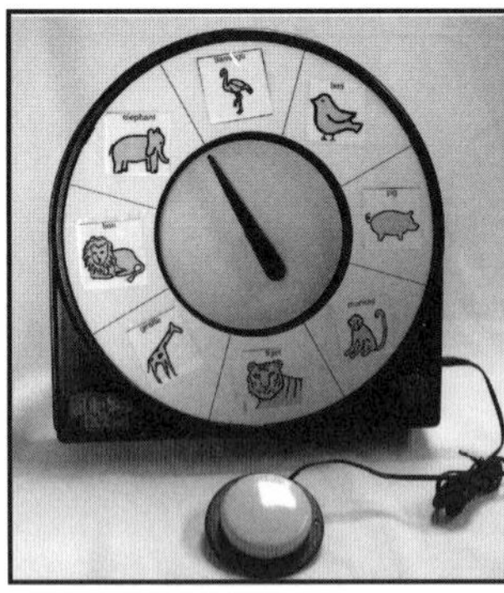

Teacher: The teacher places matching sets of pictures/symbols (letters, words, numbers, etc.) randomly on the large overlay of the All-Turn-It® spinner. The teacher instructs students to find a match.

Student: The student spins twice to randomly select two pictures/symbols. The student, or a teacher or other student, indicates if these pictures/symbols are a match or not and directs the student to keep the match or to keep one picture/symbol and spin for the match.

Solution #2: The student uses the BIG mack communicator to participate in matching activities.

BIGmack® communicator

Teacher: The teacher records on the BIGmack communicator the sentence, "These two are a match."

Student: The student is shown one picture/symbol (letter, word, number, etc.) or item and is requested to find the match. The student is then slowly shown a series of pictures/symbols or items. When the student sees the matching picture/symbol or item, he/she activates the BIGmack communicator to identify the match.

Solution #3: The student uses the iTalk2™ communicator to participate in matching activities.

iTalk2™ communicator

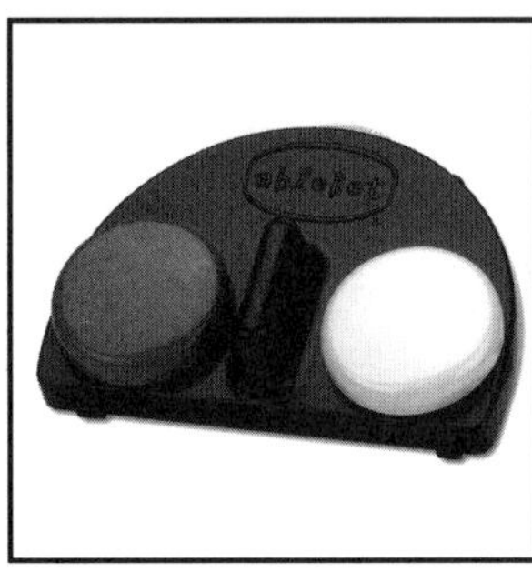

Teacher: The teacher places the MATCH and NO pictures/symbols on the iTalk2 communicator and programs the sentences, "These two are a match" and "No, these two are not a match" into the iTalk2 communicator.

Student: The student is shown two items or pictures/symbols and asked to say if they are a match or if they are not a match. The student activates the iTalk2 communicator to say if the two things are a match or are not a match.

TIPS:

1. Collect juice lids and milk/juice caps. These work well for creating matching games and activities.

2. For students just beginning to learn the concept of matching, try using different terminology such as, "Find the one that's the same" or "Find the one that looks like this one."

3. Many commercially available games popular with students, such as BINGO and Go Fish, have the basic foundation of matching. Following the principle of partial participation, students who are not able to place a BINGO marker on their card, or move a game marker along a path, or pick up a playing card may be able to identify a match and then instruct somebody else to move their marker, pick up a certain card, or put a BINGO dot on a particular square.

Solution #1: The student uses an electric mixer with a PowerLink®3 control unit and a switch to participate in a mixing activity.

PowerLink®3 control unit with mixer and switch

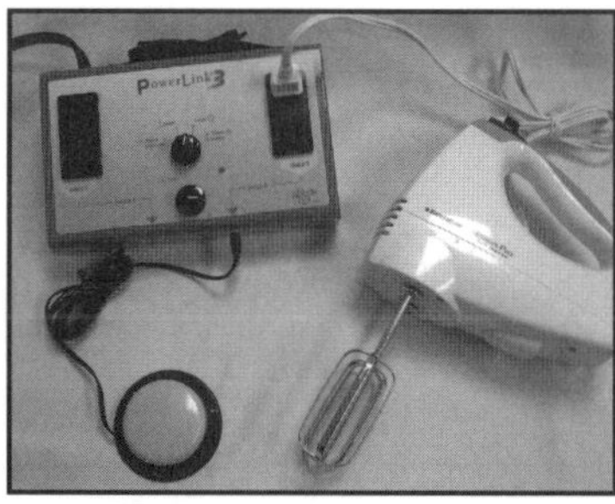

Teacher: The teacher assigns somebody to hold the mixer for the student, or secures the mixer so it remains in place while the student is mixing.

Student: The student activates the switch to turn on the mixer.

Solution #2: The student uses a LITTLE Step-by-Step communicator to participate in a mixing activity.

LITTLE Step-by-Step communicator

Example Student Script

"Let's mix up this dough."
"Turn on the mixer."
"Let's put it on a higher speed."
"I think it's almost ready!"
"Let's stop the mixer now."

Teacher: The teacher records a sequence of directions for mixing on the LITTLE Step-by-Step communicator, one direction per step.

Student: The student activates the LITTLE Step-by-Step communicator multiple times to give mixing directions to a staff or student helper.

Solution #3: The student uses a nonelectric mixing tool to participate in a mixing activity.

Wire Whisk:

Teacher: The teacher may expand the width of the whisk handle by using adhesive back, foam weatherstripping.

Student: The student may use the whisk to help beat up something simple such as eggs, pudding, or a prepared muffin mix.

Egg Beater:

Teacher: The teacher uses Velcro® or a clamp to attach the bowl to the table so it does not move around.

Student: The student turns the crank on the egg beater to mix up something simple such as eggs or pudding.

Solution #4: The student uses a shaker method of mixing ingredients.

Teacher: The teacher, or a student, puts the ingredients to something simple (eggs, a shake, pudding) into a container and tightly secures the lid.

Student: The student grasps the container and shakes it; or, if a round container, rolls it from student-to-student to shake up the ingredients inside.

TIPS:

1. When following a recipe, mix the dough or other mixture after each ingredient is added. This allows all students opportunities to mix an optimal amount of times. Mixing is highly motivational to many students.
2. It is important that all students are able to see what they are mixing. If possible, set up the mixer on a low cart on wheels so that the mixing activity can be moved around and made visible to all students.
3. Place Dycem™ matting or UltraStik™ underneath the bowl of ingredients. Using a heavier bowl also prevents the bowl from moving around.

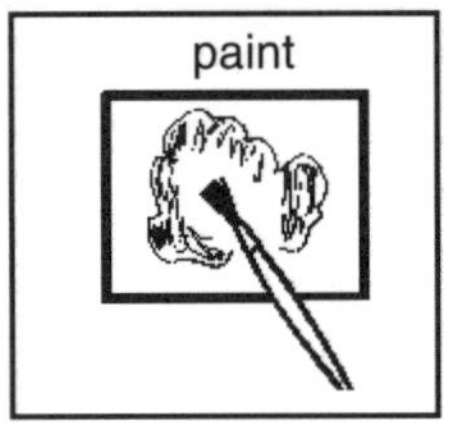

paint

Solution #1: Students use the Paint 'N' Swirl™ with a Battery Device Adapter and a switch to participate in painting activities.

Paint 'N' Swirl™ and switch

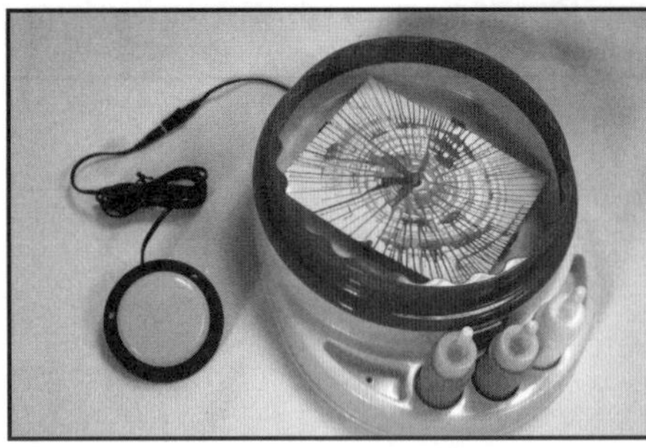

Teacher: The teacher places paper on the Paint 'N' Swirl.

Student: The student selects a color(s) of paint. The student activates the switch to spin the spinner. A few drops of the selected paint colors are put on the paper while it's being spun, and the paint is splattered on the paper.

Solution #2: Students use a LITTLE Step-by-Step communicator to participate in painting activities.

LITTLE Step-by-Step communicator

Example Student Script

"Will you help me paint?"
"I want to paint the ocean."
"We'll start with the color blue."
"Now let's paint a giant gray whale!"

Teacher: The teacher records a series of painting directions on the LITTLE Step-by-Step communicator, one sentence per step.

Student: The student activates the communicator multiple times to give painting directions to a staff or student helper.

Solution #3: Students use alternative painting methods to participate in painting activities.

Teacher: The teacher adds a handle to a sponge shape by attaching a wooden block with a hot glue gun.

Student: Students who have difficulties manipulating a paintbrush can grasp the sponge shape by it's handle, dip it into a selected color of paint, and press it on the paper.

Teacher: The teacher puts a piece of paper in the bottom of a box, with a lid. The teacher adds a few drops of each paint color selected by the student. The teacher, or student, adds marbles and puts the lid on the box.

Student: The student shakes the box around, moving it as much as possible. The lid is removed and the splattered paper is taken out of the box.

Solution #4: Students use alternative/adapted painting tools to participate in painting activities.

Teacher: The teacher puts small paint rollers in shallow containers filled with various colors of paint. The handles can be built up by using adhesive back, foam weatherstripping. The paint rollers require very little pressure to push along on a surface.

Student: The student with limited range of motion is able to apply paint to a broader area.

Teacher: The teacher adapts any paintbrush by wrapping adhesive back, foam weatherstripping around the handle to widen it.

Student: The student grasps the paintbrush and uses it to apply paint.

TIPS:

1. Put the paint in shallow containers so that students have only a minimal distance to lift the brush in order to access the paint. Sturdy paper plates also work well.
2. Attach the paint containers to the work surface using Velcro®, double-sided tape, Dycem™ matting or Ultra Stik™. This prevents the container from moving when a student is trying to access the paint container.
3. For students who are working on increasing or maintaining their range of motion, tape the paper a short distance from the student, so that he/she will need to extend his/her arm to paint on the paper.

Solution #1: The student uses a BIGmack® communicator to participate in reading.

BIGmack® communicator

Teacher: The teacher records a short passage, a book page, a piece of information, a word, or a letter into the BIGmack communicator.

Student: The student activates the BIGmack communicator to read a short passage, book page, piece of information, word, or letter.

Solution #2: The student uses a LITTLE Step-by-Step communicator to participate in reading.

LITTLE Step-by-Step communicator

Teacher: The teacher records the text from each page of the book, or a series of sentences from a written text, into the LITTLE Step-by-Step communicator.

Student: The student reads the text on each page, or each sentence of a written text, by activating the LITTLE Step-by-Step communicator one time per page or sentence.

Solution #3: The student uses the SuperTalker™ to read a book.

SuperTalker™

Teacher: The teacher places a picture/symbol representing each page of a book or section of a book on the SuperTalker overlay. The teacher programs the text from each page into each individual location.

Student: As each page is turned, the student activates the corresponding message to read the book page.

NOTE: SuperTalker™ includes keyguards for 1, 2, 4 and 8 messages.

Solution #4: The student uses the Bookworm™ literacy tool to participate in reading.

Bookworm™ literacy tool

Teacher: The teacher follows directions in the Quick Set Up Guide to adapt the book with the stickers and magnet, and records the book/text into the Bookworm literacy tool.

Student: The student reads each page sequentially by pressing on the colored sticker on that page, by pressing on the matching membrane, or by pressing the switch.

Solution #5: The student uses an adapted battery-operated tape player with a switch to participate in reading.

Tape player and switch

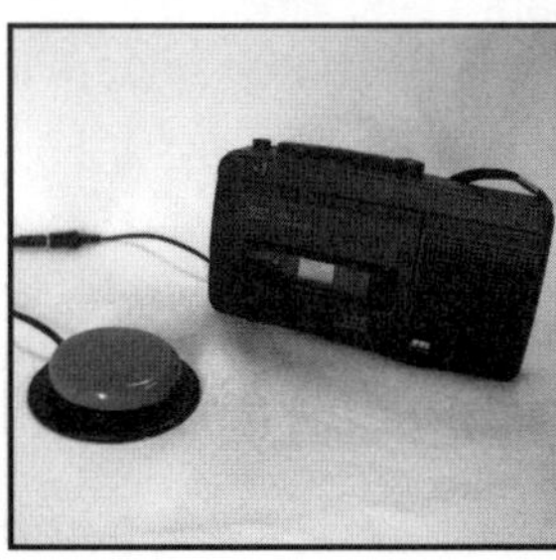

Teacher: The teacher records a book/text onto a cassette tape. The tape is put in the tape player and a switch is attached to the tape player.

Student: The student reads the book or text by pressing the switch to activate the tape player.

say

Solution #1: The student uses the BIGmack® communicator to say something to others.

BIGmack® communicator

Teacher: The teacher records a single message into a BIGmack communicator. A student may also select something to say from a choice of pictures/symbols, and that information may be recorded into the BIGmack communicator.

Student: The student activates the BIGmack communicator to say a single message.

Solution #2: The student uses the LITTLE Step-by-Step communicator to say a series of messages to others.

LITTLE Step-by-Step communicator

Example Student Script

"Do you know what?"
"My favorite kind of clothes is jeans!"
"I like old blue jeans."
"I wear jeans to the mall."

Teacher: The teacher records a sequence of pieces of information into the LITTLE Step-by-Step communicator.

Student: The student activates the LITTLE Step-by-Step communicator multiple times to say a series of different things, such as giving others multiple pieces of information.

Solution #3: The student selects and shows others a picture/symbol representing what he/she wants to say.

Display Tool

Teacher: The teacher gets a display tool and clips on pictures/symbols representing various things that students may want to say (I'm hungry, I like that, I don't like that, I want to go with you). A display tool is created by gluing clothespins onto a strip of wooden trim.

Student: The student points to or grasps a picture/symbol representing what he/she wants to say.

Solution #4: The student eye gazes at a picture/symbol representing what he/she wants to say.

Teacher: The teacher uses a piece of plexiglass to create an eye gaze communication board. The teacher puts pictures/symbols, representing various things that students may want to say, on the eye gaze communication board.

Student: The student eye gazes at the picture/symbol representing what he/she wants to say.

NOTE: Use the underlined word(s) as a key word in an Internet search to find additional information.

TIPS:

1. Whenever possible, use a voice output device with students who are nonverbal.
2. Keep one or more BIGmack communicators with the "say" picture/symbol on them readily available at all times. Encourage staff and student helpers to pick them up and record appropriate things for students to say throughout the day, giving them maximum opportunities to verbally communicate. Some of these things may include, "I'm all finished," "I'd like more," and "Please help me."
3. Encourage staff and peer helpers to respond to everything that a student says. When a student receives a response, the student gains a better understanding of the power of having a voice.
4. When students are out in the school or community, encourage staff to program voice output devices frequently, giving students opportunities to spontaneously chat with others.

Solution #1: The student uses the BIGmack® communicator to tell one or more people that they have something to show.

BIGmack® communicator

Teacher: The teacher records into the BIGmack communicator the sentence, "I have something to show you."

Student: The student activates the BIGmack communicator to tell others that there is something he/she would like to show them.

Solution #2: The student uses the LITTLE Step-by-Step communicator to tell others a series of messages about what he/she is showing.

LITTLE Step-by-Step communicator

Example Student Script

"I have something to show you."
"Do you want to see?"
"Come over here and look."
"What do you think?"
*Add additional messages about the particular thing being shown

Teacher: The teacher records the student script into the LITTLE Step-by-Step communicator.

Student: The student activates the LITTLE Step-by-Step communicator multiple times to interact with the person to whom they are showing the item.

Solution #3: The student uses a special tray or container to place something in and show it to others.

Teacher: The teacher gives the student a tray with handles, or a shallow container with handles that is easy for the student to grasp and carry.

Student: The student grasps the handles of the container to carry the item from one person to the next, showing the item to each person one at a time.

Solution #4: The student uses a tool with a handle to show others an item.

Teacher: The teacher clips the item to be shown to a pants hanger or other clip that has been attached to some kind of handle that is easy for the student to grasp.

Student: The student grasps the handle and brings the item to each person.

Solution #5: The student accesses a special "show" area and/or table to show something to others.

Teacher: The teacher sets up a special show table that is easily accessible to all students.

Student: The student puts the item on the special "show" area so that all students can see it.

TIPS:

1. When students are taking turns showing something to others, arrange the seating so that the student doing the showing needs to move a minimal distance to show the item to each student.
2. Encourage students to tell about the item while they are showing it, or before or after they are showing it.

sing

Solution #1: A student uses the tape player with a Battery Device Adapter and a switch to participate in singing activities.

Tape Player and switch

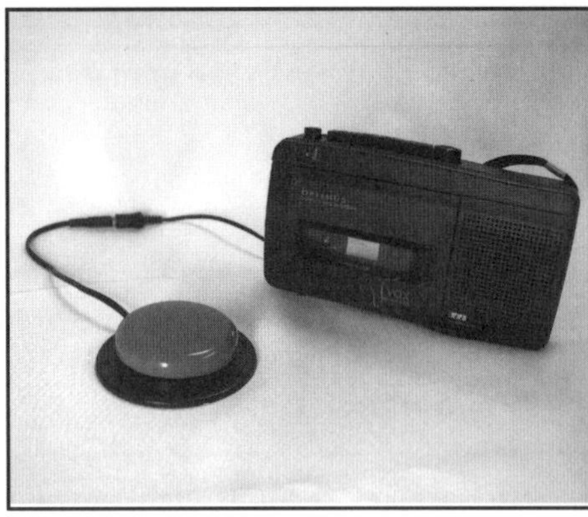

Teacher: The teacher records a song on a cassette tape and puts the tape in the adapted battery-operated tape player.

Student: The student uses the switch to turn on the tape player and play, or sing, a song.

NOTE: The Switch Latch And Timer can be used with the system and set for the approximate amount of time that each verse lasts, so that each time the student activates the switch another verse is sung.

Solution #2: A student uses a BIGmack® communicator to participate in singing activities.

BIGmack® communicator

Teacher: The teacher records a short song, a verse, or a repeated line to a song on the BIGmack communicator.

Student: The student activates the BIGmack communicator one time to sing a short song, sing one verse of a song, or sing a repeated line of a song. When a student is singing a verse or a repeated line, a representative picture/symbol can be placed on the communicator, and the student is shown that picture/symbol to cue him/her at the appropriate time to sing that verse or line.

Solution #3: A student uses a LITTLE Step-by-Step communicator to participate in singing activities.

LITTLE Step-by-Step communicator

Teacher: The teacher records the verses to a song on the LITTLE Step-by-Step communicator, one verse per step.

Student: The student activates the LITTLE Step-by-Step communicator multiple times to sing each sequential verse of a song.

Solution #4: The student uses the SuperTalker™ to sing verses of a song.

SuperTalker™

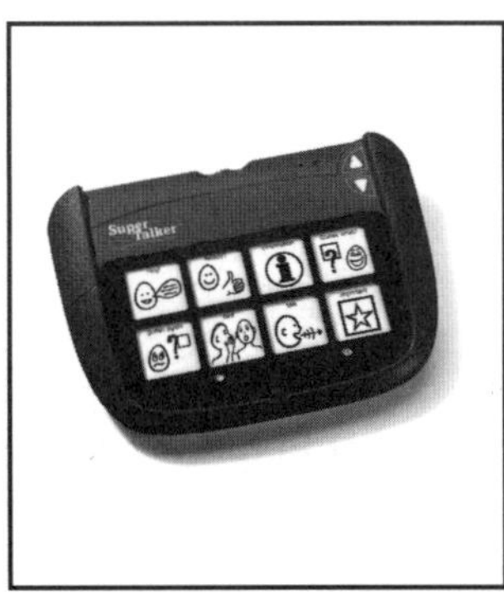

Teacher: The teacher places a picture/symbol representing each verse of a song on the SuperTalker overlay. The teacher programs the words from each verse into the device on each individual location.

Student: As each verse is sung, the student activates the corresponding message location to sing that verse.

NOTE: SuperTalker™ includes keyguards for 1, 2, 4, and 8 messages.

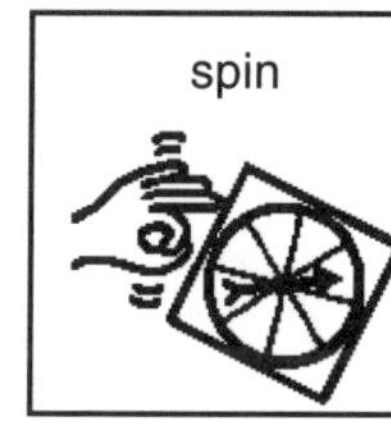

Solution #1: **The student uses the All-Turn-It® spinner with a switch to spin on their turn.**

All-Turn-It® spinner and switch

Teacher: The teacher places a dice overlay on the All-Turn-It spinner, or places pictures/symbols or real items representing what is going to be spun for, on the large overlay of the All-Turn-It® spinner.

Student: The student activates the switch to spin on their turn.

Solution #2: **The student uses the LITTLE Step-by-Step communicator with the All-Turn-It® spinner and a switch to spin on their turn.**

LITTLE Step-by-Step communicator

Example Student Script

"Time to spin!"
"I hope I get a six!"
"OK - spin away!"
"Where is it going to land?"

Teacher: The teacher follows the instructions in the Quick Set Up guide to record messages on a LITTLE Step-by-Step communicator, programming the All-Turn-It spinner to be activated on the "OK - spin away!" message.

Student: The student activates the LITTLE Step-by-Step communicator multiple times to comment on the spinning activity, and activate the spinner to spin on their turn.

Solution #3: **The student uses an adapted spinner to spin on their turn.**

Teacher: The teacher extends the length of a typical spinner dial by taping a strip of sturdy cardboard or card stock (at least an inch longer than the spinner dial) to the top of the spinner dial. The teacher, or a peer helper, holds the spinner upright in front of the student.

Student: The student puts his/her hand above the spinner dial and pushes the dial down and around.

TIPS:

1. Card games in which a card needs to be drawn may be adapted by placing the cards from the "draw" pile face down on the large overlay of the All-Turn-It spinner. When a student needs to draw a card, he/she activates the spinner.

2. Many simple learning board games that use a spinner may be created. If you have access to a die cutter, cut out some fun shapes, or shapes that go along with a theme or the theme of the game. Glue the shapes in a game path pattern on a large sheet of poster board or a sheet of lightweight wood.

3. When using the All-Turn-It spinner without a switch, set a piece of Dycem™ or UltraStik™ underneath it so it will not move, or move only a minimal amount when the spinner is activated by pressing on the button.

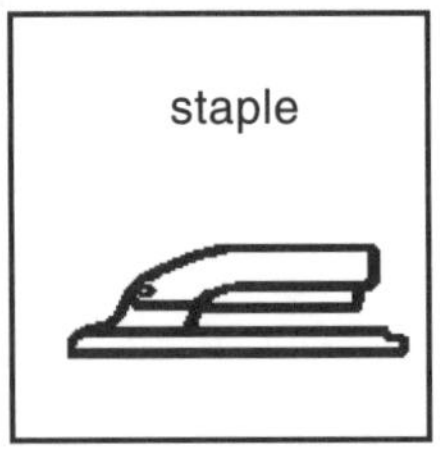

staple

Solution #1: The student uses the stapler with a Battery Device Adapter (BDA) and a switch or with a PowerLink®3 control unit and a switch to participate in stapling activities.

Stapler, Battery Device Adapter, and switch

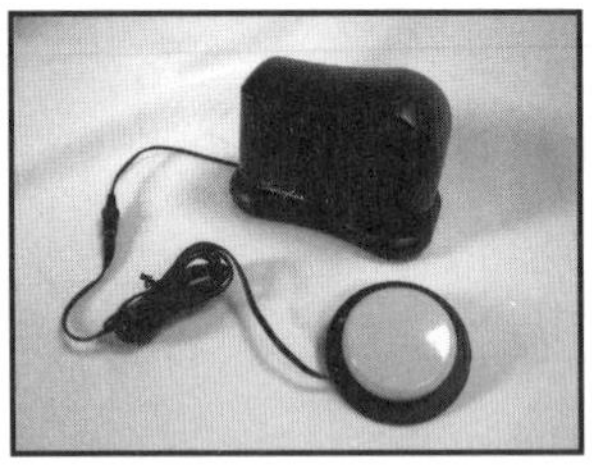

Stapler, PowerLink®3 control unit and switch

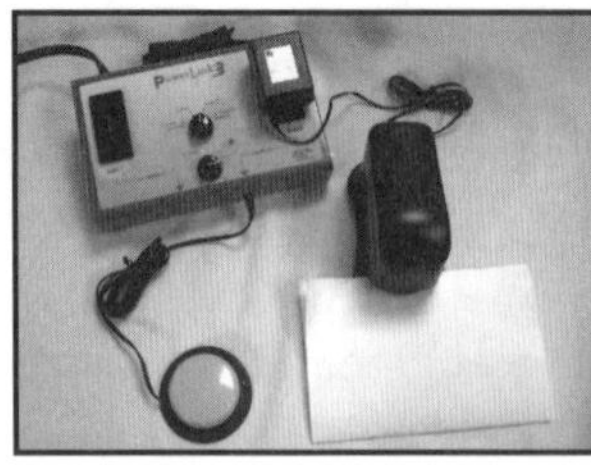

Student: The student activates the switch to staple two things together.

Solution #2: The student uses the LITTLE Step-by-Step communicator to participate in stapling activities.

LITTLE Step-by-Step communicator

Example Student Script

"We need to staple this."
"Put the paper in the stapler!"
"Let's staple!"
"Thanks!"

Teacher: The teacher records the student script into the LITTLE Step-by-Step communicator.

Student: The student activates the LITTLE Step-by-Step communicator multiple times to direct somebody through the process of stapling.

Solution #3: The student uses the iTalk2™ communicator to participate in stapling activities.

iTalk2™ communicator

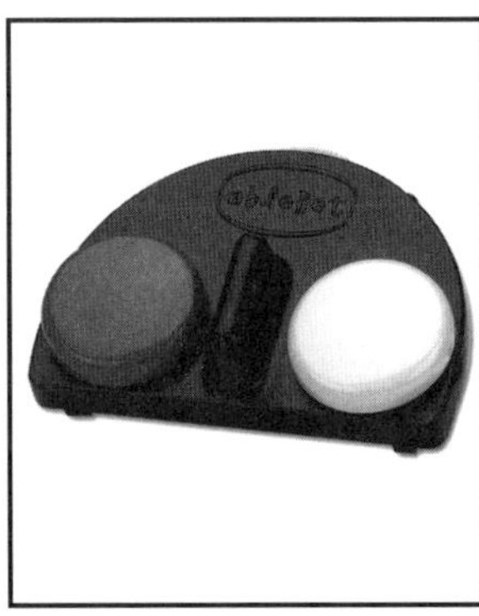

Teacher: The teacher places the STAPLE and THANK YOU pictures/symbols on the iTalk2 communicator. The teacher records the sentences "Will you please help me staple this?" and "Thanks for your help!" on the iTalk2 communicator.

Student: The student activates the iTalk2 communicator to ask somebody to help him/her staple something, and then thank that person. Use this as a teaching opportunity to direct students to first activate the STAPLE switch top and ask for help stapling, and then activate the THANK YOU switch top to thank that person for their help.

TIPS:

1. Check with teachers and/or the school office to see if they need paper packets collated and stapled. This is a great cooperative learning activity for all students, and a valuable work skill for older students.

2. If using a regular stapler that does not have rubber feet or a rubber base, put a piece of Dycem™ or UltraStik™ underneath the stapler so it will not slide around when students are using it.

3. When using the switch-activated stapler and giving directions to students, give directions such as "Please staple these papers together" rather than, "Hit the switch" so students attach meaning to the activity and are focused on the end result.

Solution #1: **The student uses a pre-adapted digital camera with a switch to participate in picture taking activities.**

Digital camera and switch

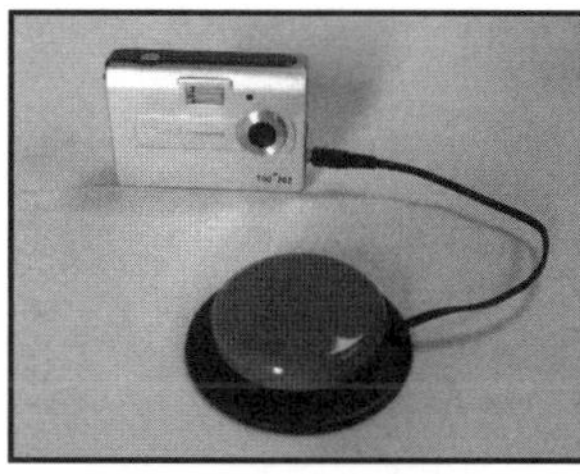

Teacher: The teacher positions the digital camera.

Student: The student activates the switch to take a picture.

Solution #2: **The student uses the LITTLE Step-by-Step communicator and the pre-adapted digital camera to participate in picture taking activities.**

LITTLE Step-by-Step communicator

Example Student Script

"Ready for a picture?"
"On the count of three."
"One, Two, Three..."
"Cheese!"
"Thanks! I'll show you the picture later."

Teacher: The teacher follows the instructions in the Quick Set Up guide to record messages on a LITTLE Step-by-Step communicator, setting the LITTLE Step-by-Step communicator to activate the camera on the "Cheese!" message.

Student: The student activates the LITTLE Step-by-Step communicator multiple times to give directions to the person who is having their picture taken, and to take the picture.

Solution #3: **The student uses an adapted 35mm camera to take pictures.**

Teacher: The teacher builds up the activation button on a camera by gluing on a small block or other object, or builds it up with Sticky Tack and attaches a hard-surfaced item to the end of it.

Student: A student with fine motor limitations will have an easier time accessing the activation button.

Teacher: The teacher clearly marks the location of the activation button on the camera by using a bright colored marker, fluorescent tape, or a bright colored paint.

Student: The student will be able to easily identify what button to push to take a picture.

TIPS:

1. Certain cameras designed especially for children have large, easy to activate buttons that some students may be able to use independently.

2. When using a switch-adapted camera, use a mounting system (such as the Universal Switch Mounting System) to mount the camera so that it is correctly positioned before the student activates the switch to snap the picture.

3. Put photos, taken by students, in the Talking Photo Album (available through AbleNet). Students may then take this album and share information about the photos with others. The Talking Photo Album may be used for reports or personal portfolios, also.

turn on/off

Solution #1: Students use any electrical device with a PowerLink®3 control unit and switch to turn the device ON/OFF.

Device with a PowerLink®3 control unit and switch

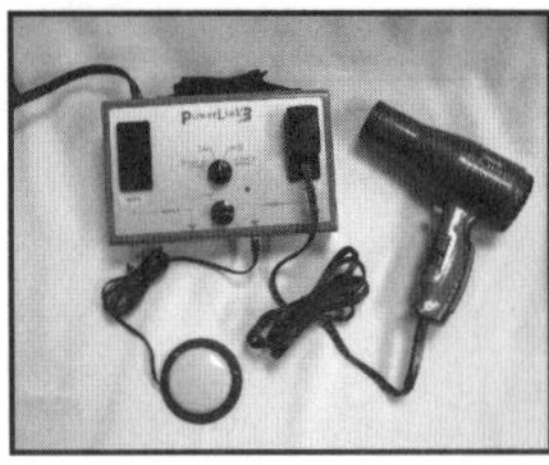

Teacher: The teacher plugs the electrical device into the PowerLink®3 control unit.

Student: The student activates the switch to turn the device ON/OFF.

Solution #2: Students use any battery-operated device with a Battery Device Adapter (BDA), a Switch Latch And Timer (SLAT), and a switch to turn the device ON/OFF.

Device with a BDA, SLAT, and switch

Teacher: The teacher attaches the Battery Device Adapter to the battery-operated device and adds a switch and the Switch Latch and Timer.

Student: The student activates the switch to turn on the device.

Solution #3: Students use an iTalk2™ communicator to ask somebody to turn a device ON/OFF.

iTalk2™ communicator

Teacher: The teacher places the ON and OFF pictures/symbols on the iTalk2 communicator and records the sentences, "Please turn (the radio) on" and "please turn (the radio) off" on the iTalk2 communicator.

Student: The student activates the iTalk2 communicator to ask somebody to turn a device ON/OFF.

TIPS:

1. Think about all of the activities your class does during the day that require something to be turned on or off. Set up those activities so they are dependent on a student turning something on and/or off.
2. Some highly motivational devices that older students might turn on and off include a hair dryer, a fingernail dryer, mixers, and blenders. Some devices of interest to younger students might include battery-operated scissors and toys, as well as mixers and blenders.

Solution #1: The student uses the BIGmack® communicator to participate in the process of turning the page of a book.

BIGmack® communicator

Teacher: The teacher records the sentence, "Please turn the page" or "Please help me turn the page" on the BIGmack communicator.

Student: The student activates the BIGmack communicator to ask somebody to turn the page, or to ask for help turning the page.

Solution #2: The student uses the iTalk2™ communicator to participate in the process of turning the page of a book.

iTalk2™ communicator

Teacher: The teacher places the TURN THE PAGE and LOOK pictures/symbols on the iTalk2 communicator. The teacher records the sentences, "I'd like to turn the page" or "Please turn the page" and "Let's look at this page for a minute" on the iTalk2 communicator.

Student: The student activates the iTalk2 communicator to either ask to turn the page or have the page turned, or to look at the page more closely.

Solution #3: The student uses book supports to aid in the process of turning the page of a book.

Teacher: The teacher sets the book on a music stand, easel, or book stand and secures the stand to the table or floor using Velcro®, clamps, or a nonskid mat. The front and back book covers are secured to the stand using clothespins or any other clamp or clip.

Student: The student is able to more easily access and turn the pages with the book in an upright position.

Teacher: The teacher creates a hand held page turner by attaching a piece of Sticky Tack, Dycem™ matting, or UltraStik™ to one end of a tongue depressor. A rubber finger may also be worn and used as a page turner.

Student: The student holds or wears the page turner and presses the sticky end down on the page, pushing the page back and over.

Solution #4: The student uses a book with adapted pages to participate in the process of turning the page of a book.

Teacher: The teacher uses tape, glue, or paper clips to attach a page extension, such as a half of a craft stick, a piece of foam, or a tab divider to the edge of each page.

Student: The student grasps the page extension and turns the page.

Teacher: The teacher puts a small piece of adhesive back, foam weatherstripping on the side of each page.

Student: The weatherstripping separates the pages, making it easier for students to slip their fingers in between the pages and turn a page.

TIPS:

1. Be sure and give students plenty of wait time to process and follow through on the request to turn the page.

2. Create high interest books that will motivate students. Use a digital camera to take photos of students engaged in school activities. Write about the photo on the bottom of that page. Print the pages onto card stock and laminate them for durability. Bind or staple them together to create a book.

3. Consider assigning roles during a book reading experience. One student may have the role of reading the book, another student has the role of turning the pages, another student has the role of asking questions, and the rest of the students have the role of answering the questions.

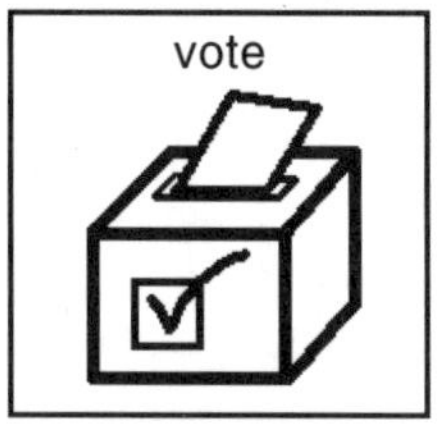

vote

Solution #1: The student uses the LITTLE Step-by-Step communicator to participate in a voting activity by counting votes.

LITTLE Step-by-Step communicator

Example Student Script

"Here's one vote."
"This makes two votes."
"Now there are three!"
"We're up to four votes!"

Teacher: The teacher records the sequential counting of votes on the LITTLE Step-by-Step communicator.

Student: The student activates the LITTLE Step-by-Step communicator one time per vote to count up the number of votes for each choice.

Solution #2: The student uses the iTalk2™ communicator to participate in a voting activity.

iTalk2™ communicator

Teacher: The teacher places pictures/symbols representing the two vote options on the iTalk 2 communicator, and records the two options on the iTalk2 communicator.

Student: The student activates the iTalk2 communicator to give their vote.

Solution #3: The student uses a voting chart to participate in a voting activity.

Voting chart

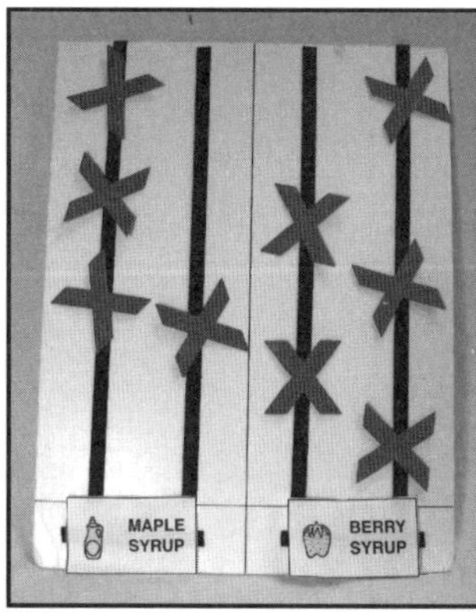

Teacher: The teacher makes a large voting chart from a piece of poster board or foam board by drawing a line down the middle of the chart, laminating it, and putting soft Velcro® on either side of the chart. The names and pictures/symbols of each vote choice are placed at the top, or bottom, of the chart. Voting markers are made out of fun foam or laminated paper, and rough Velcro® is attached to the back of each voting marker.

Student: Students physically mark their vote choice by placing a marker on the side with the picture/symbol representing their vote choice.

Solution #4: The student uses a voting ballot system to participate in a voting activity.

Teacher: The teacher makes paper ballots that show a picture/symbol for each of the vote choices.

Student: The student marks the picture/symbol representing his/her vote choice.

Teacher: The teacher gets a wide, open-mouthed container for each vote choice. A representative picture/symbol is attached to each container. The teacher gives each student a three dimensional object, such as a block.

Student: The student puts the object in the container that represents his/her vote choice.

TIPS:

1. Any time during the day that one of two activities (recipes, books, games, videos, etc.) can be used to reach the same objective, consider having students vote. Voting is a great way to work on choice-making, following directions, and counting.
2. When making a voting chart, make each side a different color so as to better differentiate one side from the other.
3. A voting chart may be placed on a flat surface and three dimensional objects may be placed on either side of the voting chart.

Solution #1: The student uses the LITTLE Step-by-Step communicator to participate in writing activities.

LITTLE Step-by-Step communicator

Teacher: The teacher records the information to be written on the LITTLE Step-by-Step communicator, one sentence, phrase, word, or letter per step.

Student: A student activates the LITTLE Step-by-Step communicator multiple times to dictate to a staff person or peer helper the information that the staff or helper will write down for that student. The student using the LITTLE Step-by-Step communicator is instructed to wait for the cue of the person doing the writing before activating the communicator again to give the next piece of information.

Solution #2: The student uses the iTalk2™ communicator to participate in writing activities.

iTalk2™ communicator

Teacher: During a writing activity, the teacher places two pictures/symbols, that represent two options for what is to be written, on the iTalk2 communicator, such as a story idea, what should happen next in the story, what a character's name should be, where a character should go or what a character should do, etc.

Student: Throughout the writing activity, the student may be asked to make one or more decisions about what will be written. A student activates the iTalk2 communicator to tell the teacher or student doing the writing what he/she would like written.

Solution #3: The student uses adapted writing tools to participate in writing activities.

Teacher: The teacher broadens the width of the writing tool by wrapping adhesive back, foam weatherstripping or foam piping insulation around it, or uses a commercially available pencil grip.

Teacher: The teacher uses a hand strap to attach a writing tool to the student's hand.

Solution #4: The student uses a writing support to participate in writing activities.

Teacher: The teacher uses a highlighter (recommend yellow) to write out the words to be written by the student.

Student: The student uses a pencil or other writing tool to trace over the highlighted letters.

Solution #5: The student uses an alternative keyboard.

Teacher: The teacher places the adapted keyboard in a location that is easily accessed by the student.

NOTE: Use the underlined word(s) as a key word in an Internet search to find additional information.

Student: The student uses an adapted keyboard (one with large keys, one appropriate for a one-handed typist, a keyboard with letters arranged in alphabetical order, etc.) to type out what they want to write.

TIPS:

1. Students may be more motivated to practice writing on surfaces other than plain paper, such as designed paper, Magna-Doodles, wipe-off boards, in shaving cream on a table top, etc.
2. Tape down the paper so it does not move while the student is writing.
3. Write words/info on labels that students place on paper.

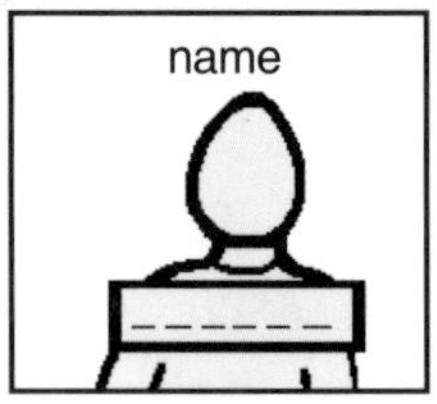

write your name

Solution #1: The student uses the BIGmack® communicator to participate in the activity of writing his/her name.

BIGmack® communicator

Teacher: The teacher records the sentence, "Will you please help me write my name? My name is __________ and It's spelled, '____, ____, ____, ____.' Thanks."

Student: The student activates the BIGmack communicator to ask somebody to help them write their name, telling that person their name and how it is spelled.

Solution #2: The student uses the LITTLE Step-by-Step communicator to participate in the activity of writing his/her name.

LITTLE Step-by-Step communicator

Example Student Script

"Will you help me write my name?"
"My name is David."
"The first letter is 'D.' "
"Next letter is 'a.' "
"Now write a v.' "
"Next is an i.' "
"It ends in a 'd.' "
"Thanks for your help."

Teacher: The teacher records the student's name and each letter of his/her name, in sequential order, on the LITTLE Step-by-Step communicator, one letter per step.

Student: The student activates the LITTLE Step-by-Step communicator, one time per letter in their name, to dictate the spelling of their name to somebody who will help them write their name.

Solution #3: The student use a name stamp to participate in the activity of writing their name.

Teacher: The teacher has a name stamp created for a student, adapting the handle as needed.

Student: The student grips the name stamp and presses it on paper to stamp his/her name.

Solution #4: The student uses writing supports to participate in the activity of writing their name.

Teacher: The teacher makes a name stencil by printing off or writing the student's name on a piece of heavy card stock and laminating it. The teacher cuts out the middle of each letter, leaving the inside open.

Student: The student uses a writing tool to trace inside of the stencil, writing each letter of their name.

Teacher: The teacher makes a row of letter shape boxes, next to each other, on a line of writing paper, one box for each letter of the student's name. The box fills the bottom space for short letters (a, c, e, i, o, m, n, r, s, u, v, w, x, z), the box takes up the bottom and top space for tall letters (b, d, f, h, k, l, t) and the box fills the bottom space and the space below that for "underground" letters (g, j, p, q, y).

Student: The student writes each letter of their name in the appropriate box.

Mary

TIPS:

1. Have students practice writing their name in highly motivational, multi-sensory ways, such as in shaving cream, in pudding, with finger paint, with gel pens on black paper, with bright markers, or with any kind of fun, different writing tool.
2. Tape down the paper so it does not move while the student is writing.
3. Give students lots of time to practice identifying the letters that are in their name and putting them in the right order. Letter scrambles and name puzzles are fun and motivational.

EARLY LITERACY AND COMMUNICATION PROGRAM

Part five

Data Collection

ablenet™

unit 2

my family

MEville to WEville

DATA COLLECTION

The Student Data Collection charts provided in this section make it easy to record and share students' growth and progress with others. Use these charts to keep track of the ongoing participation and progress of your students. These charts can also be used to collect baseline information prior to starting the program.

Blank charts have been provided for the Learning New Words/Vocabulary, Word Wall Words and Content Learning for you to report student specific Individual Educational Plan (IEP) goals/objectives that can be worked on throughout this program.

Learning New Words/Vocabulary - Unit 2 My Family

The student working toward the **highest level** would demonstrate expressive and receptive use of the vocabulary word across contexts.

Student Name: ______________________________

Current Student Goal/Objective: ______________________________

Part 1: Who Is In My Family?

DATE:														
family														
parents														
children														
dog														
cat														
INITIALS:														

Part 2: Things We Do

DATE:														
eat														
work														
go														
play														
live														
INITIALS:														

Part 3: Living With My Family

DATE:														
help														
share														
give														
laugh														
celebrate														
INITIALS:														

Date **Student Level**

_____ The student is exposed to the word within an activity.
_____ The student attends to or responds to a word within an activity.
_____ The student identifies, selects, or defines the word presented in isolation.
_____ The student identifies, selects, or defines the appropriate word within the context of an activity.
_____ The student demonstrates expressive and receptive use of the word across contexts.

(Specify the date the student level changes)

Adaptations Used by the Student

___ Voice output device to read words
___ Display tool, pictures/symbols to select a word
___ Eye gaze, pictures/symbols to select a word
___ Writing tools with adapted handles
___ Adapted computer software to write

Documentation Key

N = No attempt made, passive/non-compliant
F = Completed the task with full physical prompt
P = Completed the task with partial prompting and/or assistance
I = Completed the task independently
***** = Other ____________

Learning New Words/Vocabulary - Unit 2 My Family

The student working toward the **highest level** would demonstrate expressive and receptive use of the vocabulary word across contexts.

Student Name: ______________________________

Current Student Goal/Objective: ______________________________

DATE:														
INITIALS:														

Date **Student Level**

______ The student is exposed to the word within an activity.

______ The student attends to or responds to a word within an activity.

______ The student identifies, selects, or defines the word presented in isolation.

______ The student identifies, selects, or defines the appropriate word within the context of an activity.

______ The student demonstrates expressive and receptive use of the word across contexts.

(Specify the date the student level changes)

Adaptations Used by the Student

___ Voice output device to read words

___ Display tool, pictures/symbols to select a word

___ Eye gaze, pictures/symbols to select a word

___ Writing tools with adapted handles

___ Adapted computer software to write

Documentation Key

N = No attempt made, passive/non-compliant

F = Completed the task with full physical prompt

P = Completed the task with partial prompting and/or assistance

I = Completed the task independently

***** = Other______

Word Wall Words - Unit 2 My Family

The student working toward the **highest level** would be able to read and write the appropriate word within the context of an activity.

Student Name: ____

Current Student Goal/Objective: ____

Part 1: Who Is In My Family?

DATE:														
the														
have														
we														
INITIALS:														

Part 2: Things We Do

DATE:														
see														
are														
do														
INITIALS:														

Part 3: Living With My Family

DATE:														
work														
is														
help														
INITIALS:														

Date **Student Level**

_____ The student is exposed to the word within an activity.

_____ The student attends to/responds to the word within an activity.

_____ The student identifies the word by naming or selecting it.

_____ The student writes the word.

_____ The student reads and writes the word.

(Specify the date the student level changes)

Adaptations Used by the Student

___ Voice output device to read words

___ Display tool, pictures/symbols to select a word

___ Eye gaze, pictures/symbols to select a word

___ Writing tools with adapted handles

___ Adapted computer software to write

Documentation Key

N = No attempt made, passive/non-compliant

F = Completed the task with full physical prompt

P = Completed the task with partial prompting and/or assistance

I = Completed the task independently

***** = Other____________

Word Wall Words - Unit 2 My Family

The student working toward the **highest level** would be able to read and write the appropriate word within the context of an activity.

Student Name: ____

Current Student Goal/Objective: ______________________________

DATE:														
INITIALS:														

Date **Student Level**

______The student is exposed to the word within an activity.

______The student attends to/responds to the word within an activity.

______The student identifies the word by naming or selecting it.

______The student writes the word.

______The student reads and writes the word.
(Specify the date the student level changes)

Adaptations Used by the Student

___ Voice output device to read words

___ Display tool, pictures/symbols to select a word

___ Eye gaze, pictures/symbols to select a word

___ Writing tools with adapted handles

___ Adapted computer software to write

Documentation Key

N = No attempt made, passive/non-compliant

F = Completed the task with full physical prompt

P = Completed the task with partial prompting and/or assistance

I = Completed the task independently

***** = Other__________

Writing - Unit 2 My Family

The student working toward the **highest level** would be independently generating a word(s) during a writing activity.

Student Name: ____________________

Current Student Goal/Objective: ____________________

DATE:										
The student writes a word to complete a sentence.										
The student writes a word, phrase, or sentence to describe a person or object.										
The student writes three or more parts of a story or steps in a sequence.										
The student writes a phrase or sentence to express a personal thought, opinion, or response to an experience.										
INITIALS:										

Date **Student Level**

______ The student is exposed to providing words within a written activity.

______ The student attends or responds to a word(s) used during a writing activity.

______ The student randomly selects a word(s).

______ The student intentionally selects a word(s).

______ The student independently generates a word(s).

(Specify the date the student level changes)

Adaptations Used by the Student

___ Voice output device to read words

___ Display tool, pictures/symbols to select a word

___ Eye gaze, pictures/symbols to select a word

___ Writing tools with adapted handles

___ Adapted computer software to write

Documentation Key

N = No attempt made, passive/non-compliant

F = Completed the task with full physical prompt

P = Completed the task with partial prompting and/or assistance

I = Completed the task independently

***** = Other ____________

Literacy - Unit 2 My Family

The student working toward the **highest level** would be initiating communication during a literacy-related activity.

Student Name: ______________________________

Current Student Goal/Objective: ______________________________

DATE:										
The student makes and expresses a choice or decision.										
The student follows directions. ___ one step ___ two step ___ three or more steps										
The student responds to WH questions.										
The student expresses a personal thought, idea, or opinion in response to a literacy activity.										
The student develops and expresses a solution to a situation/problem.										
INITIALS:										

Date **Student Level**

- ______ The student is exposed to communication during a literacy activity.
- ______ The student attempts to communicate or respond during a literacy activity.
- ______ The student randomly communicates a response to a literacy activity.
- ______ The student intentionally communicates a response to a literacy activity.
- ______ The student initiates communication during a literacy activity.

(Specify the date the student level changes)

Adaptations Used by the Student

- ___ Voice output device to read words
- ___ Display tool, pictures/symbols to select a word
- ___ Eye gaze, pictures/symbols to select a word
- ___ Writing tools with adapted handles
- ___ Adapted computer software to write

Documentation Key

- **N** = No attempt made, passive/non-compliant
- **F** = Completed the task with full physical prompt
- **P** = Completed the task with partial prompting and/or assistance
- **I** = Completed the task independently
- ***** = Other______________

unit 2 my family Content Learning Areas

A blank data collection chart for the Content Learning Areas is provided for you to report students' specific Individual Educational Plan (IEP) goals/objectives, or refer to those provided below.

Part 1: Who Is In My Family?:

The student will be able to identify the features, roles, and/or activities of families and family members.

1. Student will be able to accurately identify at least one unique feature of the family to which he/she belongs.
2. Student will be able to accurately name a family member who has a certain role.
3. Student will be able to accurately identify a difference between a game that was played long ago and a game that is presently played.

Part 2: Things We Do:

The student will be able to identify and/or participate in activities that families do.

1. Student will be able to follow a series of one-step directions to complete a task.
2. Student will be able to sort food items into each of the four foods groups.
3. Student will be able to name one chore that was done many years ago that is different from chores we do now.

Part 3: Living With My Family:

The student will be able to communicate personal information, family routines, and/or solutions for problem solving within a family.

1. Student will be able to identify and say their city, address and phone number.
2. Student will be able to state one thing they can do if they are upset with a family member.
3. Student will be able to name at least one thing that their family does during a particular time of the day.

Content Learning - Unit 2 My Family

The student working toward the **highest level** would demonstrate mastery of the objective across contexts.

Student Name: ____________________

Current Student Goal/Objective: ____________________

The student will be able to identify the features, roles, and/or activities of families and family members.

Part 1: Who Is In My Family?											

The student will be able to identify and/or participate in activities that families do.

Part 2: Things We Do											

The student will be able to communicate personal information, family routines, and/or solutions for problem solving within a family.

Part 3: Living With My Family											

Date **Student Level**

____ The student is exposed to the activity.

____ The student attends or responds to the activity.

____ The student identifies, selects, or defines the objective within the context of an activity.

____ The student demonstrates mastery of the objective across contexts.

(Specify the date the student level changes)

Adaptations Used by the Student

____ Voice output device to read words

____ Display tool, pictures/symbols to select a word

____ Eye gaze, pictures/symbols to select a word

____ Writing tools with adapted handles

____ Adapted computer software to write

Documentation Key

N = No attempt made, passive/non-compliant

F = Completed the task with full physical prompt

P = Completed the task with partial prompting and/or assistance

I = Completed the task independently

***** = Other____________

Unit 2 My Family
Character Education and Community Building Outcomes

Outcomes	What Students Do	How Teachers Model and Reinforce
Students will further develop a sense of "Who I Am."	• Share meaningful things about their life • Talk about important people in their life • Express interests and preferences	• Use and have students sign their names on work. • "Our favorite things are an important part of 'who we are'. John, what's your favorite ____?"
Students will experience a sense of belonging.	• Reciprocal sharing • Cooperative projects • Take turns	• "It is great when we can all work together. Now this (project) belongs to all of us."
Students will learn to acknowledge and celebrate accomplishments, contributions, and differences.	• Clap for the winner or somebody who's accomplished something • Celebrate similarities and differences in each other	• Write ALL suggestions on chart paper or board. • "Thanks for sharing." • "Let's take a moment to celebrate our success!"
Students will experience a valued role as they learn "What we do for each other is important."	• Direct or lead the activity • Help others and be helped by others • Read and be read to • Listen	• "It really helps to have someone keep score." • "Everyone here is important and needed to get this job done!" • "You were a good listener when John told his story, which was sad."
Every student voice will be heard.	• Vote • Make a personal, relevant choice • Take turns	• Ask all students for their input. "Sue, we haven't heard from you. What do you think about _____?"

Share how these outcome have been addressed during Unit 2 My Family:

__________ developed a sense of "Who I Am" by: ______________________________

____

__________ experienced a sense of belonging by: ______________________________

____

__________ acknowledged and celebrated accomplishments, contributions, and differences by: ______________

____

__________ experienced a valued role by: ______________________________

____

__________ experienced having his/her voice heard by: ______________________________

____

EARLY LITERACY AND COMMUNICATION PROGRAM

Part six

Reproducibles

ablenet™

unit 2

my family

MEville to WEville

Dear Parents,

We are going to be working on a unit about family. The vocabulary words we will be learning about and doing activities around are: family, parents, children, cat, and dog.

We would like to share pictures of our families, and our parent(s), with each other. Would you please send in a photo of your child's family (this could be all or part of their family), and a picture of one or more of his/her parents or guardians?

Parents are some of the most important people to a child, and we want to be able to share about our parents with each other! Would you please fill out the following Parent Information sheet with your child and send it back to school.

Please send the photos and the Parent Information sheet back to school no later than

_________________________________.

Thank you so much for your help.

Sincerely,

____

- -

Student Name ___________________

Parent Information

1. My parent was born in the state of ___________________.

2. My parent likes to ______________________ in his/her free time.

3. My parent's favorite color is ___________________________.

4. My parent's favorite food is ___________________________.

5. My parent and I like to _________________________ together.

6. Something else about my parent is:

____

____

Vocabulary Picture Cards Set One

family 	parents 
children 	cat 
dog 	

parents	family
cat	children
	dog

Optional Family Member Vocabulary Picture Cards

brother

sister

grandmother

grandfather

father

mother

sister	brother
grandfather	grandmother
mother	father

FAMILY

FAMILY

grandmother	grandfather	mother	father

girl	boy	sister	brother

baby	cat	dog	fish
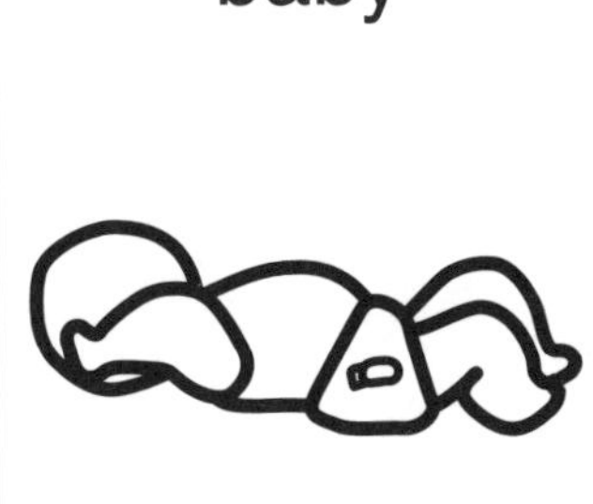			

Cat Description Pictures/Symbols

soft	mouse
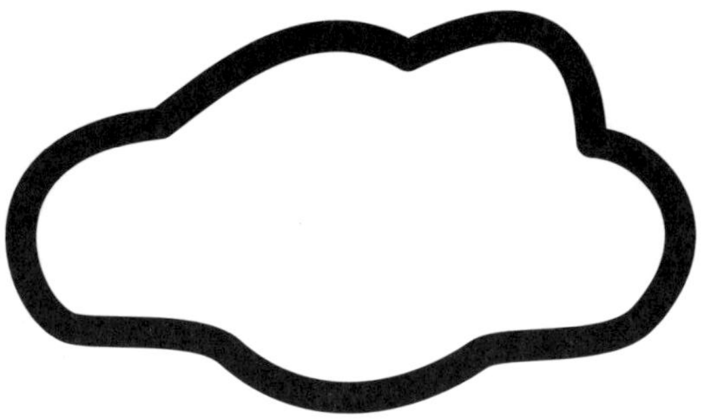	
milk	sleep

love	yarn

- A cat is soft.
- A cat chases a mouse.
- A cat drinks milk.
- A cat sleeps a lot.
- A cat gives love.
- A cat plays with yarn.

tail 	paw 
ears 	eyes 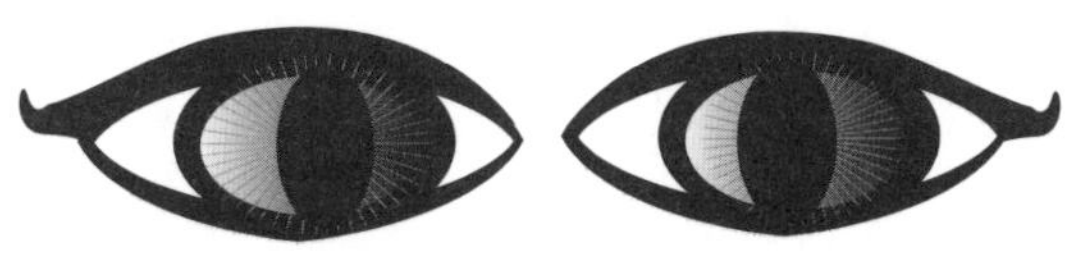
nose 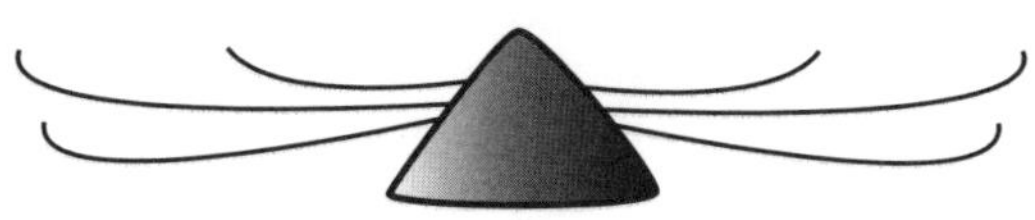	tongue 

"Is everybody ready to make a cool looking cat?"

"First, **staple** your little plate in front of your big plate. The little plate is the cat head, the big plate is the cat body."

"Next, **choose** different kinds of fabric you like."

"**Glue** the fabric squares on the back of the paper plates."

"Your cat needs to see. **Choose** two buttons for eyes. **Glue** the eyes on the cat's head."

"Your cat needs to smell. **Choose** a pom-pom for the nose. **Glue** it in the center of the cat's face."

"Next, **get** a red tongue and **glue** it on. Your cat needs to drink milk!"

"Your cat needs ears to hear! **Choose** two triangles and **glue** them on the top of the cat's head."

"The whiskers are next. **Choose** a color yarn. **Cut** the yarn into strips and **glue** them on the cat's face, near its nose. **Glue** on six whiskers."

"How will your cat run around? He needs feet! **Count** out four clothespins. Clip them onto the body of your cat, at the bottom. These are feet."

"The last thing is a tail. **Choose** a color pipe cleaner. **Staple** it on the back of the cat's body."

"Now you have a Calico Cat!"

Cat Show Award Template

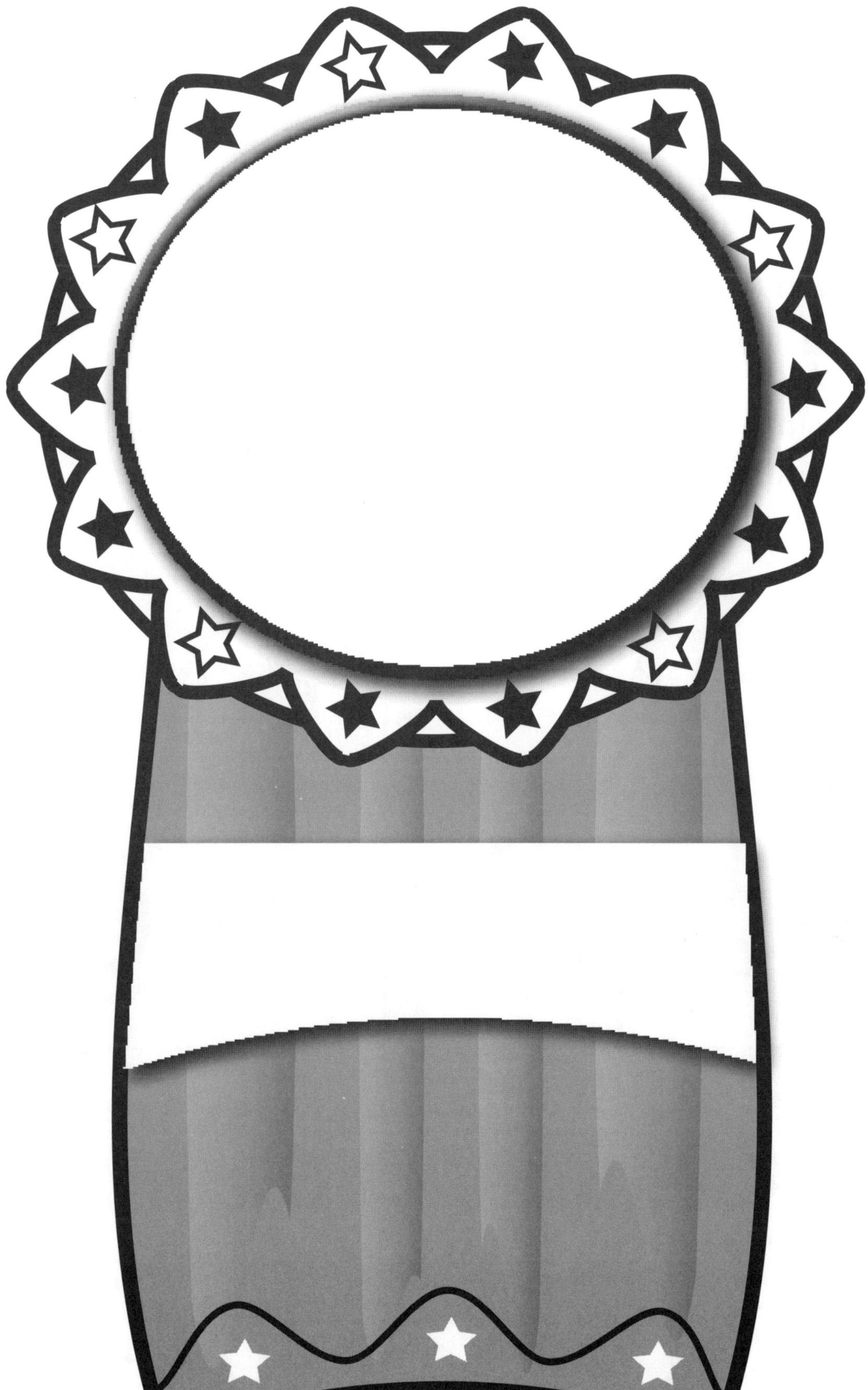

Dog Questions

- What does a dog eat?
- What does a dog drink?
- Where does a dog live?
- Where does a dog go to the bathroom?
- Who does a dog love?
- What does a dog wag when he's happy?
- What does a dog need when he's dirty and smelly?
- What do we use to take a dog for a walk?
- What does a dog use to shake your hand?
- What does a dog have that keeps it warm?

Dog Picture Cards

The Big Dog in the Pet Shop

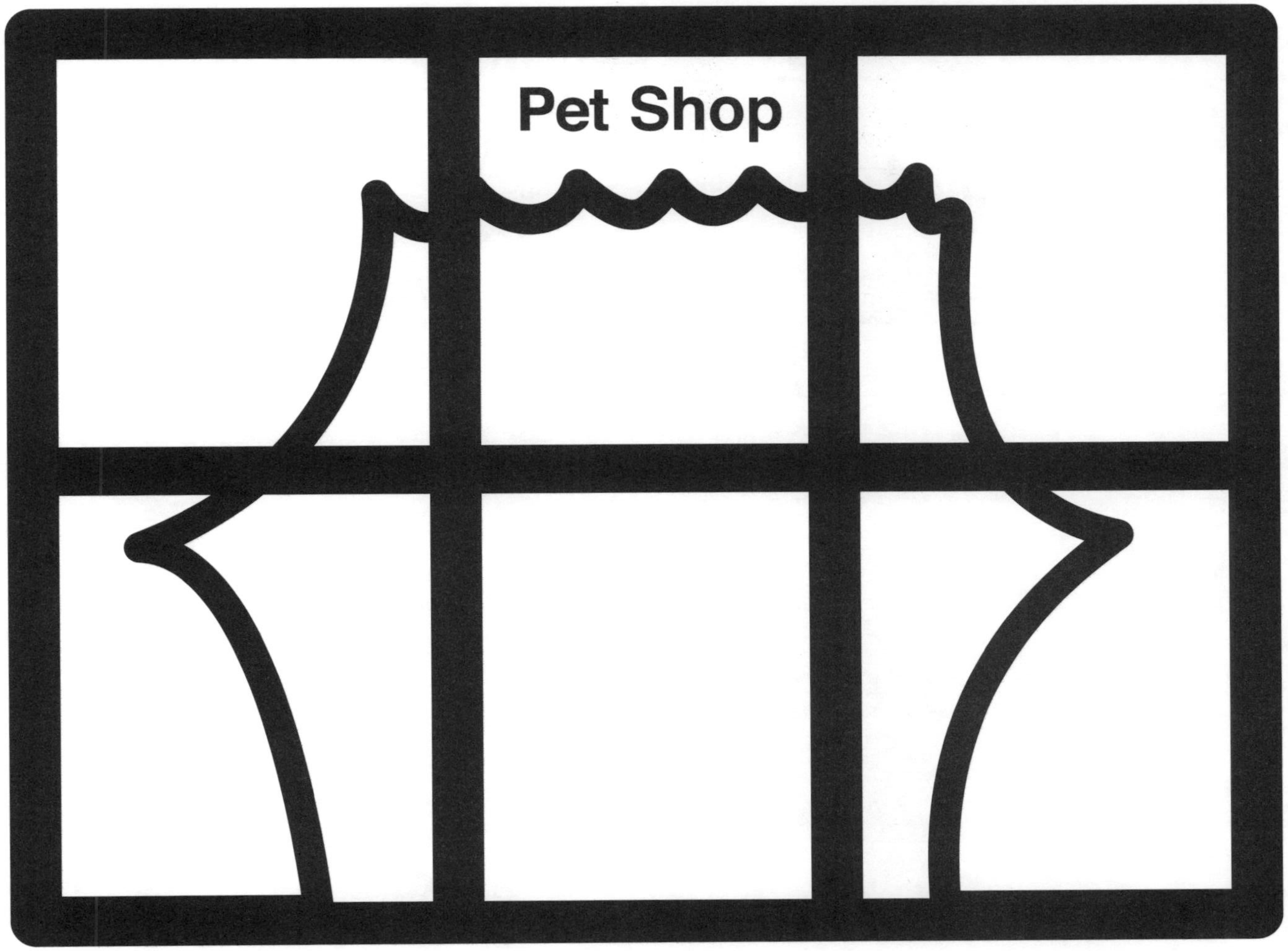

What color is the big dog in the Pet Shop?
The one with the long skinny tail.
What color is the big dog in the Pet Shop?
I do hope the big dog's for sale.

The big dog in the Pet Shop is (black).
He's the dog with the long skinny tail.
The big dog in the Pet Shop is (black).
I do hope the big dog's for sale.

Dear Parents: Please help your child write down the names of each member of their family, under the correct category heading. For the purpose of this activity, "family" may be defined as the people and pets who live with your child. Please return by ______. Thank you. Sincerely, ____________________

People in My Family

adults

____

____

____

____

____

children

____

____

____

____

Pets in My Family

dog

____

____

____

cat

____

____

____

other

____

____

Parent Interview

Dear Parents,

Our class is learning about the word "parent." Students are learning about what's different between the things children did and liked when you were a kid and what children do and like now. The students are going to interview a parent using these questions. Please help your child to write the answers that you give. Also, please take a few minutes to discuss with your child some memories that you have of your childhood. If you have any pictures of yourself as a child that you would be willing to send in for a few days, that would be great! Thanks for your help with this project.

Sincerely,

____

1. What place did you grow up in?

____

2. What did you like about school?

____

3. What chores or jobs did you have?

____

4. What music or song did you like?

____

5. Did you have a favorite food?

____

6. Do you remember something special?

____

My name is ______________________________.

The person I interviewed is

______________________________.

1. My parent grew up in a place called ______________________________.

2. Something my parent liked about school was ______________________.

3. The chores my parent had as a child were ______________________.

4. The music my parent liked as a child was ______________________.

5. My parent's favorite food as a child was______________________.

6. What my parent remembers about being a child is______________________ ______________________________.

1	The first thing I want to do is	☐ .
2	The next thing I want to do is	☐ .
3	The last thing I want to do is	☐ .

 puzzle	 books	 games
 music	 play dough	 paint
 dress up	 snack	 ball
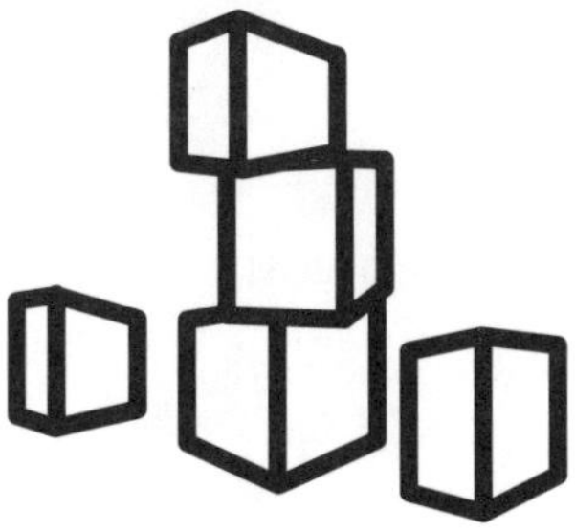 blocks	 toy cars	 make believe

A children's activity I did was ______________________________.

The children I did this with were ____________________________

____.

When I did this I felt ____________________.

The thing I liked most about the activity was___________________

____.

- -

Children's Activities Response Sheet Directions

1. **Read** the first sentence. **Select** the activity that was your favorite.
2. **Write** the name of that activity on the first line.
3. **Read** the next sentence.
4. **Say** and **write** the names of the children that were doing the activity with you.
5. **Read** the next sentence.
6. **Say** and **write** a feeling word that describes how you were feeling during the activity.
7. **Read** the next sentence.
8. **Write** what you liked about the activity.
9. On another sheet of paper, **draw** a picture of yourself doing one of the activities.

Cat Activities Script

Cat Indoor Activities Language Board

"The cat is hiding under the table."
"The cat is sleeping in the boy's lap."
"The cat is running away from the dog."
"The cat is watching the mouse."
"The cat is sleeping on the sofa."
"The cat jumps on top of the table."
"The cat is drinking some water."
"The cat is playing with the dog."

Cat Outdoor Activities Language Board

"The cat is running through the grass."
"The cat is climbing up the tree."
"The cat is jumping up to catch a butterfly."
"The cat is watching the snake in the grass."
"The cat is sleeping at the top of the tree."
"The cat is sleeping under the tree."
"The cat is watching the birds."
"The cat is rolling in the grass."

Cat Indoor Activities Language Board

Cat Indoor Activities Language Board

Cat Outdoor Activities Language Board

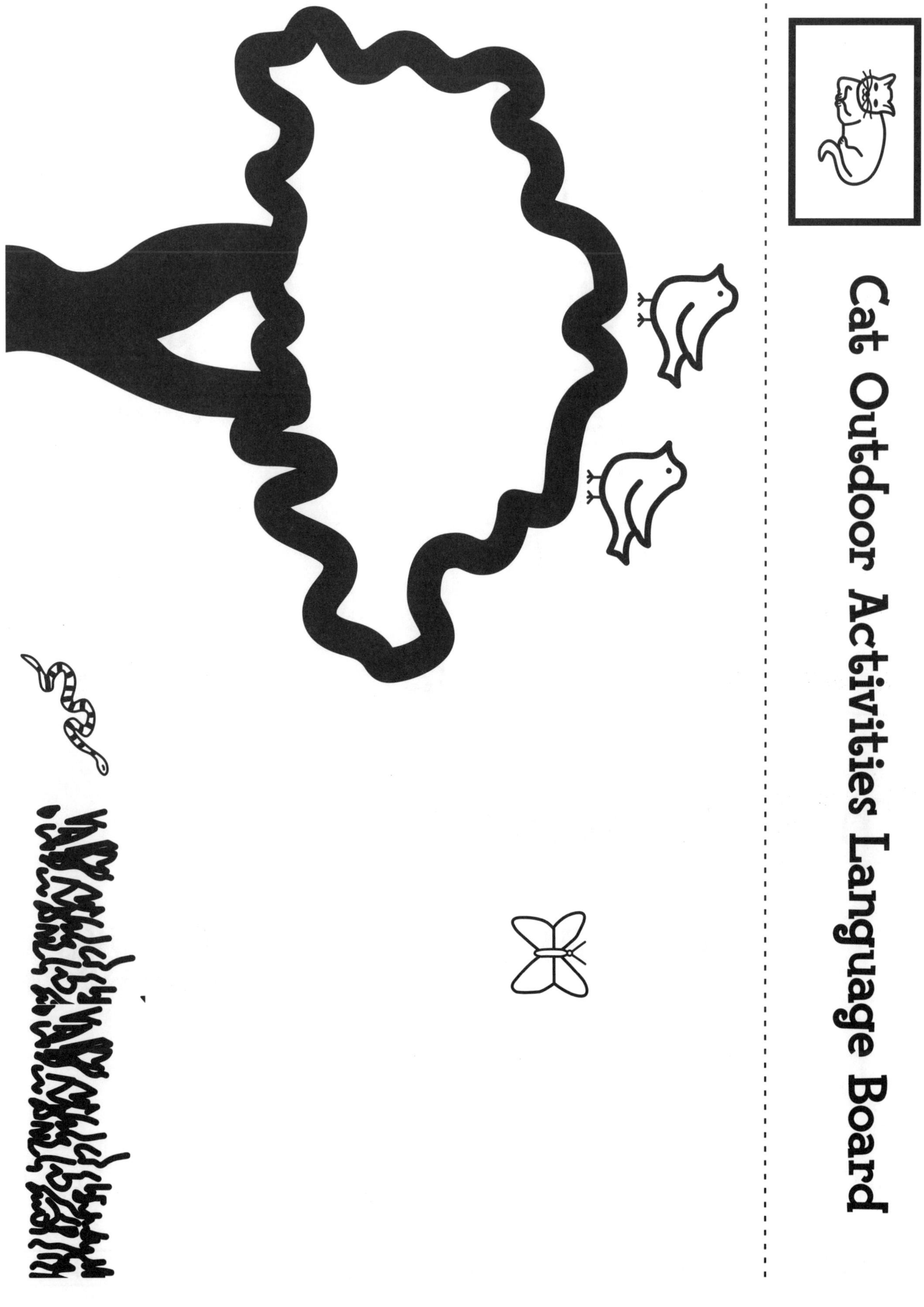

Cat Outdoor Activities Language Board

The cat is sleeping

_____ the sofa.

The cat is climbing

_____ the tree.

The cat is hiding

_________ the table.

The cat is walking

_____ the grass.

The cat is drinking

water _______ her dish.

from	under	on	in	up

Cat Activity Sentences

Dog Responsibility Cards

dog food

Feed the dog. Pour food into a dish and **tell** the dog, "Supper!"

water

Give the dog water. Pour water into the dish and put the dish on the floor.

doctor

Take the dog to the pet doctor. Pick up the dog and bring the dog to the VET sign.

brush

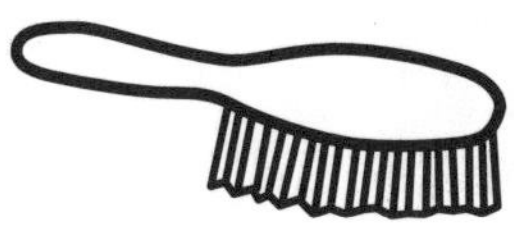

Brush the dog. Pick up the brush and brush the back of the dog.

ball

Play ball with the dog. Throw the ball and **tell** the dog, "Fetch!"

leash

Walk the dog. Put the leash on the dog and take the dog for a walk.

love

Love the dog. Give the dog a big hug.

pet

Pet the dog. Put your hand on the dog and pet the dog.

talk

Talk to the dog. Say nice things to the dog. **Say**, "Good dog!"

outside

Let the dog outside. Open up the door and **say**, "Go outside."

Dog Responsibility Cards

WORD WALL WORDS

SET ONE

we

have

the

WORD WALL WORDS
SENTENCE COMPLETION ACTIVITY

______ like to play with our new dog.

My family likes to go to ________ lake.

I __________ a black cat with gray stripes.

have	We	the

Mind Reader Script

"Are you ready for a clue for the first word?"
"It's a word on the word wall."
"This word has four letters."
"It fits in the sentence, 'I ________ one brother and a sister.' "
"This word begins with the letter 'h.' "
"Which word wall word is it?"

"Here comes the next word!"
"This is also a word on the word wall."
"This word only has two letters."
"It fits in the sentence, '__ have three people in our family.' "
"It begins with the letter 'w.' "
"Which word wall word is it?"

"It's time for the last word."
"This word is another word on the word wall."
"This word has three letters."
"The word begins with the letter 't.' "
"This word fits in the sentence, 'What is ______ name of your cat?' "
"Which word wall word is it?

"The Parent Says" Script

"The parent says, 'Pick up a red crayon and **write** the word 'we.' "

"The parent says, '**Look** at this word and **say** it in a big voice!' "
(Hold up any of the words.)

"**Look** at your words and touch the word 'have.' "

"The parent says, 'Pick any color crayon and **write** the word 'the.' "

"The parent says, '**Clap/chant** the word 'have.' "

"The parent says, '**Get** the word "we" off of the word wall and **show** it to the class.' "

"The parent says, 'Listen to this sentence: "_____ are tired."
Write the word that fits in the blank.' "

"**Count** and **say** how many letters are in the word 'the.' "

________________ likes

____________________.

________________ likes

____________________.

________________ likes

____________________.

Family Chain Pictures/Symbols

shout 	dance 	count 
laugh 	jump 	read 
write 	spell 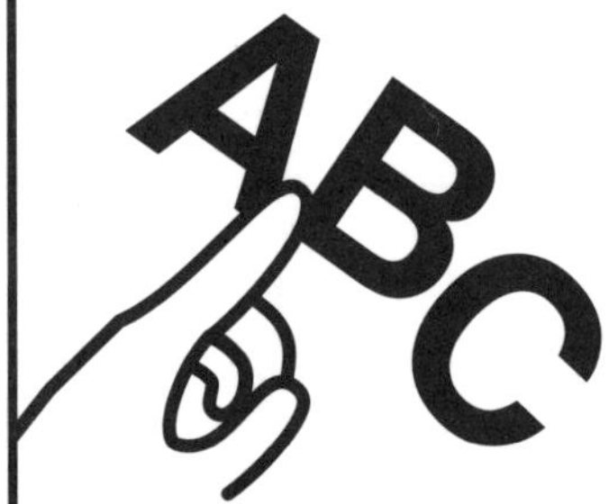	color 

Children's Activity Cards

Cat Cookie Ingredient Cards

cookies

frosting

pretzel

candy

chocolate

plate

Spread frosting on the cookie.

Put on two chocolates for ears.

Put on two green candies for eyes.

Cat Cookie Recipe Cards (1)

Put on one red candy for the nose.

Put on six pretzels for whiskers.

Put on five red candies for the mouth.

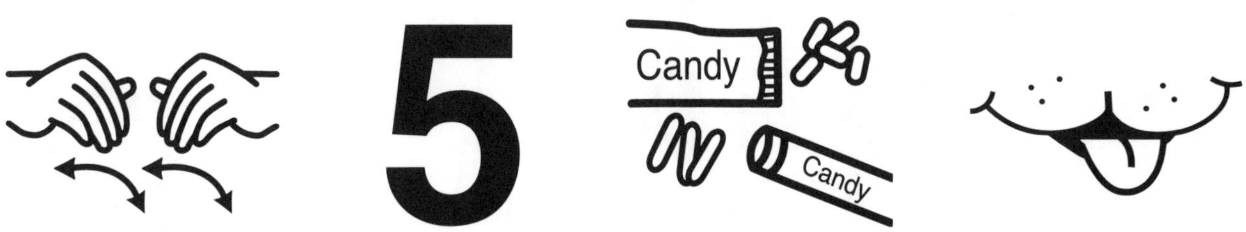

Cat Cookie Recipe Cards (2)

The Park

people

Game Piece

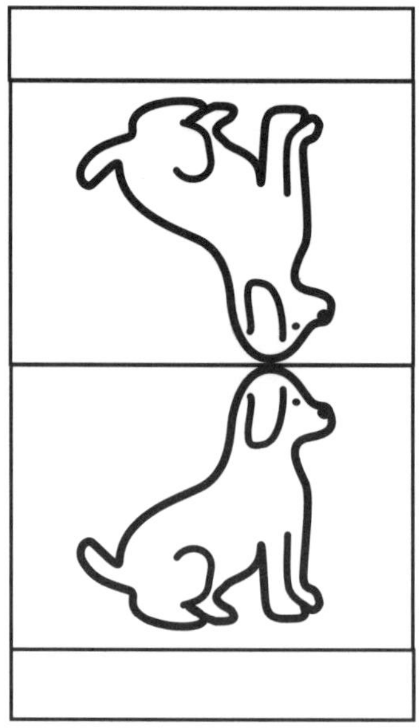

The Doghouse

dog

Sample Game Board

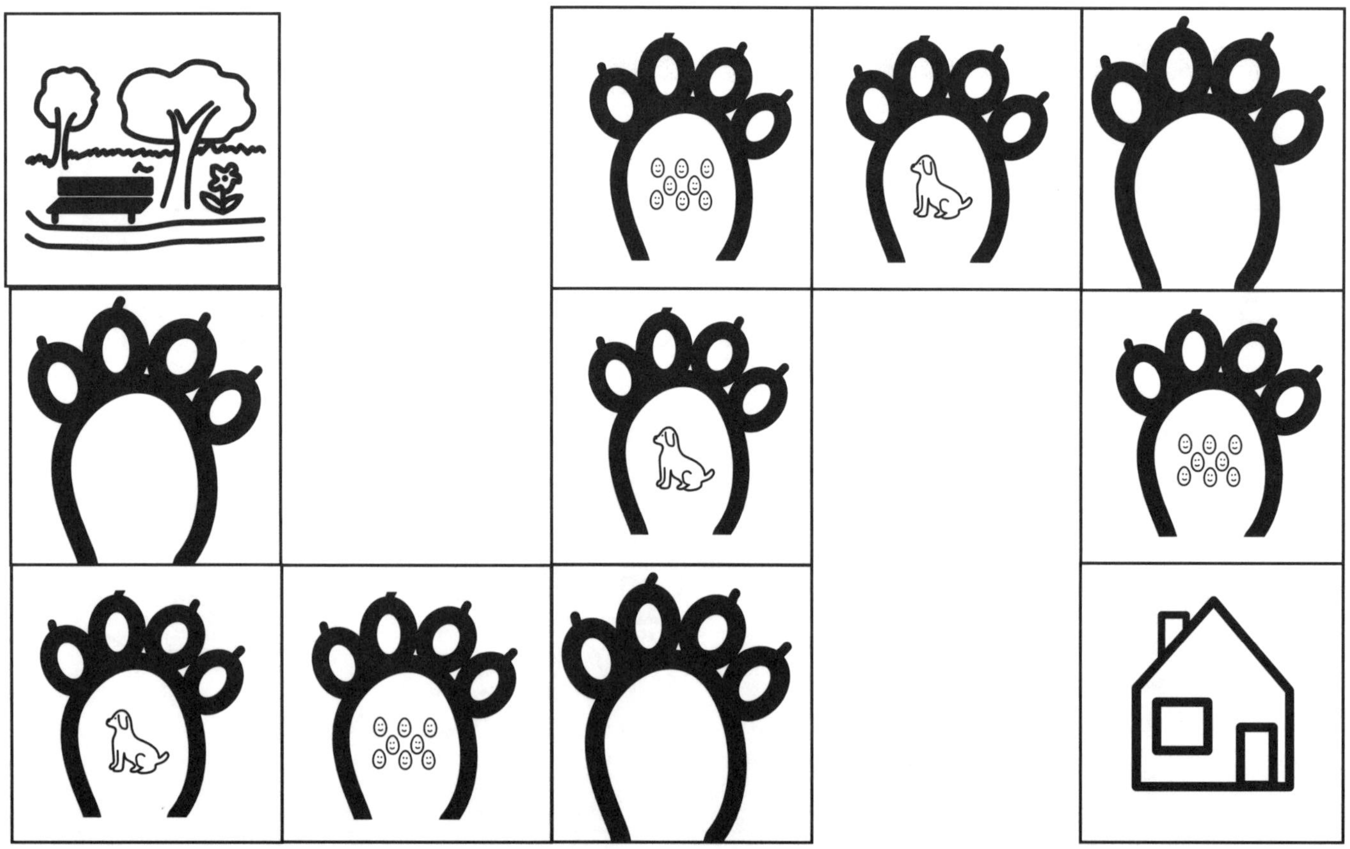

Game Patterns

You and your friends walk around looking for your dog. Move ahead 2 spaces.	Your dad puts an ad in the paper about your lost dog. Move ahead 3 spaces.
Somebody calls about your dog. You don't call them back. Move back 1 space.	You won't help your brother make posters about your dog. Move back 2 spaces.
You watch a TV show and don't look for your dog. Move back 3 spaces.	You don't let your friends help look for your dog. Move back 2 spaces.

People Game Cards (1)

You put a poster up about your lost dog. Move ahead 3 spaces.	You bring a bag of treats and call for your dog. Move ahead 2 spaces.
You call the humane society to ask about your dog. Move ahead 1 space.	You and your parent drive around looking for your dog. Move ahead 2 spaces.
You call your friends and ask them to help you find your dog. Move ahead 3 spaces.	You show people pictures of your dog and ask them to look for him. Move ahead 2 spaces.

Your dog hears you calling and runs your way. Move ahead 2 spaces.	Your dog chases a squirrel to the park. Move back 2 spaces.
Your dog stops to chase his tail. Move back 3 spaces.	Your dog sees a lake and goes for a swim. Move back 2 spaces.
Your dog digs in a big dirt pile to bury his bone. Move back 1 space.	Your dog misses you and runs toward home. Move ahead 2 spaces.

Dog Game Cards (1)

Your dog sleeps in the sun at the park. Move back 2 spaces.	Your dog sits down and scratches his ear. Move back 1 space.
Your dog comes to you when you call him. Move ahead 3 spaces.	Your dog is wearing a tag with your phone number on it. Move ahead 1 space.
Your dog does not run away when your friend calls his name. Move ahead 1 space.	Your dog runs into the woods. Move back 3 spaces.

Family Description Picture Cards

silly 	busy 	loving 
curious 	fun 	healthy 
________	________	________

My family is

__________________.

My family is

__________________.

Thank You book Direction Script

1. "Is everybody ready to make a Thank You book for your parent(s)?"

2. "Get out your scissors. **Cut** each paper down the middle on the dotted line."

3. "Now find page one. Let's **read** the sentence together."

4. "Think of something you like that your parent(s) cooks for you."

5. "**Write** that on the line."

6. "Now **draw** a picture of that food, or a picture of your parent(s) cooking that food."

7. "Now find page two. Let's **read** the sentence together."

8. "Think of a chore that your parent(s) does."

9. "**Write** that on the line."

10. "Now **draw** a picture of that chore or a picture of your parent(s) doing that chore."

11. "Now find page three. Let's **read** the sentence together."

12. "Think of a place that your parent(s) takes you."

13. "**Write** that on the line."

14. "Now **draw** a picture of that place or a picture of your parent(s) taking you there."

15. "Now find page four. Let's **read** the sentence together."

16. "Think of something special that you like to do with your parent(s)."

17. "**Write** that on the line."

18. "Now **draw a picture** of you and your parent(s) doing that thing together."

19. "We need a cover. Get out the page that says, Thank You. **Write** your parent's name on the top line, and your name on the bottom line."

20. "Use the crayons/markers to **draw** and **color** decorations on the cover. Now fold the page, so it's like a book."

21. "Let's put the book together. Find page four. Put page three on top of page four. Put page two on the top of page three. Put page one on top of page two. Put the pages inside the book cover."

22. "Get the stapler and **staple** the book together. Now bring it home to your parent!"

Dear________________

THANK YOU!

Thank you for all
you do for me.

Love,

____

Thank you for cooking

____

for me! It tastes really good!

1

Thank you for doing the

chore of ______________ for

our family.

2

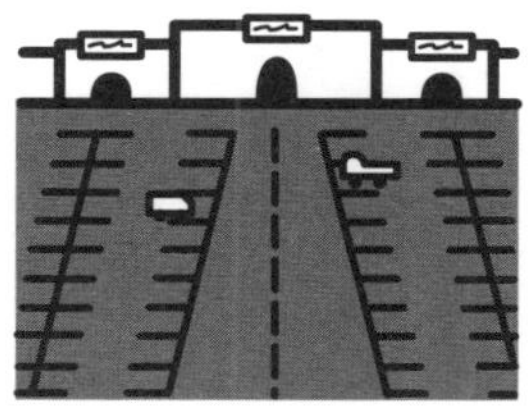

Thank you for taking me

to ______________________!

I like going there!

3

Thank you for spending

time with me and doing

____

with me.

4

Artwork Description

My name is ______________________________.

The name of my artwork is ____________________.

This is a picture of ___________________________.

I used the color(s) ___________________________.

I painted this because ______________________.

Artwork Description

My name is ______________________________.

The name of my artwork is ____________________.

This is a picture of ___________________________.

I used the color(s) ___________________________.

I painted this because ______________________.

"That Crazy Cat!" Book Direction Script

"We're going to make a book about a cat who does some crazy things!"
"First cut each of your pages in half, on the dotted line."
"Now, find the page that says, 'That Crazy Cat!' "
"**Choose** a piece of construction paper. Fold it in half, like a book."
"**Glue** the box on the front of the folded paper, so the title is near the paper fold."
"Find the word 'by' and **write** your name on the line. You will be the author."
"Set the book cover aside. Find book page one and book pictures one."
"Let's **read** page one together. 'One day the cat jumps in a ______. That crazy cat!' "
"**Look** at the pictures. Those are all things your crazy cat can jump in to go someplace."
"**Choose** a kind of transportation you want your cat to jump in."
"**Color** that picture, and **cut** it out. **Glue** it in the box on the page, and **write** the word on the blank line."
"Now flip that page over. Find book page two and book pictures two."
"Let's **read** page two together. 'The cat goes for a ride to the _____. That crazy cat!' "
"**Look** at the pictures. Those are all places your crazy cat may want to go."
"**Choose** a place that you want your cat to go."
"**Color** that picture, and **cut** it out. **Glue** it in the box on the page, and **write** the word on the blank line."
"Now flip that page over. Find book page three and book pictures three."
"Let's **read** page three together. 'The cat eats lunch at __________. That crazy cat!' "
"**Look** at the pictures. Those are all places where your crazy cat may want to eat lunch. This cat is crazy because this cat eats in restaurants!"
"**Choose** a place where you want your cat to eat lunch."
"**Color** that picture, and **cut** it out. **Glue** it in the box on the page, and **write** the word on the blank line."
"Now flip that page over. Find book page four and book pictures four."
"Let's **read** page four together. 'The cat sleeps on ________. That crazy cat!' "
"**Look** at the pictures. Your crazy cat is tired and will want a cat nap! Where will your cat sleep?"
"**Choose** a place where your cat will sleep."
"**Color** that picture, and **cut** it out. **Glue** it in the box on the page, and **write** the word on the blank line."
"Now we need the cat. **Color** and **cut out** the cat picture. Put rough Velcro® on the back."
"Flip through each page, including the title, and put a piece of soft Velcro® on each black X."
"Now put the cat on the black X on the title page."
"Who wants to **read** your story first? When you **turn each page**, pick up your cat and move it to the X on the next page."

That Crazy Cat!

X

By ____________________

One day the cat jumps on a

________________.

That crazy cat!

X

1

The cat goes for a ride to the

________________.

That crazy cat!

X

2

The cat eats lunch at

______________.

That crazy cat!

X

3

The cat sleeps on the

______________.

That crazy cat!

X

4

"That Crazy Cat!" book pages

book pictures 1

book pictures 2

book pictures 3

the sandwich shop 	the ice cream shop 	McDonald's
the pizza parlor 	the coffee shop 	Taco Bell

book pictures 4

couch 	rug 	desk 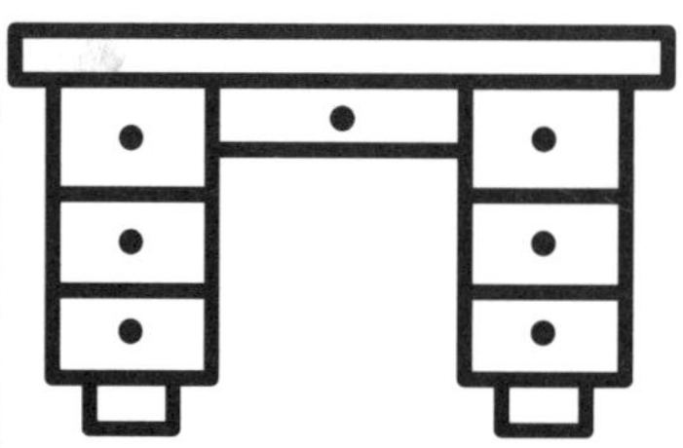
chair 	bed 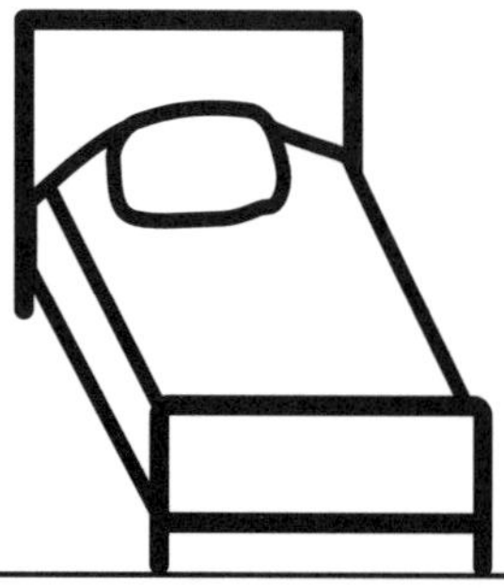	stairs 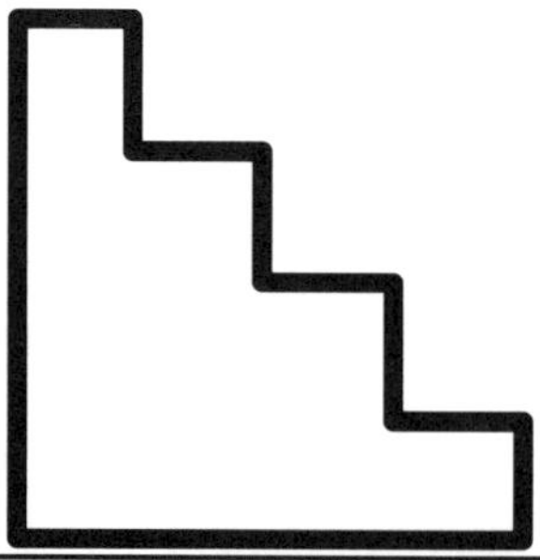

Dog Care Picture Cards

brush 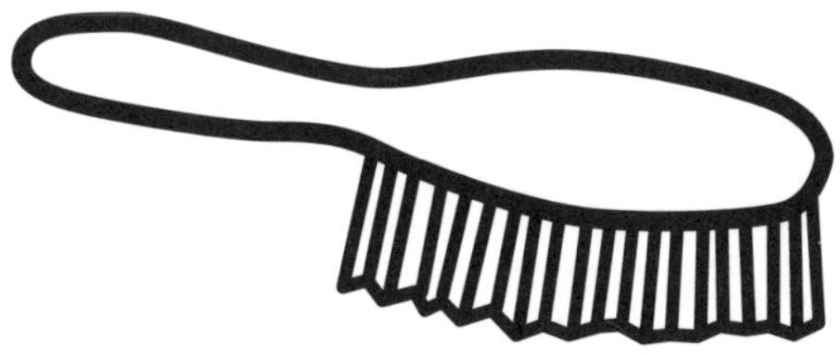	water 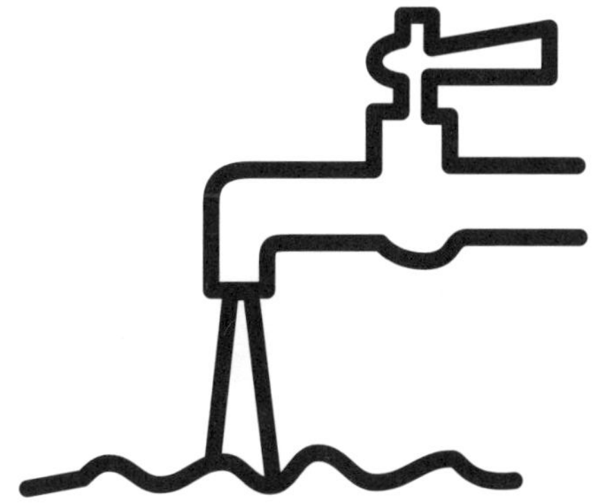
outside 	time 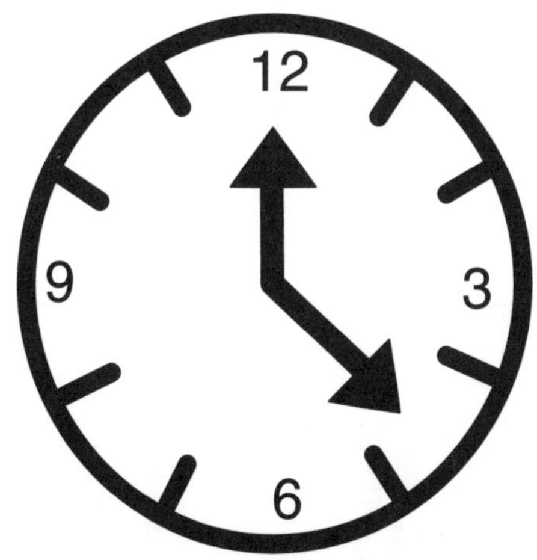
dog food 	walk 

1

Your dog has lots of fur.

You need to __________

your dog.

2

Your dog gets thirsty.

You need to give your

dog __________ every day.

3

Your dog gets hungry.

You need to give your

dog ________ every day.

4

Your dog needs

exercise. You need to

__________ your dog.

5

Your dog needs to go to the bathroom. You need to open the door and let your dog go ________.

6

Your dog needs love.

You need to spend

________ with your dog.

Vocabulary Picture Cards Set Two

Vocabulary Picture Cards Set Two

eat

work

go

play

live

work	eat
play	go
	live

Parent Letter

Dear Parents,

We are going to be learning about the things that we do with our families.

In one of our lessons, we will be telling each other about one place we go with our family. Would you please talk with your child about the places your family goes and help him/her decide on one of those places they would like to share with the class? Please help your child write down the name of the place, and the transportation used to get there, on the bottom of this form. If you have a photo of that place, a photo of your family on an outing to that place, or an item related to that place (such as a McDonald's bag if your family loves to go to McDonald's), please send that in with your child as well. All items sent in will be returned.

In another lesson we will be sharing with each other about the places we live, and the people who live with us. Please send one or more photos of the home in which your child lives. It could be a photo of the outside of the home or a photo of any part of the inside of the home. Please also send in one or more photos of the person or people that live with your child. On the bottom of this form there is a place for you and your child to write his/her address and one special thing about the place where they live. This could be anything your child would like to share, and can be about the things in their home, the people in their home, their neighbors, or the things that their family does together in their home.

Thank you so much for your help.

Sincerely,

____

- -

Student Name ____________________

A Place I Go With My Family

A place I go with my family is ______________________________.

The transportation we use to get there is ______________________________.

I like to go here with my family because ______________________________.

The Place Where I Live With My Family

The address of where I live is ______________________________.

One special thing about the place where I live is______________________________

____.

wash dishes	wipe table	sweep

dust	laundry	clean room

Work Stations Materials and Preparation

MATERIALS:

- **Wash dishes**: dishes with something to make them "dirty" such as mustard and ketchup
- **Wipe table**: sponge or cloth with bucket and soapy water
- **Sweep**: broom and dustpan
- **Dust**: dust cloths or duster
- **Laundry**: clothes basket with items that need to be folded
- **Clean room**: various toys, books, etc. to scatter

PREPARATION:

- **Wash dishes**: Put the dirty dishes in a bin, and put them near the sink, or near a bin of clean water if a sink is not available. Have a towel or drying rack that the dryer can put the dishes on after the dishes have been dried.
- **Wipe the table**: Put the sponge or cloth in a shallow bucket of soapy water. Designate a table that needs to be washed.
- **Sweep:** Set out broom and dustpan. Put some visible items to be swept on the floor, like wrappers.
- **Dust**: Make a list of things in the classroom that need to be dusted.
- **Laundry**: Set out a basket with easy to fold items, such as towels and washcloths that need to be folded.
- **Clean room**: Scatter some things around the room so they are visibly out of order.

Student Script

"Hi! Our job is to (wash and dry the dishes)."
"How about you (wash) and I (dry)?"
"Are you ready?"
"OK - (here's the first dish)!"
"Be sure and (rinse it good)!"

Place Picture Cards #1

Place Picture Cards #1

Place Picture Cards #2

play 	motel 	museum 
fishing 	parade 	fireworks 
city 	cabin 	campground 
Taco Bell TACO BELL®	circus 	Target TARGET.

Place Picture Cards #2

Transportation Picture Cards

Transportation Picture Cards

train 	airplane 	motor home 
boat 	bus 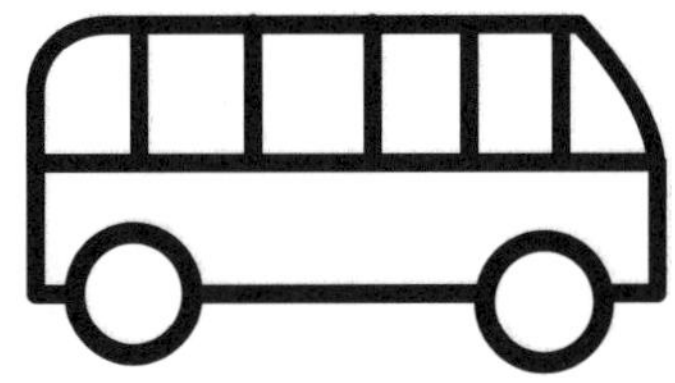	taxi 
van 	car 	pickup truck 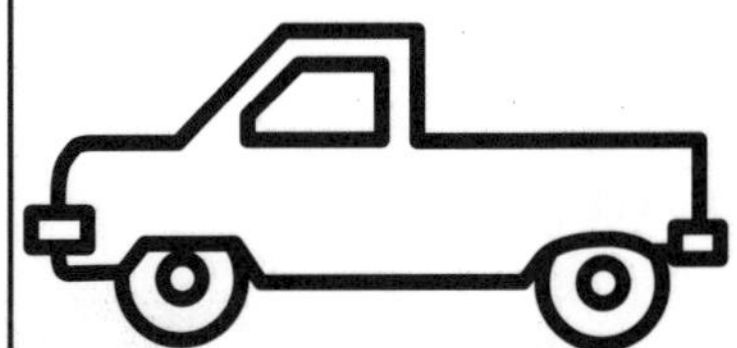
walk 	roller blades 	bicycle 

catch	cards

game	puzzle

build	play dough
	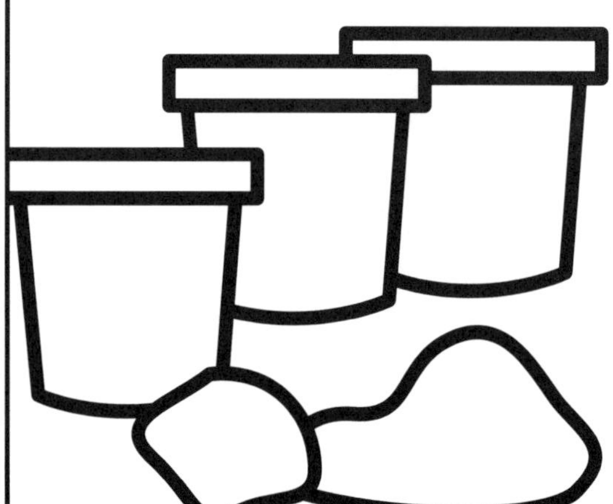

Tableware Picture Cards

plate

glass

knife

fork

spoon

napkin

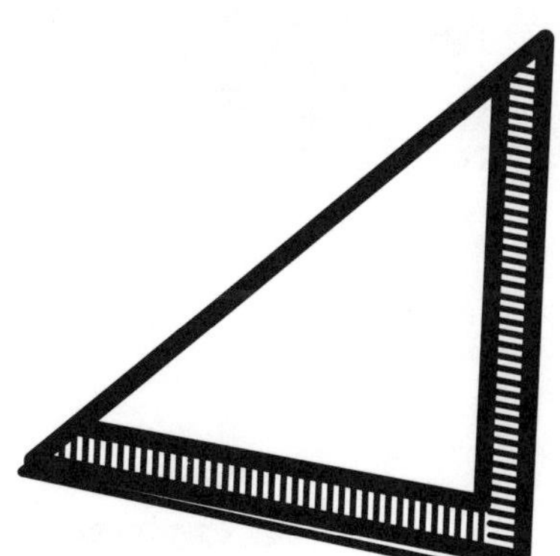

Tableware Templates

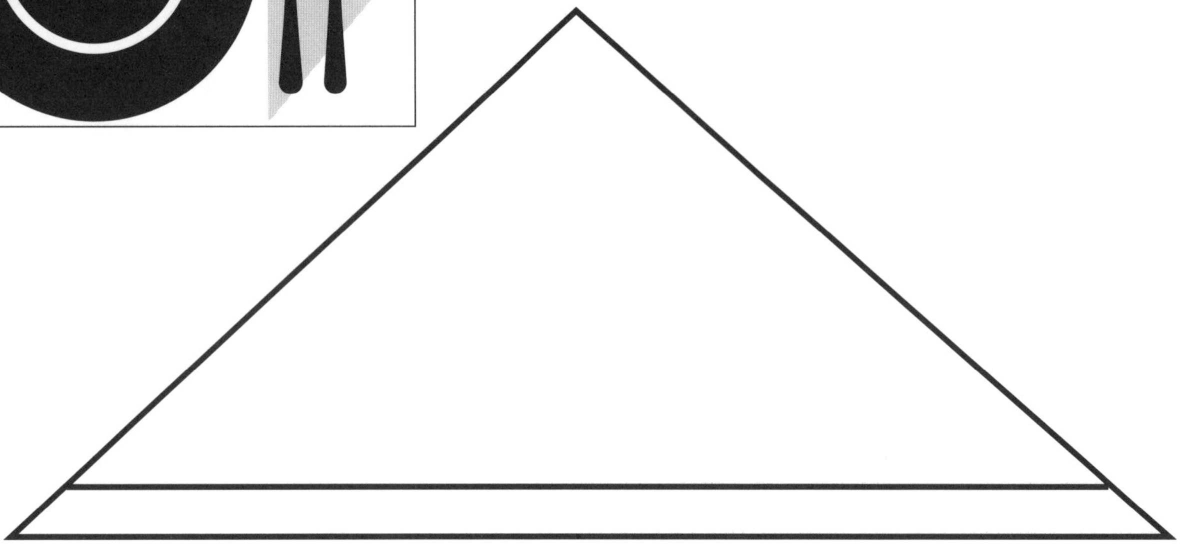

Game #1 - Sack Pack

"The first game is called Sack Pack."
"When your family goes to the grocery store, you need to pack the groceries in the grocery sack."
"Each family team will get a paper grocery sack and a grocery list."
"Before we start, let's **read** the name of each food on the grocery list."
"When it's your turn, go up to the grocery table."
"**Look** at the first food picture on the grocery list. **Identify** that food."
"Pick it up and put it in the grocery sack."
"**Mark** an X on that food picture on the list."
"**Tell** the next person, 'It's your turn now.' "
"The first team to get all their food items in the grocery sack wins the game."
"Line up single file with your team!"
"We'll have a practice round to learn what to do, and then a real round!"
"Are you ready?"
OPTION: After the student identifies the item, put it on the edge of the table and the grocery bag on the floor. A student can push it over the edge of the table and into the grocery sack.
A switch-adapted, battery-operated moving toy can also be **turned on** and used to push the item off of the table and into the sack.

Game #2 - Laundry Toss

"This next game is called Laundry Toss."
"Dirty clothes go in the laundry basket so they can be washed."
"Each family team will have a list of clothes that are dirty and need to got in the laundry basket."
"Each family team will have a laundry basket that the dirty clothes go in."
"When it's your turn, **look** at the clothes picture on the list. **Identify** that type of clothing."
"Pick it up and put it in the laundry basket."
"**Mark** an X on that clothes picture on the list."
"**Tell** the next person, 'It's your turn now.' "
"The first family team to get all of the dirty clothes on their list put in the basket wins the game!"
"Gather around your team's pile of clothes."
"We'll have a practice round and then a real round."
OPTION: Roll and tie up shirts, pants, socks, etc. so they are in more of a three dimensional shape. Put the clothing item on the edge of the table and have students push the item off of the table and into the laundry basket.

Grocery List

cereal

bread

ketchup

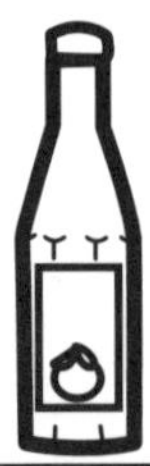

soup

potato

butter

Laundry List

T-shirt

pants

socks

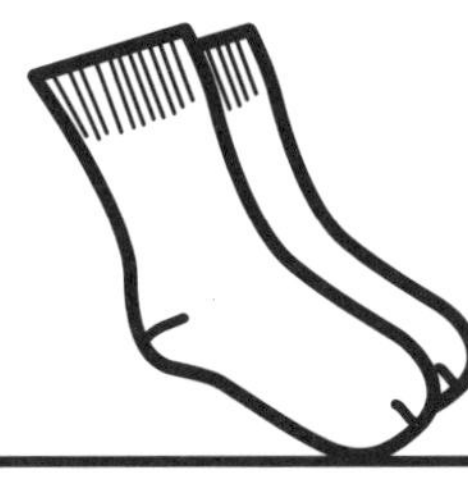

sweater

shorts

jacket

book page 1

We put ____________ in the ____________.

We put ____________________

in the bag.

book page 2a

We put ________________

in the basket.

park

grocery store

library

movies

zoo

mall

Treasure Hunt Place Pictures/Symbols

Clue #1

Go to the park and

pick up trash on the ground.

Under an old soda can,

is where a clue will be found.

Clue #2

Go to the library and

look for a book.

6

The clue is on page six,

that's where you should look.

Clue #3

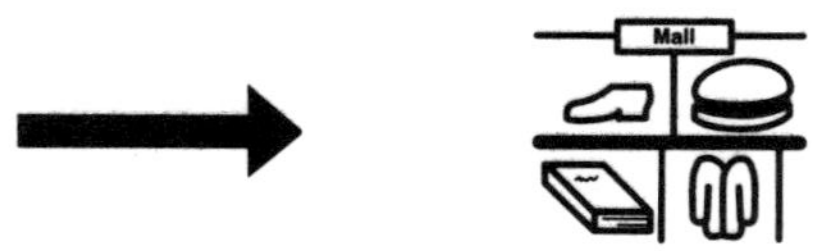

Go to the mall and

find a shoe.

Look inside,

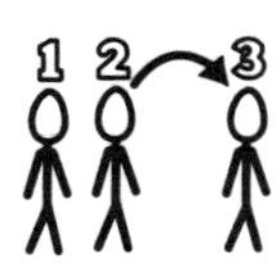

for the very next clue.

Clue #4

Go to the grocery store and

pick up the bread.

Look close and you'll find,

a clue to be read.

Clue #5

Where's the next clue?

Do you want to know?

Then the movie theatre,

is the place you need to go.

Clue #6

Go to the zoo and

find a big, fat bear.

Look behind him,

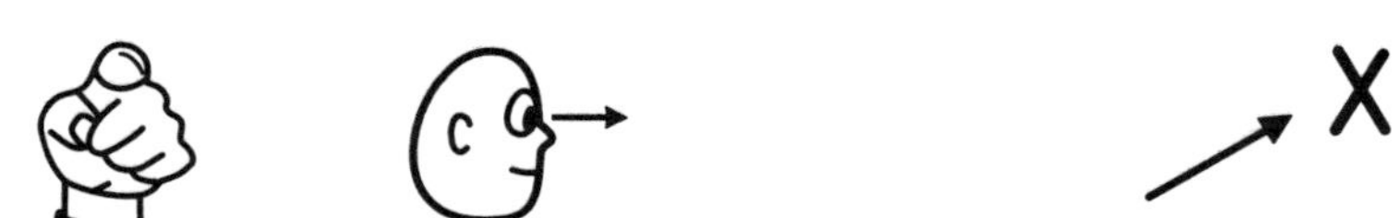

you will see treasure there!

Red Light Green Light

1. The children pretend to be cars on a road.
2. There is one traffic officer.
3. The traffic officer will show a red or green light.
4. If the cars see a green light, they can go and move toward the FINISH line.
5. When they see a red light, they need to stop.
6. If the traffic officer sees a car moving during a red light, that car has to go back to START.
7. The first car to get to the FINISH line wins the game.

Musical Chairs

1. The children begin in a circle, in a chair or on a piece of colored paper on the floor.
2. One child turns on the music.
3. An adult takes a chair away.
4. The children move around the inside of the circle.
5. When the music stops, the children sit down or move to a piece of colored paper.
6. The child without a chair or paper is out of the game.
7. The game continues until there is only one student.

Drop the Handkerchief

1. The children begin in a circle on chairs or on the floor.
2. Children spin or draw for a child name.
3. That child takes the handkerchief and moves around the outside of the circle.
4. When the child arrives at the student of their choice, he/she drops the handkerchief in their lap.
5. The child who received the handkerchief gets up and chases the first child around the circle.
6. The child who now has the handkerchief moves around the circle and drops the handkerchief.

WORD WALL WORDS

SET TWO

do

see

are

WORD WALL WORDS
SENTENCE COMPLETION ACTIVITY

I _____ not like to wash the dishes.

Do you want to _______ my new bike?

We ____________ going to the zoo today.

see	do	are

Mind Reader Script

"I'm ready with a clue for the first word!"
"It's a word on the word wall."
"This word has three letters."
"It fits in the sentence, 'There ______ three people in my family.' "
"This word begins with the letter 'a.' "
"Which word wall word is it?"

"Get ready for word number two!"
"This is also a word on the word wall."
"This word also has three letters."
"It fits in the sentence, 'I _____ a cat up in the tree!' "
"It begins with the letter 's.' "
"Which word wall word is it?"

"This is the very last word."
"This word is another word on the word wall."
"This word has only two letters."
"The word begins with the letter 'd.' "
"This word fits in the sentence, 'What ___ you want to eat for lunch?' "
"Which word wall word is it?"

more	help	thank you

You ate all the food on your plate and you are still hungry. What do you say?	You would like another bowl of soup. What do you say?
You drank all of your milk. You would like another glass of milk. What do you say?	You ran out of ketchup for your French fries. What do you say?
You dropped your napkin and you can't reach it by yourself. What do you say?	Your grandma says that she likes the hat you have on. What do you say?
You would like some salad, but can't reach it. What do you say?	Somebody passes you the butter that you asked for. What do you say?
You want butter on your bread but can't spread it by yourself. What do you say?	Your dad just put a big piece of cake on your plate. What do you say?
You have meat on your plate and can't cut it by yourself. What do you say?	You ask your mom for more milk. She pours you another glass. What do you say?

I've Been Working With My Family

home song sheet

(sung to the tune, "I've Been Working on the Railroad")

**I've been working with my family, all the morning long.
I've been working with my family, as we laugh and sing this song.
Can't you see us with our work rags? We make quite a crew!
Can't you hear my grandma saying, "We've got lots of work to do!"
Family work together, family work together, family work togeth-eth-eth-eth-er.**

**We've been working in the bathroom, all the morning long.
We've been working in the bathroom, as we laugh and sing this song.
Can't you see the bathtub shining, it's getting nice and clean!
Can't you hear my mother saying, "Scrub that mold it's green!"
Family scrub the toilet, family scrub the toilet, family scrub the toi-oi-oi-oi-let!**

**We've been working in the garden, all the morning long.
We've been working in the garden, as we laugh and sing this song.
Can't you hear my father asking, "Who wants to help me dig?"
Can't you see the veggies growing? They're getting nice and big!
Family pull those weeds, family pull those weeds, family pull those we-ee-ee-ee-eeds.**

**We've been working in the kitchen, all the morning long.
We've been working in the kitchen, as we laugh and sing this song.
Can't you see the cookies baking? Are they almost done?
Can't you hear my brother asking, "May I have just one?"
Family are you hungry? Family are you hungry? Family are you hun-un-un-un-gry?**

family	bathroom	garden	kitchen

Dear Parents,

We are studying about family, and learning about different chores that families need to do.
We are going to be learning, singing, and acting out this fun song about working together as a family!
Please read through and practice this song with your child.

We need some props for this song! Could you please send in a set of old chore clothes for your child? Also, if you have any of the following props that you could loan us for a few days, that would be great! We will need work rags, bathroom scrub brushes, garden gloves/hats, garden tools, fresh garden vegetables such as whole carrots, aprons, kitchen tools such as spatulas, and a cookie sheet with cookies! Please send them in by ____________________.

Thanks for your help!

Sincerely,

____

I've Been Working With My Family

class song sheet

(sung to the tune, "I've Been Working on the Railroad")

I've been working with my family, all the morning long.
I've been working with my family, as we laugh and sing this song.
(Sing while linking arms together, moving back and forth)
Can't you see us with our work rags? We make quite a crew!
(All students hold up a work rag)
Can't you hear my grandma saying, "We've got lots of work to do!"
(Female student says this line)
Family work together, family work together, family work togeth-eth-eth-eth-er.
(Sing while linking arms together, moving back and forth)

We've been working in the bathroom, all the morning long.
We've been working in the bathroom, as we laugh and sing this song.
(Sing while holding scrub brushes)
Can't you see the bathtub shining, it's getting nice and clean!
(Turn on and shine a flashlight)
Can't you hear my mother saying, "Scrub that mold it's green!"
(Female student says this line)
Family scrub the toilet, family scrub the toilet, family scrub the toi-oi-oi-oi-let!
(Sing while holding scrub brushes)

We've been working in the garden, all the morning long.
We've been working in the garden, as we laugh and sing this song.
(Sing while wearing garden gloves and hats, holding garden tools)
Can't you hear my father asking, "Who wants to help me dig?"
(Male student says this line)
Can't you see the veggies growing? They're getting nice and big!
(Hold up the veggies and show them to the audience)
Family pull those weeds, family pull those weeds, family pull those we-ee-ee-ee-eeds.
(Sing while wearing garden gloves and hats, holding garden tools)

We've been working in the kitchen, all the morning long.
We've been working in the kitchen, as we laugh and sing this song.
(Sing while wearing aprons, holding kitchen tools)
Can't you see the cookies baking? Are they almost done?
(Show cookies on a cookie sheet)
Can't you hear my brother asking, "May I have just one?"
(Male student says this line)
Family are you hungry? Family are you hungry? Family are you hun-un-un-un-gry?
(Sing while wearing aprons, holding kitchen tools)

family

bathroom

garden

kitchen

"I've Been Working With My Family" Teacher Directions

1. Direct students to put on their chore clothes.
2. Select one student to **say** the speaking line during the "can't you hear" verse and give that student the paper with the line written out.
3. Select another student to **show** the prop during the "can't you see" line and give him/her the prop. **NOTE:** During the family stanza, give each student a work rag to show during this line.
4. Show the students the sign indicating which stanza they are going to sing. Direct students to go to that sign area and get the props they will need for that part of the song. **NOTE:** Have a staff or student helper at the prop area, assisting students with the props.
5. Lead the students in **reading** through the song sheet, explaining to them what they are going to do while they are singing each verse. (See the class song sheet for specific directions.)
6. Students put on or hold the props as suggested in the class song sheet, and **sing** each verse.
7. During the "Can't you hear" line, cue the selected student to **read** the appropriate line.
8. During the "Can't you see" line, cue the selected student to **show** the appropriate prop.
9. Continue this same process for each of the other stanzas.

Song Picture Cards

"Name That Place" Game Directions Script

"Is everybody ready to play a fun game?"

"This game is called, 'Name That Place.' "

"You are going to play in a team."

"We'll take turns being the game show host."

"The game show host is going to **read** a description of a place to both teams."

"The description will tell you when or why you would go to this place with your family, and what you might do at that place."

"When the description has been read, the host **says**, 'Go!' "

"When each team knows the place that is being described, they should ring their bell."

"The host calls on the team who rang their bell first."

"That team has a chance to **say** the name of the place they think is being described."

"If they get it right, they get the point."

"If they don't get it right, the other team gets to **say** an answer."

"If that team gets it right, they get a point. If they don't, then the teams keep taking turns until a team **answers** correctly."

"When all of the places have been described, the game is over."

"Each team will **count** up their points."

"The team with the most points wins the game."

"Don't forget to **clap** for the winning team."

"Name That Place" Game Questions Script

"This is a place a family goes when they want to swing or go down a slide. This is a good place for a picnic. This word rhymes with the word 'dark.' What is this place?"

"A family goes to this place when they want to go swimming. There is a lifeguard. This word rhymes with the word 'school.' What is this place?"

"This is a place a family might go when they want to go out for dinner. This place serves hamburgers and french fries. What is the name of this place?"

"This is a place a family will go if they need to buy some chicken, bread, and carrots to cook supper. You give money to a cashier to buy your food. What is this place?"

"This is a place a family might go if somebody is celebrating a birthday. There is cake, ice cream, presents and music. People have a lot of fun here. What is this place?"

"A family will go here to have fun! A family can ride scary rides, play fun games, and eat cotton candy. This word rhymes with the word 'scare.' What is this place?"

"This is a place a family will go if they want to watch people play a sport. You can buy snacks and soda. There are cheerleaders to cheer on players. What is this place?"

"This is a place a family will go to look at animals. They can see a tiger, a zebra, and a bear. This word rhymes with the word 'new.' What is this place?"

"This is a place a family will go to listen to music. There may be people singing or playing instruments, or both. Sometimes a family will dress up. What is this place?"

"This is a place a family will go if they want to read books and bring books home. There are chairs and tables where you can read. What is this place?"

"This is a place a family will go if they want to watch something on a big screen. The family may eat popcorn here. There are soft seats to sit in. What is this place?"

"This is a place a family will go to shop for different things and buy things. There are many different stores at this place, all under one roof. What is this place?"

"Catch a Rhyme" Game Directions

1. Take the fish cards, picture cards, and pole out of the envelope on the back of the folder.
2. Open the folder. Put the fish face up on the lake.
3. Put the picture cards in a stack, face down.
4. Draw a picture card and read the word.
5. Look at the fish in the lake.
6. Find a fish that rhymes with the picture card.
7. Touch the fish with your fishing pole.
8. Use your pole to drag the fish in.
9. When you catch a fish, put it next to you!
10. Give the pole to somebody else for a turn.

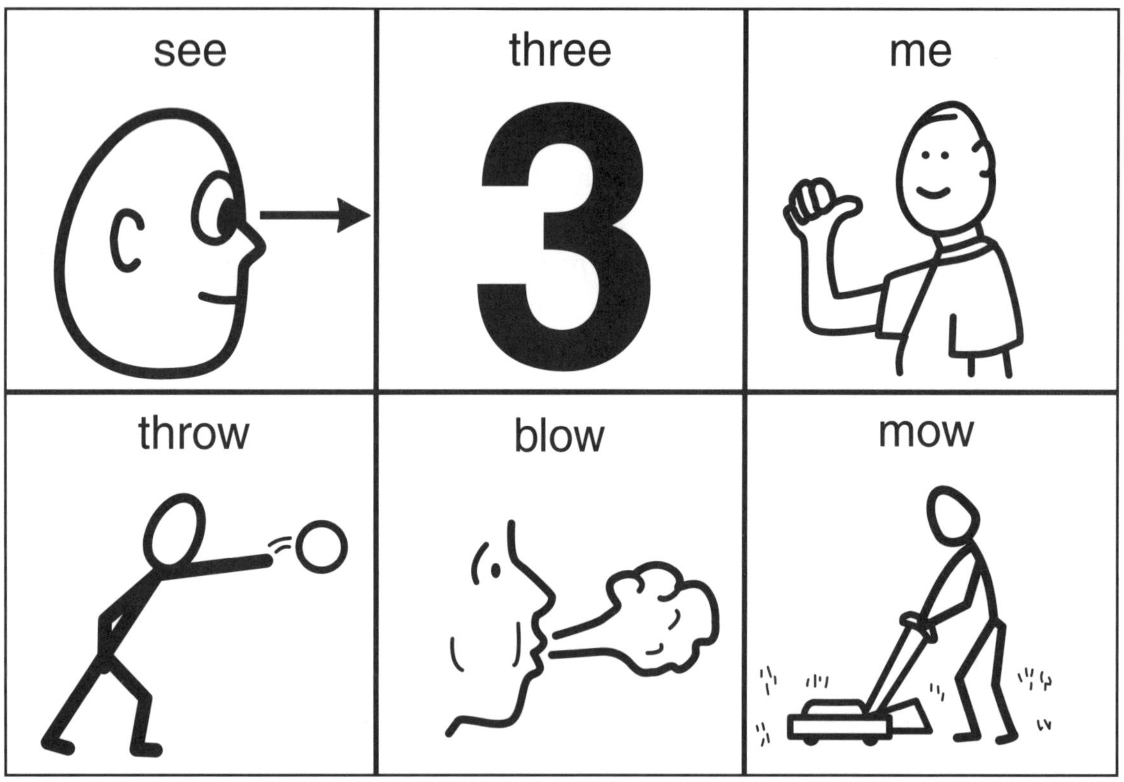

key

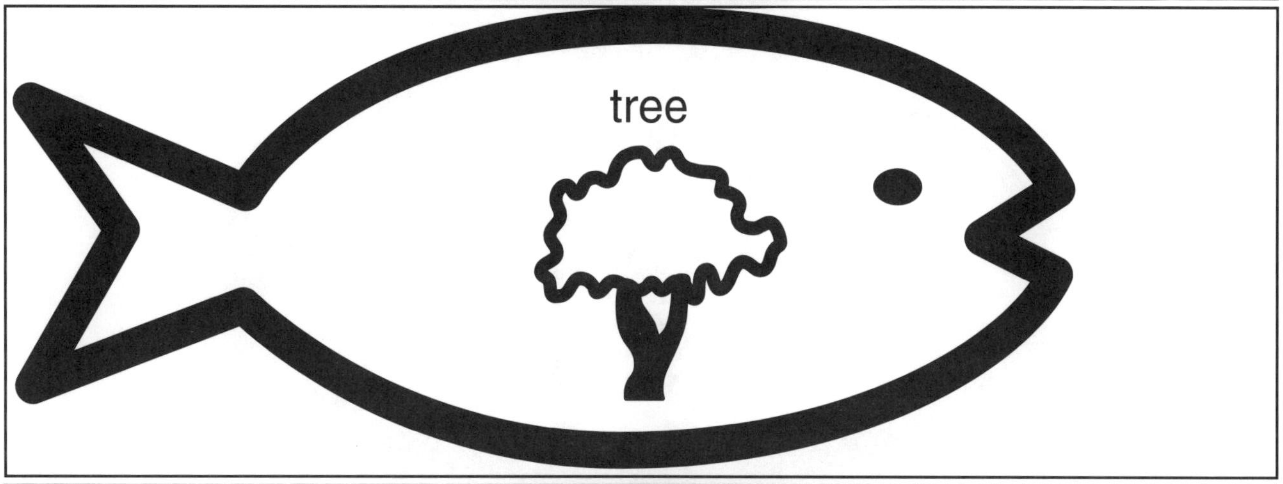
tree

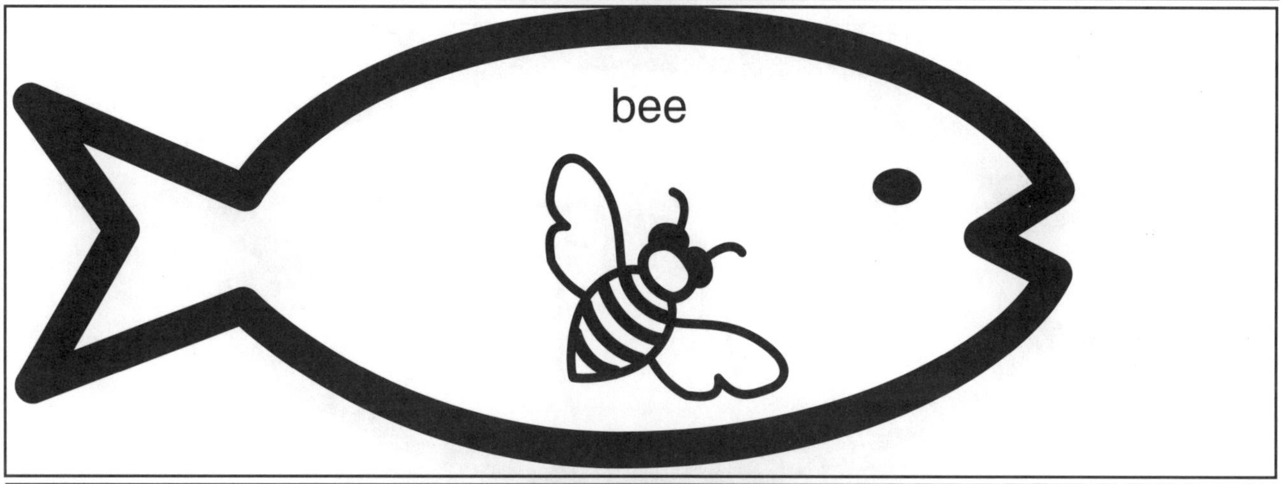
bee

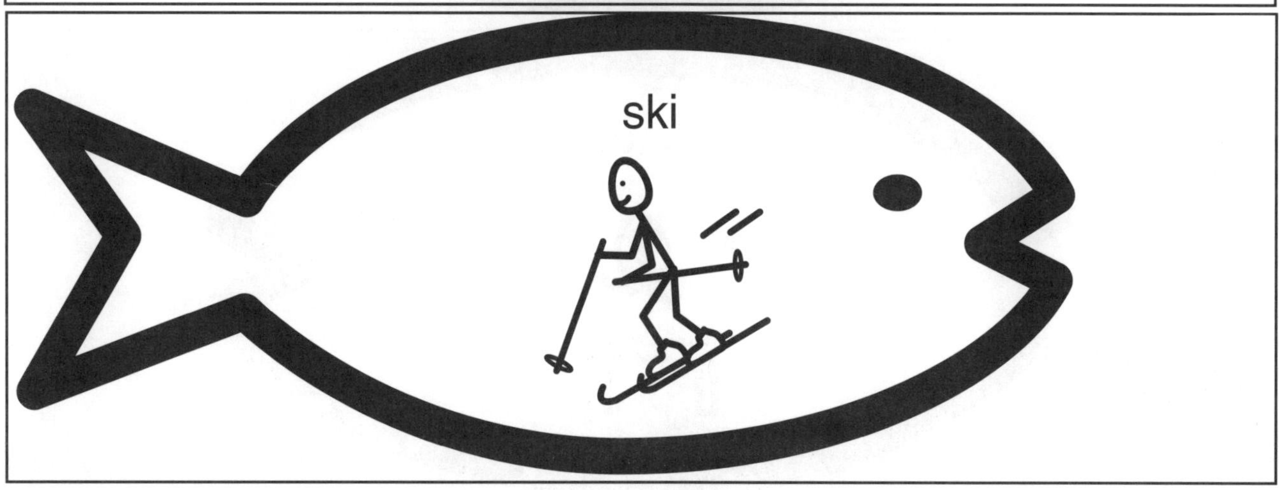
ski

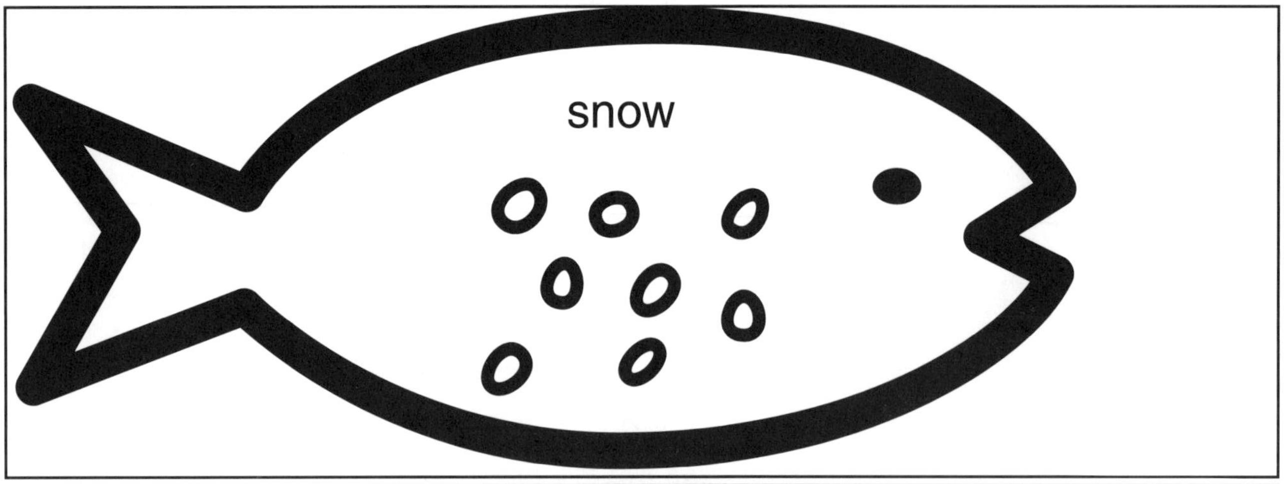
snow

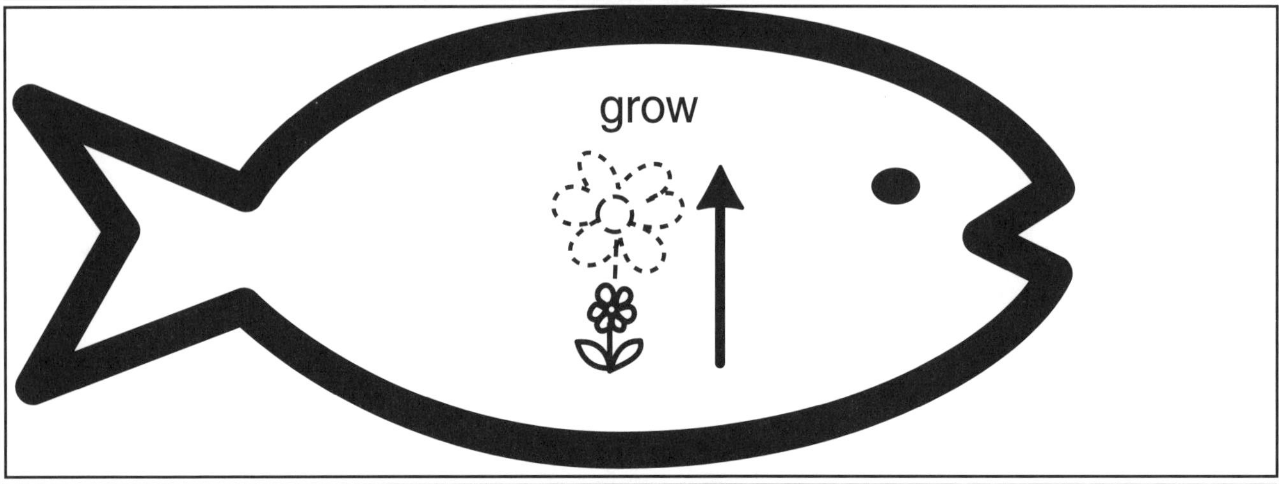
grow

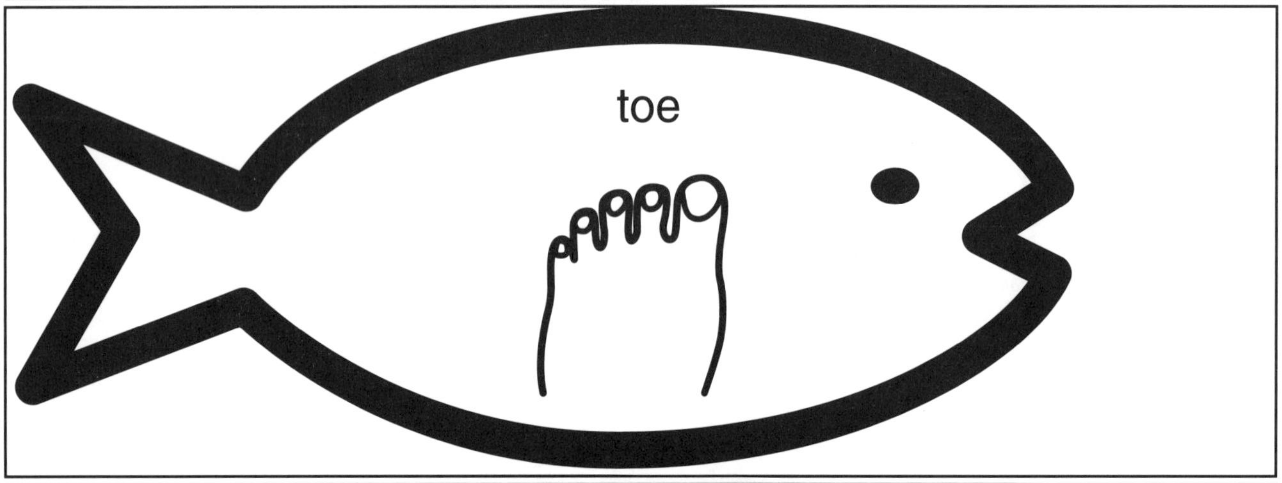
toe

know

Family Game Response Sheet

Dear Parents,

We are learning about family and learning about the word "play." Your child made their own game, called "Catch a Rhyme." Please take a few minutes to follow the directions on the front of the game folder and play the game with your child. An alternative way to play this game would be to work on picture identification only. Name a picture on a fish and have your child find that fish, or select (by touch or eye gaze) the fish with that picture from several fish you put on display. Then somebody can help them reel that fish in!

Please help your child fill out this response form and send it back to school by ______________.
Thank you for your help. Enjoy playing this rhyming game with your child!

Sincerely,

____

My name is ________________.

I played Catch A Rhyme with these people:

____

This is how I felt when we were playing:

This is what our family said about the game:

____

Do I want to play this game again?

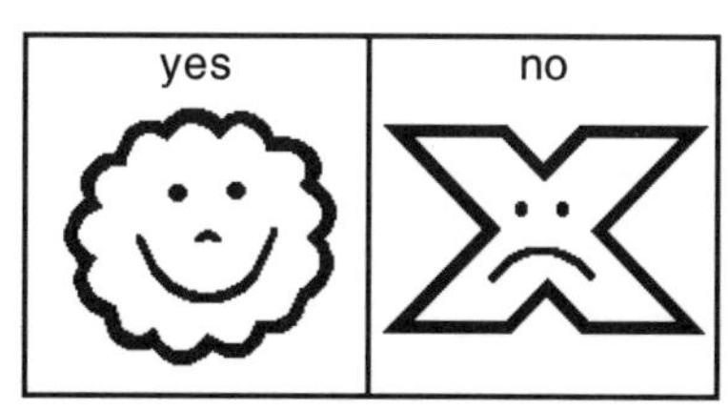

Families live together and do

things together. This family is

____

______________________together.

Large Food Group Picture Cards

meat/fish

grains

fruits/vegetables

dairy

Fruits/Vegetables

applesauce	orange juice

grapes	carrots

salad	corn

Meat /Fish

chicken	fish
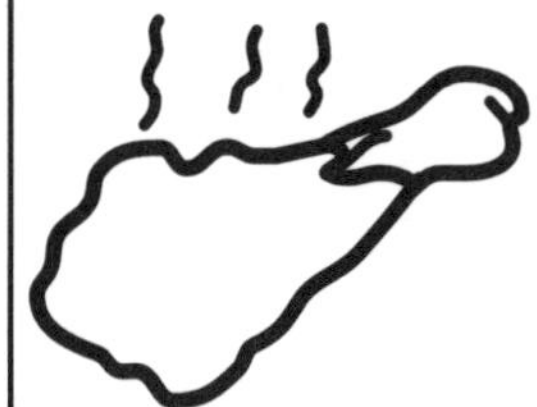	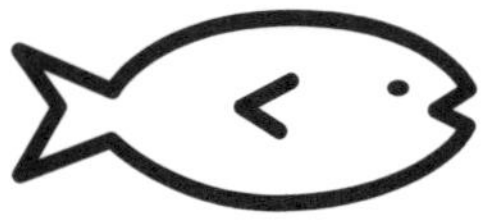
hot dog	hamburger

peanut butter	egg
	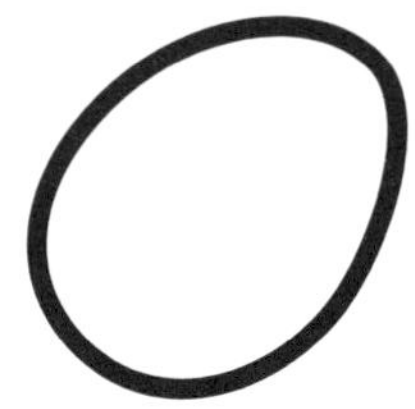

Grains

toast	cereal

macaroni and cheese	pretzels

pancakes	waffle

Dairy

milk	cheese

yogurt	ice cream

cottage cheese	pudding

Menu for:

breakfast
lunch
dinner

meat/fish

____

grains

____

fruits/vegetables

____

dairy

____

cream

jar

bowl

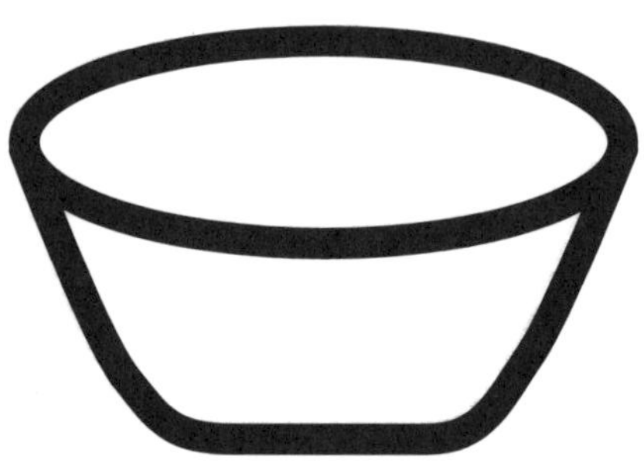

spoon

knife

bread

Butter Making Materials Picture Cards

food

clothes

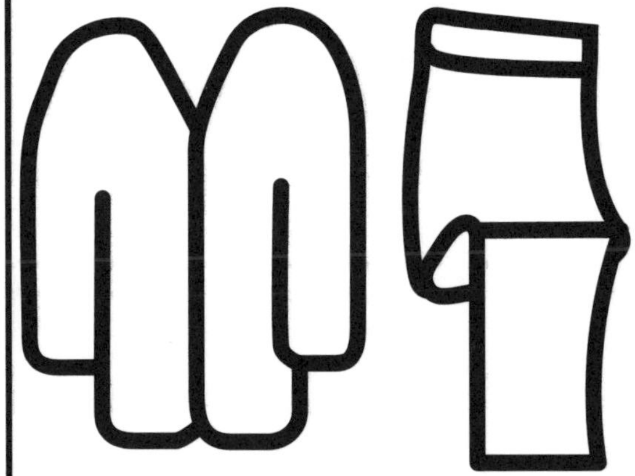

office

tool

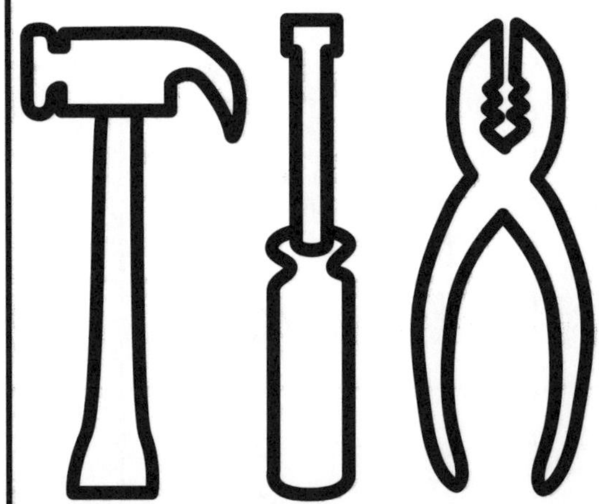

toy

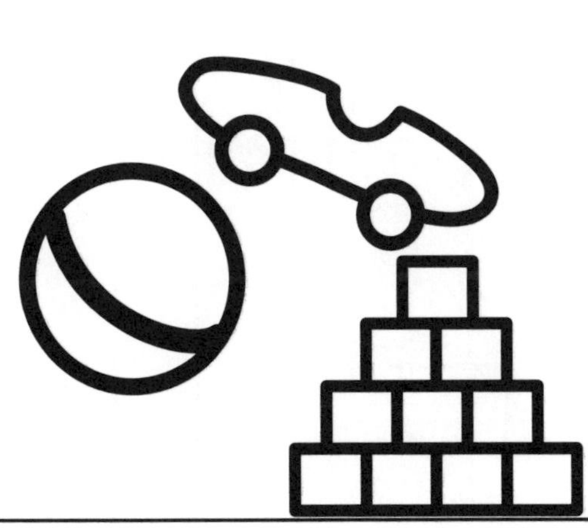

book

Store Picture Cards

"Crazy Rules" rule cards (1)

1		If you get a 1, ______________ ______________ ______________
2		If you get a 2, ______________ ______________ ______________
3		If you get a 3, ______________ ______________ ______________

4

If you get a 4, ______________________

____

____

5

If you get a 5, ______________________

____

____

6

If you get a 6, ______________________

____

____

"Crazy Rules" pictures/symbols

jump - jump up and down
clap - clap your hands
pig - oink like a pig
lion - roar like a lion

laugh - laugh out loud
dance - dance to music
cow - moo like a cow
bear - growl like a bear

sing - sing a favorite song
shake hands - shake hands with a friend
duck - quack like a duck
monkey - scratch like a monkey

"Crazy Rules" pictures/symbols

"Where Do You Live?" Book Teacher Directions

Tell students they are gong to make a book about places where people and animals live.
Direct students to **cut** out each of the animal and place picture cards (below) and put them in separate piles.
Pile 1 - snow, lake, zoo, dirt *Pile 2* - giraffe, worm, fish, polar bear *Pile 3* - giraffe, worm, fish, polar bear
Lead students in **reading** the animal book page.
Name one of the animals. Direct students to **identify** that animal picture card and **glue** it on the first blank.
Lead students in **reading** the sentence, "A (giraffe) lives in the_______."
Direct students to **select** the place picture card where that animal lives and **glue** it on the second blank line.
Continue this process for each of the four animals.
Direct students to **read** the student book page and **write** their address on the blank line.
Direct students to make a picture for each book page (see Teacher Script).

Teacher Script

"Find the book page that says, 'A fish lives in the lake.' "
"Use the blue paint to **paint** a lake on that page. Put the fish picture on the lake. Set it aside to dry."
"Now find the book page that says, 'A giraffe lives in the zoo.' "
"**Glue** the giraffe picture on the page. Now **glue** craft sticks on to make bars, like in a zoo."
"Next, find the book page that says, 'A polar bear lives in the snow.' "
"Spread some glue on the page. Sprinkle sugar over the glue to make snow. **Glue** on the polar bear picture."
"The next page says, 'A worm lives in the dirt.' "
"Spread some glue on the page. Sprinkle dirt over the glue. **Glue** on the worm picture."
"The last page tells where you live! **Cut** a house out of construction paper. **Glue** it on the box. Now **glue** your picture on the house."
"We need a title page. **Choose** a color of paper. Let's **read** the title that's on the board. The title is, 'Where Do You Live?' Now use a marker to **write** that on the construction paper."
"When the pages dry, we will **staple** the book together."

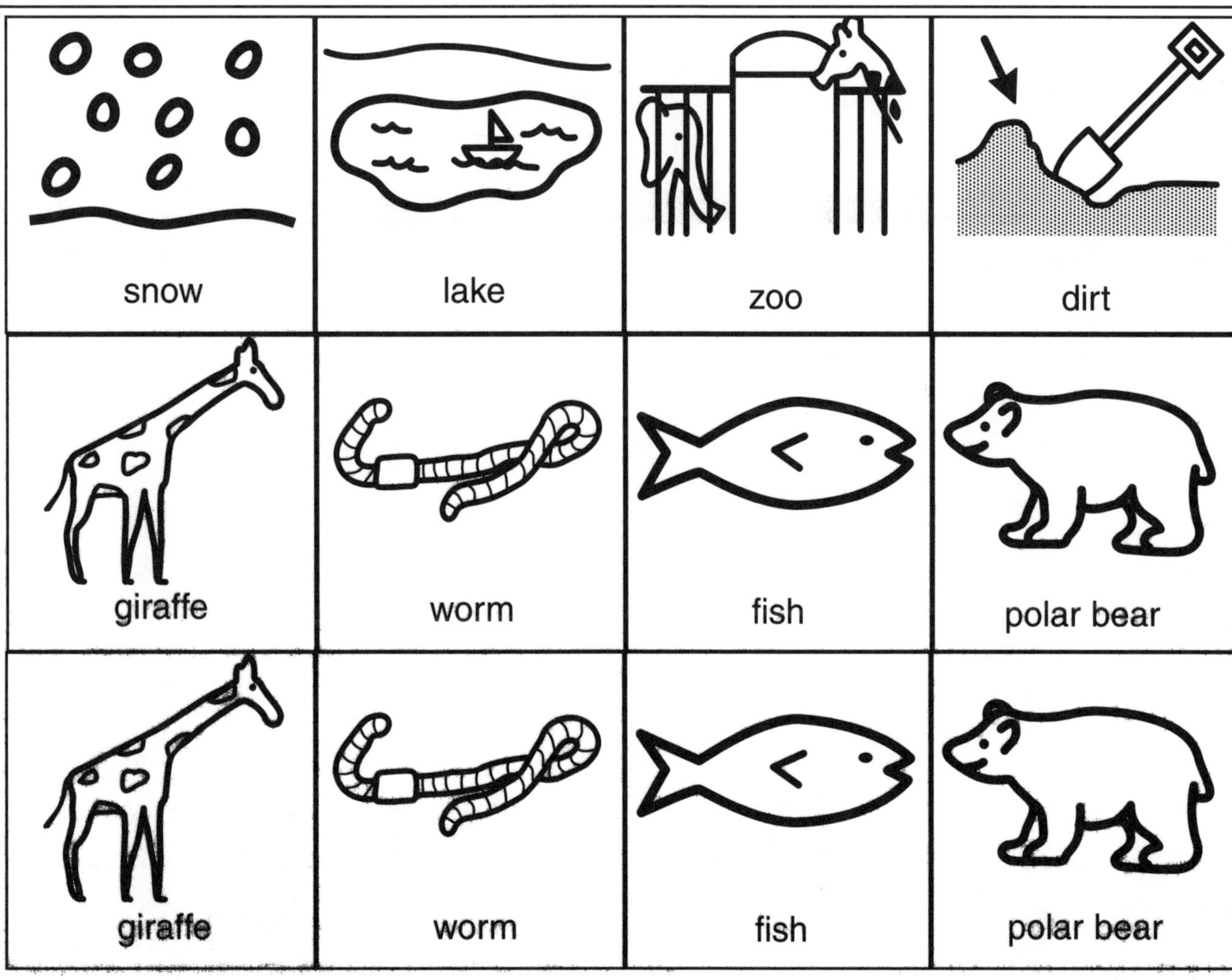

"Where Do You Live?" Animal Book Page

A _______ lives in the________.

I live at ______________________

______________________________.

help

give

share

celebrate

laugh

Vocabulary Picture Cards Set Three

give	help
celebrate	share
	laugh

Smiley Jar Tag

The Smiley Jar

This jar is full of Smileys, created just for you.
If you find yourself without a smile, here's what you should do.

The Smileys can be bashful, in fact they like to hide.
So carefully take off the top, and reach down deep inside.

Pull out your favorite Smiley, and hold it in your hand.
Soon, upon your face, a great big smile will land!

Keep your Smiley with you throughout your busy day.
When you feel a frown approaching, just look your Smiley's way.

Put the top back on the Smiley jar, don't let the others out,
For you will need them later, of this there is no doubt.

The other Smileys in your jar are for you to give away.
It's amazing how a Smiley can brighten someone's day!

When you look at someone's face and see no smile there,
Here's what you can do, to let them know you care.

Reach back inside your Smiley jar and grab a Smiley tight,
Then slip it in that person's hand and wait for their delight!

Smiley Faces

Laugh Cards

silly

Make a silly face.

joke

Tell a funny joke.

pig

Oink like a pig.

dance

Dance the crazy dance!

sing

Sing a silly song.

read

Read a fun book.

costume

Put on a silly costume.

bubbles

Blow bubbles.

touch

Touch something slimy.

puppet

Make a puppet talk.

hair dryer

Blow things around.

take pictures

Take a fun class picture.

What We Use to Celebrate

What We Do to Celebrate

SET A - I need help to learn.

I don't know how to do my math homework.
I don't know how to read all the words in this book.
I don't know how to play UNO. I want to learn.

SET B - I need help with a decision.

I wonder what I should cook for dinner tonight?
I don't know what to wear today.
I'm bored! I don't know what to do.

SET C - I need help to feel better.

Today has been a really bad day.
I got in a fight with my friend. I'm upset.
Ouch! I fell off my bike and scraped my knee.

SET D - I need help to do something.

I can't reach the cup on the top shelf.
Wow! There sure are a lot of dishes I have to wash tonight.
The car is so dirty, but I don't have time to wash it today!

Date ___________

Dear Parents,

We have been learning about the word share. We have learned about what it means to share, and have practiced sharing with each other. In class we made instruments and shared materials.

Your child is bringing home a Family Sharing Bag. As we have also been learning about families, students will have an opportunity to work together with their family, sharing materials inside this Family Sharing Bag, to make a special project.

This project is called, "Family Creature." Inside the bag you'll find crayons, glue, construction paper, and other assorted materials to use. Please find a time within the next week that you can gather your whole family, and work together to make a Family Creature! This creature can be anything your family wants it to be. Have fun with this! Be creative! You may use any other materials you have. The important part of this project is that everyone shares the materials in the Family Sharing Bag. If your child wants to use something that someone else is using, or has already used, help them understand that they need to share, and need to wait their turn. Please name your Family Creature. You may also want to take pictures of your Family Creature with different members of your family.

Students will share their finished Family Creatures at school. Please send your Family Creature back to school, with its name and any pictures you have taken, no later than ______________. The Family Creature will be sent back home after being shared at school.

Thank you so much for your help! Enjoy your Family Creature making experience!

Sincerely,

____

This card is coming directly your way, to bring you cheer, and to BRIGHTEN your day!

Without you, What would I do? Hey, friend, here's LOOKING at you!

Your friend-ship always lifts me high, just like a RAINBOW in the sky!

You're my friend. I like your style. When I'm around you, I always SMILE!

Just a little NOTE that I wanted to send, to tell you "Thank You" for being my friend!

I like being with you! You're so much fun! Hanging with you is like being in the SUN!

Card Directions

Rainbow - Choose colors you like. Glue them around the top and sides of the expression box.
Light bulb - Decorate the front of the card with neon crayons. Spread glue on and add gold glitter.
Note - Glue a long and short piece of yarn, and a pom-pom, on the card to make a music note.
Look - Glue wiggle eyes on the front of the card.
Smile - Glue two pom-poms on for eyes and the yarn on for a wide smile.
Sun - Glue a yellow pom-pom in the center, and short lengths of yellow yarn around the outside.

Joke Survey Script

- Hi!
- Do you like jokes?
- Can we tell you a joke?
- OK - Here it is!
- Our Information Giver will tell you what rating that joke got.
- Do you want to hear another joke?
- Listen up - this is it!
- Let's ask the Information Giver what score this joke got.
- Thanks for your help!
- Have a great day!

Laughometer Instructions

1. Cut out the Laughometer.
2. Cut out the arrow.
3. Insert a brad through the black dot in the arrow, then through the black dot on the Laughometer.
4. Now your Laughometer is ready for action!

WORD WALL WORDS

SET THREE

work

is

help

WORD WALL WORDS
SENTENCE COMPLETION ACTIVITY

Will you ____________ me with my homework?

Today ____ a cold and windy day.

My mom is going to ________ in her office.

work	is	help

Mind Reader Script

"I'm ready with a clue for the first word!"
"It's a word on the word wall."
"This word has two letters."
"It fits in the sentence, 'What ____ your name?' "
"This word begins with the letter 'i.' "
"Which word wall word is it?"

"Get ready for word number two!"
"This is also a word on the word wall."
"This word has four letters."
"It fits in the sentence, 'I am going to _______ hard to get good grades!' "
"It begins with the letter 'w.' "
"Which word wall word is it?"

"This is the very last word."
"This word is another word on the word wall."
"This word also has four letters."
"The word begins with the letter 'h.' "
"This word fits in the sentence, 'Can I _____ you bake the cookies?' "
"Which word wall word is it?"

Dear Parents,

As we continue on in our family unit, we are now learning about how our family lives together. We are studying the words help, share, give, celebrate, and laugh. We are going to make Family Celebration Mobiles. We need your help!

1. Would you please send in a photo of your child's family, either their entire family or part of it.
2. Would you also please help your child complete each of the sentences below with a statement about your family, something special about your family. For example, "My family eats pizza on Friday nights" or "My family likes to watch Star Trek together."

Please send this completed form and the photo to school by ________________.

Thank you.

Sincerely,

____

My family ____________ ____________ ____________.	My family ____________ ____________ ____________.
My family ____________ ____________ ____________.	My family ____________ ____________ ____________.

Situation Cards

Your little brother is really bored.	Your brother was going to help your mom wash the car, but he had to leave.	You and your sister get in a big fight. You are both mad at each other.
You're playing with the Legos and your brother wants to use them.	You got mad at your brother and said something mean. You feel bad.	Your little sister fell down and hurt her knee. She's crying.
You fixed yourself a snack and your little brother comes in.	Your sister is sad because her best friend moved away.	You want to play with your dad, but he's busy doing paper work.

Solution Cards

share 	talk 	play 
help 	I'm sorry 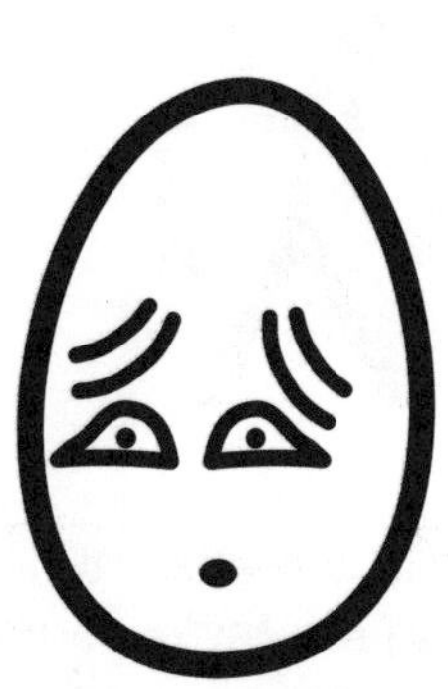	hug 

Celebration Day Cards

music

1. Play our favorite music.
2. Make up a family song.
3. Make instruments.

hugs

1. Give away extra hugs.
2. Make and give hug coupons.
3. Give away Hershey® hugs.

animals

1. Watch a movie about animals.
2. Visit a zoo or pet store.
3. Read books about animals.

chocolate

1. Make a new chocolate recipe.
2. Make smores!
3. Paint with chocolate pudding.

books

1. Take a trip to the library.
2. Have family reading time.
3. Make a family book.

breakfast

1. Fix breakfast for dinner.
2. Kids help make breakfast.
3. Cut pancakes in fun shapes.

friends

1. Make a card for a friend.
2. Invite friends over for a fun day.
3. Take fun pictures with friends.

exercise

1. Go on a scavenger hunt walk.
2. Set up an obstacle course!
3. Dance to some fun music.

art

1. Make and bake clay creations.
2. Color a picture and frame it.
3. Use junk to make a sculpture.

Celebration Day Cards

TODAY WE CELEBRATE

Dear Parents,

Today your child is coming home with a Celebration Day poster. In class we have been talking about family, and ways we can celebrate as a family.

Use this poster with your child to turn any day into a day to celebrate!
Attached to the back of this poster is a bag of different Celebration Day Cards. Each of these cards shows a picture of something to celebrate, such as art or music or chocolate, and three ideas of ways to celebrate this.

Consider choosing one day a week that will be a Celebration Day. Prior to that day, you or your child select a Celebration Day Card. Read the ideas on the card, and think about what specific ways your family can celebrate that. Write additional ideas on the back of the card. Or come up with your own ideas and make your own cards. Prepare anything you may need for celebrating.

On Celebration Day, clip the Celebration Day Card on the poster. Show your family, and talk about how you might celebrate this special day. Throughout the day, whenever possible, celebrate!

Have fun celebrating with your family!

Sincerely,

____

Dear Parents,

We are learning about family, and about sharing. Please help your child read to their family the information they wrote below to share about their day. Then, please help your child to read the sentences at the bottom of the page to ask a family member about their day. Thank you!

Sincerely,

____

	In school today I studied and learned ____.
	In school today I read about ____.
	Something fun I did in school was ____.
	Something important that happened was ____.

Now tell me about your day!

Tell me about something good that happened today.

Was there anything bad that happened today?

Please tell me something else about your day.

Thanks for sharing!

Questions

fun 	What did you do for fun this week?
movie 	Did you see any good movies?
place 	Did you go any special place this week?
family 	What's new with your family?

Information

friend 	The friends I've spent time with are ______________________________.
movie 	A movie I've seen and really liked is ______________________________.
family 	Something I've done with my family is ______________________________.
place 	One place I went this past week was ______________________________.
game 	A game I've had fun playing is ______________________________.

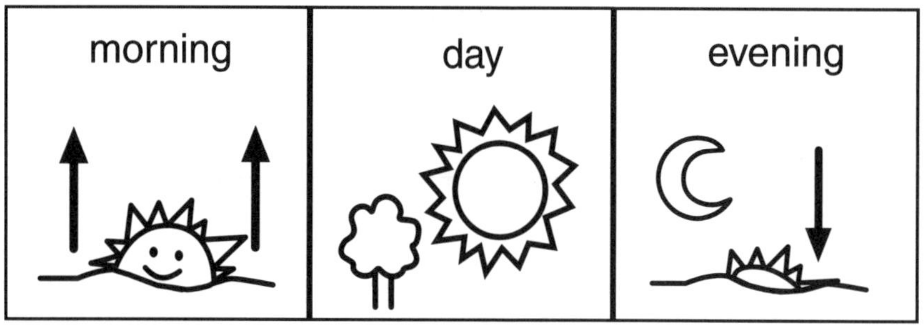

Book Pictures

In the ______________,
people in my family
do lots of things.

My family ______________
______________________.

My family ______________
______________________.

My family ______________
______________________.

My family ______________
______________________.

R#123 REPRODUCIBLES

Important
Information
About ME!

____

I live in
the city of

__________________.

1

My home
address is

__________________.

2

My phone
number is

__________________.

3

"Important Information About ME!"

Dear Parents,

We have been learning about the word "help" and how we help each other out in our families.

Our class will be doing a project in which we write about the different ways that we help our family members.

Would you please help us prepare for this project by working with your child to think about and write three different ways that he/she helps in your family.

Attached are three note cards. For each sentence, please have your child draw a picture of himself/herself helping out in the way written in the sentence. Your child could have a family member help him/her draw the picture, or a family member could take a picture of your child helping out in this way and your child could glue it on the note card.

Thank you so much for your help. We will be using these pages to make a book, and your child will bring the book home at the close of our unit about family.

Please return this sheet and the pictures to school by

____________________________.

Sincerely,

____

In my family, I help by

____.

In my family, I help by

____.

In my family, I help by

____.

Personal Piñata Making Directions

1. **Count** out ______prizes and put them in your bag.
2. **Count** out three sheets of newspaper. Crumple them and put them in the bag.
3. Fold down the top of the bag several times.
4. Punch two holes on either side of the folded part.
5. Lace yarn through the holes. Make a large loop above the paper bag, to hang the piñata.
6. **Choose** colors of streamers you like.
7. **Cut** the streamers into strips.
8. **Glue** the streamers on the paper bag.
9. **Color** decorations on the paint stirring stick to make a piñata paddle.
10. Set the piñata and piñata paddle aside to dry.

Personal Piñata Breaking Directions

1. Hang the piñata from the ceiling.
2. **Turn on** some fun music!
2. Draw or **spin** for the person who will have the next turn.
3. That person holds the piñata paddle and hits the piñata one time.
4. When the piñata breaks, wait for an adult to say, "go."
5. You may collect prizes and put them in your prize bag.
6. Remember to share your prizes with people who didn't get any, or didn't get as much as you.
7. Pick up the pieces of the piñata and throw it away.